THE SILENCE OF MEMORY

THE LEGACY OF THE GREAT WAR
A Series sponsored by the Historical de la grande guerre Péronne-Somme

General Editor
JAY WINTER

Other titles in the series

Antonie Prost
IN THE WAKE OF WAR
'Les Anciens Combattants' and French Society

Patrick Fridenson
THE FRENCH HOME FRONT 1914–1918

Stéphane Audoin-Rouzeau
MEN AT WAR 1914–1918

Gerald D. Feldman
ARMY, INDUSTRY, AND LABOR IN GERMANY 1914–1918

Rosa Maria Bracco
MERCHANTS OF HOPE

THE SILENCE OF MEMORY
Armistice Day 1919–1946

ADRIAN GREGORY

BERG
Oxford/Providence, USA

First published in 1994 by
Berg Publishers
offices:
150 Cowley Road, Oxford, OX4 1JJ, UK
221 Waterman Road, Providence, RI 02906, USA

(c) Adrian Gregory

Library of Congress Cataloging-in-Publication Data
A catalogue record for this book is available from the
Library of Congress.

British Library Cataloguing in Publication Data
A catalogue record for this book is available from the British Library.

ISBN 0 85496 955 1 (Cloth)
1 85973 001 9 (Paper)

Printed in the United Kingdom by Short Run Press, Exeter.

Contents

Contents

Acknowledgements

My first acknowledgement should be to the Provost and Fellows of King's College for lifting the burden of financial and career insecurity by electing me to a Research Fellowship during the writing of this book.

I would like to thank the staff of all the organisations, libraries and archives mentioned in the notes and bibliography. The Historial de la Grande Guerre provided financial support at a crucial moment, Queen Mary and Westfield College provided the priceless assistance of a month's free accomodation in London.

In the acknowledgements to my thesis I have mentioned all the many people whose support has been so valuable. If I edit the list here I hope I shall not give offence. Thanks to all the following; Gareth Stedman Jones, George Mosse, Peter Clark, John Barber, Miles Taylor, Jon Lawrence, Annette Becker, David Lloyd, Catherine Moriarty, Pat Thane, John Shaw, Andrea Smith, Padma Anagol, Jon Hall, Patrick McGinn and Sarah Cohen. Particular thanks to Morgen Witzel for heroic copy editing, to Jaqueline at Collindale for help finding the illustrations and to Sara Everett for overseeing the publication. Many thanks to my parents for love and support. Finally, thanks to Jay Winter who has been so very important in making this book possible.

Introduction

The First World War made an indelible impact on those who lived through it. No event since the Black Death, neither revolution, religious upheaval or war, had touched the lives of Europeans in such a general and far reaching manner. The guns of August echoed far beyond Europe, bringing anxiety and news of loss to remote villages, from Hawke's Bay to Newfoundland, but it was in Europe that the upheaval of war was felt most immediately in the lives of whole populations. Such an event would be remembered in a multiplicity of ways. The way it was remembered in one nation is the subject of this book.

At the outset I wish to apologise. Like most English historians I have written a history of England disguised as a history of the British Isles. In doing so I am aware that I have perpetuated the injustice of a hegemonic history which has ignored the particularities of the other constituent nations of these islands. I have found the problem insoluble. To ignore the Scots, Irish and Welsh in this book would have been a perpetuation of blinkered arrogance. I have therefore referred, perhaps superficially, to some interesting features of commemorations outside England.

At the same time to do justice to the specificity of these cases would have involved entering into discussion of many things of which I am ignorant and which would have overburdened the book with indispensable but bulky contextual explanation. Historical events such as Welsh Disestablishment, traditions such as those of the Unionist and Nationalist communities of Ireland, theological details such as those of Scottish Calvinism and long term historical trends such as the decline and revival of Welsh and Gaelic languages would need discussion.

Fortunately, Jane Leonard, Fiona Douglas and Angela Lambert are currently undertaking work on the memory and commemoration of the war in Ireland, Scotland and Wales and hopefully the combined impact of our studies will lead to a genuine understanding of the memory of the impact of an event which was not limited by the confines of Offa's Dyke, the Irish Sea and Hadrian's Wall, any more than it was by the English Channel.

In recent years the memory of war has become a topic which has attracted substantial interest from authors both within universities and outside. Three schools of thought are beginning to emerge and it may be time to initate a debate as to how the memory of war was related to popular culture in the inter-war years.

The first approach to the memory of war is neatly summarised in Paul Fussell's title for his very influential work, *The Great War and Modern Memory*. Fussell views the First World War as a fundamental moment in breaking the cultural traditions of the pre-war period. Although the war did not create modernism, it created the conditions in which modernism was to flourish by undermining the authority of the older order. The artist would henceforth have to rebel to be taken seriously.

This approach has its mirror image in the work of Modris Eksteins. In *The Rites of Spring: The Great War and the Birth of the Modern Age,* Eksteins to some extent reverses the causality by seeing the Great War as in many respects the product of modernism, rather than its cause. Furthermore his version of modernism differs substantially from Fussells by stressing the urge to 'value' commitment rather than rebellion and protest in modernism. Nevertheless the link between the First World War and 'modernism' remains the theme of the book. Both these approaches stress the 'culture clash' of the war with modernism ranged against the moral certitudes of an earlier epoch.

The theme of culture clash is central to a third influential work on the topic by Samuel Hynes, entitled *A War Imagined*. In this book, Hynes explores the ways in which the war was perceived by both the combatant and non-combatant populations. he stresses both continuity and change, pointing to modernist elements in culture prior to 1914 and the persistence of older cultural forms after 1918. The war is located in a longer perspective and is not the sole motor of change in perspective, but it still relates to a new way of seeing the world.

Each of these works concentrates on 'high culture'. This is strong theme in the fascination of North American historians with twentieth century Europe. Fussell and Hynes are literary critics by training, Eksteins a cultural historian in the traditional sense, interested in landmarks of art. This represents a strength and a limitation in these works. Although all three demonstrate an interest in popular culture, it tends to act as a backdrop for the discussion of the 'culturally significant. The second approach to the memory of war is quite different.

George Mosse in his book, *Fallen Soldiers,* takes a very different view of the memory of war. Far from representing a break in European history, the First World War becomes a way station on the route to an unthinkable enormity, the Holocaust. Building on his work on the cultural roots of nationalism, Mosse sees the First World War as a moment of brutalisation in the nationalist tradition. The memory of war, far from being subversive, was one which glorified conflict, through the twin impulses of sacralisation and kitsch(there are some clear similarities with Eksteins here, although the starting points are rather different.) The constructed memory of war generally served the purposes of the nationalistic forces of the European far-right for whom it was a congenial discourse.

The weakness in Mosse's work is best illustrated by the work of Bob Bushaway on remembrance in the United Kingdom. Like Mosse, Bushaway sees war commemoration as an important element in explaining inter-war politics. Also like Mosse, he sees it as tending to operate to the disadvantage of the political left. Both authors take a position similar to what might be called a traditional Marxist analysis of false consciousness, where an 'ideology' is used to prevent the oppressed from seeing the reality of their situation. However, whereas Mosse stresses the advantages of the memory of war to the most radical and extreme right wing forces, Bushaway claims it as a force for integration, beneficial in averting political polarisation and therefore most useful to the moderate conservative. Both writers tend to generalise their theory, claiming the extreme importance of the memory of war in determining politics, but their positions are inherently contradictory. The memory of war cannot lead 'naturally' to extreme nationalism in Italy and Germany and at the same time 'naturally' to political moderation in the United Kingdom. Of course, it can be objected that the former cases deal with a nation which lost and a self-perceived loser nation after the war whilst the latter case deals with a 'winner'. But once that is admitted, the broader political and social context must also be readmitted as well, because the simple causal relationship between war experience and the memory of war has been undermined.

Mosse and Bushaway begin with war commemoration and posit a theory about the influence of the memory of war on inter-war political culture. Three works, on Britain, France and Germany respectively reverse the process and can be taken as representative of the third approach. Antoine Prost has written extensively on the veterans movement in inter-war France. His work, now summarised in an English translation as *In the Wake of War: Les Anciens Combattants and French Society 1914-1939*, provides a fine example of what can be done by paying close attention to the context in which the memory of war was constructed. Moving away from stereotypes of the veteran created by the activities of an unrepresentative right wing minority, Prost has uncovered the every-day attitudes of a vast range of ex-servicemens' organisations. The most common ideology of these organisations was a subtle blend. The war experience was central but it was mediated by the previous experience of these men, an experience of civic indoctrination by the institutions of the Third Republic, particularly the schools. The result was a civic minded 'patriotic pacifism', often incoherent, but neither the militant nationalism of Mosse nor the numbed acceptance of the *status quo* postulated by Bushaway. Although they were not a major organised force in French politics, veterans had a distinct voice and were capable of activism and influence. These veterans had a distinctive effect on the way that the war was remembered both in their writings and more significantly in their actions, pariculary in the annual pilgrimages to Verdun and in the local commemorations of *l' Onze Novembre*.

The subtlety of Prost's analysis is appealing and is in some respects mirrored by a recent thesis on ex-servicemen in Britain by Charles Kimball of Stanford University. Kimball similarly views British ex-servicemen 'on the ground', concentrating on the associational level. Like Prost, he found that the context in which the veterans functioned was of enormous significance. Thus the British Legion in the countryside tended to mirror the society around it, conservative and hierarchical. By contrast veterans in urban areas with a radical associational tradition were more likely to have left-wing politics and to clash with the conservative veterans' leaders. Unfortunately Kimball ends his thesis in nineteen thirty and does not explore at length the symbolic constructions of memory which were fruitfully examined by Prost. Part of the reason for this is that British veterans were not the principal custodians of the memory of war, a point I intend to discuss at length.

A third representative of the 'contextual' approach is Robert Whalen's book, *Bitter Wounds: German Victims of the Great War 1914-1939*. Dealing with the associations of both the wounded and the bereaved, Whalen places equal stress on the war experience and the political and economic traumas which followed the war. In dealing wih the German experience, Whalen walks the tightrope with some sucess, balancing the pre-determination implied by the *Sonderweg* view of German history, with a refreshing stress on diversity and contingency in the 1920s, whilst never losing sight of the terrible and disastrous outcome.

To summarize, of the three approaches outlined my prefence tends towards the third. In other words, if forced to choose I would argue that the memory of war was determined by existing predelictions in the culture, political, religious and 'communitarian', rather than the other way around. Furthermore, I would stress that the memory of the war was not constant and that in fact it was being reshaped by political, diplomatic and economic events during the inter-war period, rather than shaping them. However, I am aware that this is to simplify a complex problem. The memory of war and the divisions it created both internationally and within nations, as well as the unity it fostered, did play an independent role in shaping 'discourse'. In one respect the second approach has a point, there was a conservatism inate in the effect of the war. To justify mass death and equally to justify mass killing, it was necessary to extol the values that were being defended, whether German 'Kultur' or British 'Civilization'. Wars in this sense define nationality, they licence the killing of national enemies and the suppression of anti-national subversives. As such they raise the question of what the nation is and what it stands for. Such heightened 'national sentiment' does not disappear when the shooting stops. A language which justifies death in wars will continue to justify those deaths afterwards and there are good psychological reasons why this should be the case.

Conservative tendencies are inherent in justifying modern wars, just as utopian dreams of reconstruction or apocalyptic visions tend to arise out of the strains of fighting them. Yet 'conservative' means different things in different contexts. The French ex-servicemen described by Prost were conservative in their vision, yet their vision of a perfected pacific republic was radical in its implications. The 'conservative' vision of the British in fighting the war was of a society which stood for decency, order, peace, fairness and social harmony. Absurd though much of this was in the context of a racial empire and a class division, this was how the war against Prussianism was defined. Paradoxically the fight to 'conserve' these values gave them a certain amount of real force as a transformative language for society. An idealistic benchmark had been set, and the performance of governments was measured against it.

In Germany, by contrast, this conservative vision turned sour; the impulse was turned against a new regime with shallow roots in German society. The memory of the war became a weapon against those who had made the peace, 'The November Criminals' who had betrayed the united and victorious German people. That this image was totally false meant little against the comforting myth that it provided to absolve German society from responsibility for defeat. It was better to blame the un-German, the traitor.

The book that follows is implicitly comparative. Why was British commemoration of the war markedly different from French or German commemoration? This was the first question I set myself. This has meant taking a genuinely comparative view, rather than assuming British exceptionality. I start with the assumption that there is no normative model of war commemoration. Indeed, were I to undertake this work again, I might stress even further the diversities within the national community as Ken Inglis has done in his recent work on Anzac Day in Australia. Nevertheless, the nation, in this case fairly narrowly defined is the best unit with which to start. The discourse of memory was a national discourse.

There remains one important qualification. In line with the academic fashion of the 1980s, I have placed a great deal of stress on the importance of language in the shaping of consciousness. In examining ritual, I paid a great deal of attention to how the ritual was explained by contemporaries and which tropes they used. Because the discourse surrounding the ritual was so rich and so diverse in its political and social implications, I was content to accept that all of the memory of the war would be shaped and reflected by the languages I have presented. I am no longer so confident. A wonderful study by Geoffrey Moorhouse of the memory of the First World War in the town of Bury suggests that beneath all of the varied public discourse there remained a 'hidden transcript' about the war, a memory preserved at a familial and personal level which was at odds with the rhetoric about the war. More studies are needed at a local level to penetrate this memory, although the problems of uncovering it are methodologically profound. I happily leave those studies to others. Even so, this memory remains a language, one that is undoubtedly related to the languages I present (much of my material is drawn from a level deeply personal to those involved).

There still remains a deeper concern. My study centres on a silence. I have written a book which places words, and through words, thoughts, into that silence. I have interpreted the silence as a space filled by discourses and as a profoundly multi-vocal ritual. But sometimes silence was simply a silence. Some experiences could not be expressed. Some went mad because of the war and some had moments of despair bordering madness. For them the silence signified the inexpressible. It signified everything and nothing. This was the worst silence of memory.

1

Lest We Forget: The Invention and Reception of Armistice Day

Nations must justify mass killings, if only to support the feelings of the bereaved and the sanity of the survivors.

Pierre Berton [1]

The Two Minutes Silence

The two minutes' silence to commemorate the first anniversary of the ceasefire of 11 o'clock on 11 November 1918 was almost as much of a surprise to the general public as the ceasefire itself had been. The decision to mark the first anniversary of the Armistice with a silent pause in the life of the nation was taken very close to the anniversary itself. As late as 15 October 1919 there is evidence to suggest that the government had not considered the first anniversary of the Armistice as being a natural moment to consider the war and its human cost. In a minute discussing the replacement of the temporary Cenotaph[2] in Whitehall, Alfred Mond, who as head of the Board of Works was responsible for the Cenotaph, made a revealing comment:

> I consider that the placing of flowers, memorial wreaths etc, at all times on the Cenotaph should be discountenanced and the break between the demolition of the temporary memorial and the erection of the permanent structure should make such a policy comparatively easy.
>
> A mass of decaying flowers needs almost daily attention besides tending to attract crowds in a crowded thoroughfare.
>
> I suggest that permission to lay floral tributes be restricted to one or perhaps two days in the year, say, the 19th July, the date of the Peace procession and some other day such as Easter Monday.[3]

This minute is revealing because it shows that less than a month before the anniversary of the cease fire, 11 November was not even

Notes for Chapter 1 can be found on page 41.

being considered as an appropriate date for the laying of wreaths by the public at the Cenotaph, let alone an official ceremony.

There was one man, outside the Cabinet, who had no doubts about the appropriateness of 11 November as a day for public commemoration. Sir Percy Fitzpatrick had served as High Commissioner in South Africa during the war. In early November he submitted a memorandum to Lord Milner for the consideration of the Cabinet:

> In the hearts of our people there is a real desire to find some lasting expression of their feeling for those who gave their lives in the war. They want something done now while the memories of sacrifice are in the minds of all; for there is the dread – too well grounded in experience – that those who have gone will not always be first in the thoughts of all, and that when the fruits of their sacrifice become our daily bread, there will be few occasions to remind us of what we realise so clearly today.
>
> During the War, we in South Africa observed what we called the " Three minutes' pause." At noon each day, all work, all talk and all movement were suspended for three minutes that we might concentrate as one in thinking of those – the living and the dead – who had pledged and given themselves for all that we believe in...
>
> Silence, complete and arresting, closed upon the city – the moving, awe-inspiring silence of a great Cathedral where the smallest sound must seem a sacrilege...Only those who have felt it can understand the overmastering effect in action and reaction of a multitude moved suddenly to one thought and one purpose.[4]

The origin of the two minutes' silence (or Silence; it was often to be capitalised in the inter-war years) is this memorandum.[5] It did not come into being without precedent, it was based on an existing model drawn from a Dominion. There would be other reasons why a silent pause would prove to be an extraordinarily successful way of commemorating the Armistice, but the South African example was the specific model. What did Fitzpatrick see as the purpose and meaning of the ritual he was proposing? He was quite specific in the proposal:

> ...it is not in mourning, but in greeting that we should salute them on that day. When we are divided it may serve to remind us of the greater things we hold in common. When we are gone it may help to bring home to those who come after us the meaning, the nobility and the unselfishness of the great sacrifice by which their freedom was assured.[6]

This appears to be a classic case of what Hobsbawm has described as the 'invention of tradition'.[7] In the immediate post war period, the danger of the example of the Russian Revolution spreading was a continuing preoccupation. The mood of returning servicemen was to some extent unknown, but there had been mutinies in bases in France caused by anger and uncertainty about demobilisation. In Germany, the extreme right and the extreme left appeared to be equal threats to the state and each had recruited returning soldiers and sailors in large numbers. If ever there was a time when rituals of integration and unity appeared to be required, it was the autumn of 1919.

The Silence could also be seen as a ritual of legitimation.[8] A public commemoration of the war would inevitably seem to strengthen the position of 'the man who won the war', as Lloyd George was being called by his supporters. This may be the reason why the Prime Minister seems to have enthusiastically supported most ideas for commemoration.

Fitzpatrick had given an idea of what the silence was supposed to achieve. He also gave an account of who it was for:

> It is due to the women who have lost and suffered and borne so much, with whom the thought is ever present. It is due to the children that they know whom they owe their dear bought freedom. It is due to the men and *from* them as men. But far and away above all else it is due to those who gave their all who sought no recompense, and whom we can never repay – our Glorious and Immortal Dead.[9]

The intended subjects of the silence were outlined here: first, the bereaved, characterised significantly as women; second, children for whom the silence was intended to be pedagogic; third, the men, by which it is clearly meant veterans, to whom the silence was both a tribute and a reminder of fallen comrades; finally, the dead. These four categories marked out in this memorandum would be the ones that would be used repeatedly in discussion of the purpose of Armistice Day throughout the inter-war period and it is interesting to see them clearly defined in the original proposal for the silence.

The proposal was discussed by the War Cabinet on 5 November 1919. It was the opinion of the majority that the 'realisation of the nation of its deliverance from the great perils of the war', was more important than the objection that, 'a precedent would be established, which, in remote years, after the passing of the present generation, might conceivably prove inconvenient'. It was decided that a pause of three minutes would be too long and that a pause of one minute, 'as adopted in the United States of America on the occasion of President Roosevelt's funeral', would be 'more impressive'.[10]

The idea was accepted by the War Cabinet subject to the approval of George V. That approval was forthcoming and it was agreed to announce a silence of two minutes. The request for a national pause was carried by all newspapers on 7 November, as a personal request from the King:

Tuesday next, November 11, is the first anniversary of the Armistice, which stayed the world wide carnage of the four preceding years and marked the victory of Right and Freedom. I believe that my people in every part of the Empire fervently wish to perpetuate the memory of the Great Deliverance, and of those who have laid down their lives to achieve it. To afford an opportunity for the universal expression of this feeling, it is my desire and hope that at the hour when the Armistice came into force, the eleventh hour of the eleventh day of the eleventh month, there may be for the brief space of two minutes a complete suspension of all our normal activities...

No elaborate organisation appears to be required. At a given signal, which can easily be arranged to suit the circumstances of each locality, I believe that we shall all gladly interrupt our business and pleasure, whatever it may be and unite in this simple service of Silence and Remembrance.[11]

On 11 November newspapers carried reminders and editorials discussing the silence:

In quiet graves beyond the seas sleep a million British men who paid the price of victory... It is our duty to see that they did not die in vain, and for the accomplishment of that duty all classes must combine as they did to win the war, unselfishly and harmoniously. There must be a truce in domestic quarrels, an end to industrial strife. We must all pull together lest the rewards of victory be thrown away.[12]

This editorial, from the *Daily Express*, shows how the objects of the silence were presented to the public. The concern with unity, with over-ruling dissent and with legitimating the government and more broadly the existing order of society, are implicit. The two minutes of silence was to symbolise a harmony which would overcome conflict. This meant that the commemoration would, in practice, be a defence of the existing order.

Nonetheless, it is vital to qualify this picture of the operation of an 'invented tradition'. Ritual may be defined by those who invent it as having a certain significance and a certain meaning, but it is not always going to mean exactly the same thing to those who practice it. In a plural society there can be alternative definitions of meanings. Armistice Day would always produce competing discourses surrounding the ritual. The *Daily Herald* welcomed the idea of a silence, but placed a very different interpretation on what the silence should mean:

> You are asked to be silent for two minutes to-day, to be silent and pause in your labours, to remember this day and this hour last year...
>
> What will you remember and what will you forget? You will remember, mothers, the gay sons you have lost; wives, you will think of the husbands who went out in the mist of the winter morning – the mist that sent cold chills round the heart – never to come back. And brothers will think of brothers and friends of friends, all lying dead today under an alien soil.
>
> But what will you forget? The crime that called these men to battle... The war that was to end war and in reality did not?..
>
> Make the most of this day of official remembrance. By the sacred memory of those lost to you, swear to yourself this day at 11 o'clock, that never again, God helping you, shall the peace and happiness of the world fall into the murderous hands of a few cynical old men.[13]

The *Daily Herald* took the view that the 'peace' of 1919 was far from complete. Allied forces were still involved in the intervention against Soviet Russia which was in the throes of civil war. A murderous guerilla campaign was being fought in Ireland.[14] The RAF was bombing Kurdish tribesmen in Northern Iraq; Germany was being blockaded to prevent supplies of material for heavy industry.[15] Until such injustices were rectified and all the violence ended, the two minutes' silence would be an aspiration towards a genuine international peace rather than a celebration of its reality.

The two minutes' silence from the very beginning had both behavioural and ideational elements. What people did during the 'national pause' was important, but great significance was also placed on what they thought. During that two minutes people were not expected to be empty of all thought and emotion. It was expected that the time would be filled with private contemplation of the meaning of the war, with prayer, with a renewed commitment to certain goals. The next section of this chapter will describe what people did during the first silence, how it was signalled, how it was organised and how it was received. However in many ways the most significant part of the silence was the language that surrounded it and which shaped what it meant to people. The success of the competing languages surrounding Armistice Day would depend to a great extent on their ability to define the groups to which these languages appealed. This will be dealt with in subsequent sections.

A Silent Pause

For two minutes after the hour of eleven had struck yesterday morning Plymouth stood inanimate with the nation... Two minutes before the hour the maroons boomed out their warning in one long drawn out note... As the hour struck a great silence swept over the town. People halted in their walks chatter ceased as if by magic, traffic stopped and the rumbling note of industry stayed.[16]

Silence was something that many of the inhabitants of urban Britain may have barely known. By the early twentieth century there existed the continuous background noise of a modern society; the constant sound of people talking and moving in densely populated areas and the sounds of traffic, motorised and horsedrawn, would have been ever present, varying only in intensity. It would have been difficult to imagine what a city would be like without deliberate noise; 'Nobody can imagine what a silent London – still for two minutes – is like. No Traffic, no business no talking – nothing for a brief but sacred space of time'[17], as the *Daily Express* stated on the day of the first silence. It was urban Britain which felt the sensation of silence most powerfully. For example in Belfast, 'it was particularly impressive. The sudden hush of great industrial works could almost be felt'.[18] Although rural areas seem to have observed the silence equally faithfully, the impact of the first silence appears to have been a great deal less overwhelming.

The silence was signalled in various ways. Four principal means existed for alerting the population that 11 a.m. had arrived. Maroons were both visible and audible; they were used in London in 1919 [19] and in other centres such as Plymouth, Birmingham and Bradford. They were also used in some east coast communities, where the lifeboat stations and coastguards provided the signal, for example at Cromer and Mandesley. Artillery gunfire, which was clearly audible over a wide distance, was used in Leeds and in Edinburgh. Sirens were not much used in 1919, although the use of sirens was to grow in popularity, they were used in 1919 only where such devices were available, coastal communities such as Devon and Cornwall fishing villages, at the port of Yarmouth, and in mining and quarrying communities. Some large port cities such as Newcastle and Swansea also made use of harbour sirens. The most common form of signalling the silence was the use of bells, particularly church bells, but also the bells of town hall clocks (which was the subsidiary signal in Leeds). Cathedral towns such as Truro, Exeter, Durham and

York used the Cathedral or Minster bells as the main signal, as did Glasgow. In Norwich, the 'time ball' of the town clock was used despite some doubts as to whether it would be sufficiently audible.[20]

The silence could be observed in one of two ways. It could be observed as a pause in the every-day business of life, in which regular activities were carried on up to the moment of the silence. Alternatively it was possible to go to some specific site, either sacred or secular, to be with a crowd of people who had gathered for the purpose of marking the silence. For many, if not most, it would be impossible to leave everyday responsibilities in order to join in a crowd, so the silence would be observed either in transit or in the place of work. For those who, for whatever reason, did have freedom of action, there was a choice of possible venues at which to gather in cities and large towns.

Very few permanent war memorials had been built by November 1919, and most of those that had been built were probably the simpler memorials in the smaller communities. The choice of where to assemble was between the civic centre or a place of worship. In Leeds, 'a large gathering of citizens assembled in the square and on the steps of the Town Hall'. In Bradford many people laid wreaths at the temporary cenotaph in Victoria Square.[21] Such temporary monuments acted as a focus in a number of places.[22] At Bridlington:

> A large white cross was erected near Wellington Gardens, Prospect Street, and at eleven o'clock there was a large company of men and women present. The mayor, councillor Lambert, who lost his elder son Lieut S. Lambert in the war, placed a beautiful wreath on the cross, and the local branch of the Discharged and Demobilised Soldiers, Sailors and Airmen paid a like tribute to their fallen comrades. The company sung the hymn, "Peace, Perfect Peace", followed by " O God Our Help In Ages Past" and a verse of the National Anthem.[23]

In Exeter, the Salvation Army band headed a parade to the Guildhall, 'where an enormous crowd assembled'; there was also a crowded congregation at Matins in the Cathedral.[24] Many people attended church services throughout the country, but the *Daily Express* considered that those who did so had missed the more impressive demonstration of feeling: 'There was no mechanism of ritual or service – those who went to church missed the stupendous thrill and mystery of the greater service in which men and women, confronting their God, held communion without the hindrance of formula.'[25] In Birmingham the silence was described as 'an occasion for high simplicity rather than elaborate ritual, for the tribute of the heart rather than outward show'; ceremonial additions, 'marred more than they emphasised the solemnity of the event'.[26]

As this suggests, the informality should not be exaggerated. In London there was certainly a mechanism of ritual, albeit a secular one (prayers were not said at the Cenotaph in 1919). Royalty and politicians rather than religious acts were the focus. Early in the morning the King and Queen sent a wreath to be placed at the foot of the Cenotaph; crowds gathered around the temporary Cenotaph in anticipation:

> By half-past ten there was a great gathering round the Cenotaph, and the bearers of wreaths had difficulty passing them on to be placed at the base of the column. The mounted police, with great skill and courtesy diverted the crowd from the main road to the foot paths, and here the sightseers stood until the murmur passed down from Whitehall, "Lloyd George is coming". There was a slight rush forward. Few of those assembled saw the Prime Minister with bent white head, carrying a wreath of orchids and roses with a background of laurels... Then the hush came ... There is nothing under heaven so full of awe as the complete silence of a mighty crowd.[27]

Bill Grant, an Australian serviceman present at the Cenotaph ceremony, described the scene in a long letter to his family. Clearly impressed and moved, he mentioned the wreaths of the King and Queen and the Prime Minister and the wreath sent by the French. Then, 'eleven struck & the maroons & Guns crashed out their signals. Men bared their heads. Soldiers stood at the salute & women bowed their heads. Traffic stopped and everything became silent.' Near to where he stood, 'a child started to cry but was quieted by its mother – but that cry sounded 100 times louder than ordinary because of the great hush, who knows but the mother there whether or not the father of that child was represented in that Column of Stone'. He went on to imagine, 'a Great Phantom army' passing the Cenotaph, 'Swiftly, Silently & singing as they went a song of triumph or victory'.[28]

Even those who had discussed the silence before the public announcement and might have anticipated public reaction were stunned by the response. King George V wrote that, 'It was most impressive'.[29] Sir Henry Wilson described the crowd at the Cenotaph as 'a wonderful sight' whilst H.A.L Fisher noted of the Prime Minister that 'LG was much impressed' and had engaged his fellow cabinet members in a discussion on 'the moral value of silence' as they had returned to work.[30]

Yet it was not so much these deliberate gatherings of people as the abrupt interruption of everyday life that was truly impressive. A description of the impact of the silence for 1921 in the shops of Edinburgh would have been equally applicable to 1919: 'At the booming of the gun buyers immediately stopped buying, servers stopped serving, parcels in the process of parcelling were laid aside and money for the moment ceased to pass between buyers and sellers... For two minutes everyone stood with bowed head. Then the tide of business rolled on, marketing was resumed and thoughts came back to material things like butter, boots and bacon.'[31] In a striking simile, *The Nation* compared the abrupt halt in London to 'the mechanical scene in a Swiss toy show after the penny in the slot had done its work'.[32] Newspapers throughout the country tried to describe the impact of people stopping suddenly during their everyday business:

He must have a strangely cold heart who was not moved by the impressive scenes witnessed in Leeds yesterday... As eleven o' clock drew near there was a certain hesitancy in the movements in the streets. The day was a market day, and the centre of the city was thronged...a distant signal gun was heard and immediately men uncovered their heads and women bowed their faces and all stood silently until the two minutes had passed.[33]

Perhaps the most impressive manifestation of this interruption of ordinary life came on the railways:

And so on that winter morning a great silence fell over the North British – a silence symbolic of the stillness that had fallen over the battlefields when the guns had stopped firing a year ago to the very minute. All over the system from Northumberland to Inverness-shire, on mainlines and branches, in sheds and yards, passenger trains, goods trains and shunting engines stopped wherever they happened to be. Engine crews stood bare headed at their footplates, passengers sat silent in their compartments. Great stations fell suddenly silent, travellers froze into immobility. People had much to remember; few in those trains and stations had not lost a friend or relative in the recent war. Of the 4,836 NB men who joined the armed forces 775 had not returned.[34]

It was not only transport that came to a stop. Telephone exchanges ceased putting through calls.[35] All over the industrial north, textile mills stopped the machinery for the two minutes.[36] In the Midlands, engineering firms halted. In the south west, the naval dockyard at Devonport stopped still, at the other end of the country Rosyth did likewise. In many schools a special assembly was called:

Just before eleven o'clock, the boys of Bradford Grammar School assembled in the main hall and members of the school O.T.C were drawn up on the terrace. The King's proclamation was read and upon the first maroon being fired from the Town Hall, the cadets were brought to attention, and their officers saluted as the Union Jack was dipped. After the period of silence the boys sang the national anthem.[37]

In the mining community of Huthwaite, 'opportunity was taken of presenting commemoration mugs to the scholars to the number of 1,600', after which, 'The scholars attending the church schools were taken to church where the vicar conducted service', then, 'a procession was formed and joining the council school scholars, they all assembled in the market where the National Anthem was sung. The children were then dispersed and were given a half day's holiday'.[38]

The silence struck individuals with an irresistible force. People were swept into the collective emotion. A correspondent of *The Times* described how he had been travelling on a bus with friends through southwest London. In the minutes before the silence, they had been 'discussing with a forced cynicism of which each of us was secretly ashamed, some supposedly humurous sides of the proposed standstill'. Just before eleven o'clock the bus pulled to a halt outside a small factory. The correspondent saw, '10 or a dozen factory workers wearing their overalls but not their caps, standing rigidly at attention. Glancing along the road we saw at irregular intervals perhaps twenty people, mostly women...some with children in perambulators. Without exception they stood still... It was then that we four cynics...realized that we too were on our feet with our heads uncovered'. At the end of the silence the factory workers gave three cheers for victory and the four 'scoffers' on the bus, three of whom, significantly, were ex-soldiers, joined the cheering.[39]

The impact of the 'Silence' had been enormous. It was immediately obvious that the general public had universally responded to the appeal and that furthermore it seemed to many people that the Silence (as it was soon to be called) ought to become a regular act of commemoration, occurring annually: 'Do not let us neglect so fine an instrument. Let us at the eleventh hour of the eleventh month of every year hold this service of pity and thanksgiving'.[40]

The success of the Silence as a means of commemoration drew on several sources. It could be taken to symbolise perfectly the moment when the guns ceased firing on the Western Front, signalling the end of the slaughter and the return of the prospect of life. It also carried a religious sense of 'silent prayer' and communion between the living and the dead.[41] In Birmingham, one newspaper described the silence as 'emphatically a moment for the Quaker ideal of worship to predominate'.[42]

The lasting appeal of the Silence rested, above all, on its double nature as public and private commemoration. The Silence enforced public unity of action; everyone had to stop and silently pay their respects at the eleventh hour.The solidarity of the community was enforced by the fear of shame. This is close to Durkheim's concept of mourning as a public duty enforced regardless of the 'affective state' of the individual.[43]

Paradoxically, the Silence was also an intensely *private* activity. Each individual was alone for two minutes with his or her own thoughts. It is difficult as a historian to reconstruct that experience for any one individual, let alone for millions over a period of twenty years. Nonetheless, to refuse to attempt to do so would be to describe the ritual of Armistice Day only in the most superficial terms and to fail to address the issues that contemporaries believed to be most important.

The only way to attempt to discover these deep private meanings is, paradoxically, to examine the public legacy. Through an examination of the discursive context in which Armistice Day occurred, it should be possible to gain an insight into what those two minutes meant to people. It seems improbable that there would be many people capable of finding new and original meanings in the observance of Armistice Day year after year. It is more probable that most of the time they would be guided by the public language surrounding the ceremony.

The discourse surrounding Armistice Day was directed at particular groups. Appeals were made on behalf of these groups to provide legitimation to various interpretations of what Armistice Day should mean. Various religious, political and social meanings were expressed, but ultimately most appeals based their legitimacy on their construction of the image of one of two groups, the bereaved families or the veterans of the war. The test of possible meanings would be their ability to be seen to be meeting the needs of one of these groups in society. It is therefore necessary to examine what those needs were likely to be.

And I Think My Heart Was Broken by the War[44]

Armistice Day was part of a sustained and creative effort to give meaning and purpose to the terrifying and unexpected experience of mass death.[45] To quantify such an experience seems cold-blooded. Nonetheless, an attempt ought to be made to do so. Somewhere in the region of three million Britons lost a close relative in the First World War, a substantial number in a population of under 42 million.[46] This figure represents only the 'primary bereaved', (parents, siblings, widows and orphans). In addition, the 'secondary bereaved' ought to be considered, those who lost a cousin, uncle, son-in-law, a colleague, a friend or a neighbour.[47] This category, those who would have under normal circumstances, attended the funeral of the deceased, encompassed virtually the entire population. Most poignant of all of these, looming large in the post war imagination, were the young women who lost their fiancés.[48]

Another category of bereaved must be considered; the war veterans themselves. Every frontline soldier experienced loss, the loss of comrades who were often intensely bonded with those who survived. The combination of this loss, often horrific and witnessed at close range, with the more general effects of surviving the 'carnival of death' (memories of living with the dead, memories of the fear of death, close escapes from death, memories of killing) produced a complex experience of bereavement, possibly even more intense than the loss of a close relative (and many veterans may have suffered that in addition). Somewhere in the region of five million men served and survived. Of these, perhaps three million had some experience of the quintessential horror, trench warfare on the western front.[49]

Mourning and Meaning: Some Thoughts on Grief and its Expression.

> War creates wounds – figuratively as well as literally... These wounds are acknowledged as the war is discussed and clarified and as we work toward understanding individual losses, personal tragedies in the light of positive national experience. Healing occurs as we bestow meaning on the war experience.[50]

For the sake of clarity, a distinction will be made between grief, mourning and bereavement. Bereavement refers to the objective situation of someone who has experienced the loss of someone significant to them through death. Grief is the emotional(affective) response to that loss. It includes psychological and somatic reactions. Mourning refers to acts expressive of grief. Mourning is shaped by the customs of a given social or cultural group, which create expectations of the correct behaviour for one bereaved.

It can be seen from these definitions that grief, the emotional, psychological and medical aspects of which are stressed, is seen as the realm of the psychologist, whereas mourning, the cultural determinism of which has been stressed since Durkheim, has been the realm of anthropologists. Recent trends which stress the social and cultural construction of personality and personal psychology represent a challenge to this view.

The neo-Durkheimian model of such 'cultural' activity as mourning would see it as mediating between social structure, which varies from society to society, and the psychological imperatives (distancing from the corpse, release from affective bonds, coming to terms with separation) which are universal. This form of analysis is described by Geertz as being 'widespread to the point of orthodoxy in social anthropology, social history and social psychology.'[51]

Such a model can easily incorporate wide variations in mourning practice. It acknowledges that an Irish wake would be intensely offensive to a Balinese and that the controlled dispassion of a mourning Balinese would be equally strange to an Irish family. These differences are related to the structures and codes of the societies involved.

What this model is less successful in illuminating is the possibility of wide variations in the reactions of individuals in different societies to the death of close relatives. It is not simply that a Navajo and a Japanese behave differently with regard to the dead, it seems unquestionable that they *feel* differently.[52] The Navajo horror of anything to do with corpses and pervasive terror of ghosts[53] would be considered pathological in Japanese society. Not only individual behaviour but the individual's thoughts and emotions would be maladjusted. Likewise, reverence for one's (immediate) ancestors would seem a form of madness amongst the Navajo. It is not just mourning practices but the dynamics of grief itself which are culturally variable. The components (separation, distancing from the corpse etc.) are arranged so differently that they present completely different profiles of what grief is. Acceptable amounts of emotional display, length of mourning and reverence for the memory of the departed are only the visible signs, but what is socially permissible, circumscribes what is psychologically possible (at least in the sense that deviation from those norms is seen as madness or sickness, rather than as legitimate grief). This is not to say that everyone in a society will react to death in the same way; this is manifestly untrue. Some will adhere more closely to the cultural ideal than others, showing more or less of the classic grief symptoms which reflect the state of mind. It is merely to point out that there are different sets of personal responses possible in different cultures. Presumably a more plural culture can tolerate a wider variety of grief than a monolithic one.

What is true of different societies may also be true of the same society in different periods. For example, Queen Victoria's prolonged mourning for her deceased husband unquestionably reflected an intense personal grief. Although some Victorians may have considered her reaction excessive, the majority seem to have found it legitimate, even admirable.[54] Today such a prolonged and extreme period of grief would certainly be considered pathological and 'a suitable case for treatment'.[55]

The example above is directly relevant to this study. It seems probable that the First World War marks a watershed in attitudes to death. The requirements of national morale prevented extravagant mourning in wartime, forcing prominent people to mourn for only a short time in public and with as stoic an attitude as they could muster.[56] This set a standard of public behaviour to be expected. It can be argued that after some time had passed, the limitations on acceptable public behaviour began to have an influence on the psychological structure of grief. This was not simply repression of emotion as some psychologists[57] and many historians of death have argued[58], but a changed set of parameters in the psychologically possible, a new *emotional* reaction to death.[59] As Robert Solomon argues, 'an emotion is a system of concepts, beliefs attitudes and desires, virtually all of which are context-bound, historically developed and culture specific.'[60]

However, there is a countervailing factor to be considered. This process of 'denial of death' was only beginning during the period of the war. For at least one group of the bereaved, the unexpected nature of bereavement represented a profound emotional shock. Falling rates of infant mortality since the 1880s had created for the first time the situation which we now consider to be natural, the expectation that children would outlive their parents. Perhaps for the first time in history, parents were emotionally unprepared for the death of their children. Attitudes that have become common-place in modern society had come into being. Children became a way for parents to vicariously fulfil their ambitions, they satisfied cravings for family continuity and personal immortality. The emotional defences that had reconciled previous generations to the loss of children, not least of which was the feeling that an experience so commonplace was in some sense 'natural', had been broken down. The loss of a child had become a peculiarly traumatic experience, as it has remained to this day.[61]

The parents of those who were killed in the First World War suffered emotional stress to an unparalleled degree, victims of a transitional moment in the history of attitudes towards death. Their affective state was miserable, a combination of the worst of Victorian grief and modern sense of loss, but without access to the defensive strategies of either period, extravagant public mourning or 'denial of death.' As noted above the needs of wartime morale prevented the former, yet the latter, the long term internalisation of processes in the mores of mourning, would not be effective for at least a generation.

The severity of the experience of parental bereavement is amply documented. Herbert Asquith described his feelings on hearing of the death of his son Raymond in a heartbreaking fashion, 'The war has sucked up so much of what was loveable and full of promise... Whatever pride I had in the past and whatever hope I had for the future – by much the largest part was invested in him. Now all that is gone'.[62] Bonar Law lost two sons in the war. Lord Blake describes Bonar Law's reaction with striking metaphors, 'Night seemed to have descended upon him. For the moment he was incapable of work and could only sit despondently, gazing into vacancy. All those dark clouds which were never far below the horizon of his thought came rolling up obliterating light and happiness.'[63]

It was not only amongst the political elite that such devastation was felt. Many of the middle-class and the more secure segment of the working-class had become practitioners of family planning, limiting their families to one male child. The result between 1914 and 1918 was all too often devastating:

> Every spare farthing had been spent on his upbringing since childhood. He was to be the pride and assistance of his parents when they attained old age. Then from all the terraces and villas which occupy the hills around great cities came the news that no blood sprinkled on the lintel

or door post had been of any avail against the Angel of Death. A house had been left henceforth forever desolate.[64]

Sir Harry Lauder might stand as emblematic of these people:

> I could not bring myself to open the telegram. I knew what it contained. God! the agonies I suffered that bright New Year's morning... hundreds of thousands, aye, millions of fathers and mothers will know just what I passed through for many hours and for many weeks. My only son. The one child that God had given us.[65]

These examples of extreme trauma can be multiplied by thousands. Kipling was haunted for the rest of his life by the death of his son John and expressed it in his poetry. Sir Arthur Conan Doyle tirelessly promoted spiritualism after the death of his son.[66]

Britain during the 1920s and 1930s was a country with millions of its population trying to come to terms with the death of loved ones, particularly in the case of parents trying to deal with severe emotional shock and lasting grief. The process of coming to terms with death had two interrelated elements. There are two ways in which sudden death is coped with, in making the necessary movement on to the phase of 'acceptance'. The first is discovering the ability to face up to memories of the deceased. Being able to see the body, for example, is a useful component of the grieving process. The use of the name of the dead person by the bereaved and others is also a stage in coming to terms with the death.

The second element on the road to recovery from the trauma of bereavement is overcoming the inevitable guilt feelings when a loved one dies. The best way of doing this is to find meaning and purpose in the death. In this respect it is necessary to construct a story which makes sense of the death and finds some good in the event.[67]

Both of these needs were catered for by the process of memorialisation. Physical memorials were created in huge numbers in Britain during the 1920s. The majority of these memorials were lists of names, names which were often read out on Armistice Day. Cathedrals and churches took possession of Books of Remembrance which also listed names. Both of these methods revived the names of the dead and encouraged a public *naming* of the dead. This is seen by psychologists specialising in bereavement as crucial to the process of recovery. Another form of memorial was the Tomb of the Unknown Warrior which provided a surrogate *body* for those who could not hope to ever see the body of the family member lost.

These physical memorials were given meaning by a language of memorialisation, which gave meaning to the loss. This language during the 1920s drew heavily on pre-war rhetoric of God, Empire, King and Country, on notions of sacrifice and on presenting the war in terms of a crusade for human dignity and liberty. The 'Big Words' were used in abundance because they were the best form of giving comfort to those who grieved.

Comforting and supporting those suffering from grief was the principal rationale for Armistice Day in the United Kingdom. In describing the ritual as collective mourning it is important to give nuance to the actual meanings involved. Many were mourning a close personal loss, but many were not. The majority of those who commemorated the war dead on 11 November were doing so in solidarity with those who had lost family members. In acknowledging and honouring their sacrifice, particularly the loss of children, they may have made it more possible to bear. The two minutes silence, the first and pre-eminent ritual of mourning, was perfect as a demonstration of mute solidarity with the bereaved.[68] But the healing process would require words and actions as well as silence and inaction.

Memorialisation

Carry our lowly, our meek, our innocent dead;
Saying to each and all our silent mourners,
Mother or widow or sister, 'This is your loved one.'
This is life you gave.[69]

Mute and immovable, and with bowed head we stood:
Two minutes passed: words rose, dreams, fears
Chaos and quiet, old pain and sudden tears
But we remembered and for this were glad.[70]

Armistice Day in 1920 was centred on a funeral. On that day an 'Unknown Warrior of the Great War' was buried at Westminster Abbey. Within a week somewhere between 500,000 and a million people had paid homage at the tomb. It was one of the most striking public demonstrations of emotion in British history.

The story has been told in detail elsewhere,[71] but in outline it is as follows. In early October 1920 the Dean of Westminster Abbey, apparently acting on a suggestion by the wartime padre, David Railton, wrote to George V suggesting that an unknown body from the battlefields of France and Flanders should be disintered and reburied with full military honours in Westminster Abbey. The King did not approve of the idea, believing that it would be distasteful and 'would reopen the war wound which is gradually healing'.[72] The Dean, undeterred, approached Lloyd George who was enthusiastic. The Prime Minister persuaded the King and Lord Curzon was placed in charge of arrangements. A Committee chaired by Curzon planned the ceremonies of the day. The Committee comprised Curzon, Lord Lee, Winston Churchill, Walter Long, Alfred Mond, Mr Shortt and Colonel Storr (secretary).[73] It was attended by service representatives, by Sir Douglas Dawson (Lord Chamberlain's office, to liaise with the King) and by Dean Ryle of Westminster Abbey. It is clear from reading the Committee reports and conclusions that the bulk of the ceremony was Curzon's personal inspiration. For example, Churchill was assigned committee duty but did not attend any of the meetings.

On 9 November 1920, according to most press accounts, six bodies were exhumed from Ypres, the Somme, Cambrai, the Aisne, the Marne and Arras. The bodies were taken to Ypres where a blindfolded officer selected one of the coffins.[74] The body was returned to Britain on HMS *Verdun*, in a great coffin made of oak from a tree at Hampton Court palace. It was delivered to Dover and brought in a special railway carriage to Victoria Station where it rested in a temporary chapel overnight.

On the morning of 11 November the pall-bearers arrived to accompany the coffin. They were Admirals Meux, Beatty, Jackson, Sturdee and Madden; Field Marshals French, Haig, Methuen and Wilson; Generals Horne and Byng and Air Marshal Trenchard. At the Abbey, 100 holders of the Victoria Cross lined the nave. The Royal Family had pride of place, but the congregation was primarily composed of widows and mothers who had lost sons.[75] There was no foreign representation at the service. The coffin was interred at the foot of the statue of the 'great commoner', Chatham. After the committal the grave was filled in with a hundred sandbags of earth from all the main battlefields and a large slab of Tournai marble, a gift from the Belgian people, was placed on top, inscribed simply, 'An Unknown Warrior'.

The archetypal nature of the ritual was uncanny. Thirteen years previously Robert Hertz had written on the collective representation of death, drawing on studies of secondary burial rites in Borneo. The picture he drew could be applied almost without adaptation to the events of 11 November 1920. Peter Metcalf and Richard

Huntington summarise his conclusions: 'many peoples conceive of a period when the mortal is neither alive or finally dead.' This reflects precisely the uncertainty embodied in the words 'missing in action'. At the end of the 'intermediary period' there is a 'great feast' during which, 'the remains of the deceased are recovered, ritually processed and moved to a new location... the irreducible minimum is the time required for the bones to become dry and free of decaying flesh'. This accords well with the lapse between the war and 1920, particularly as there was a clear bias in selection for an older body. During the intermediate period, the souls of the dead are an uncomfortable presence in need of propitiation by elaborate ceremonial. Once again there is a parallel, the two minutes silence fits well in this context. The dead threaten illness and social strife, which in the context of 1919–20 seems interesting. Finally, 'the "great feast" terminates this miserable period by honouring the now dry bones of the deceased, confirming the soul's arrival in the land of the ancestors and marking the *reestablishment of normal relations among the survivors* '.[76] (My italics)

The event touched the nation in a way that few other events have ever done. The *Daily Mirror* special edition, which was bought for its superb photographic coverage, sold 1,907,685 copies, a record for a single issue of that paper.[77] The same paper reported that on the 15 November there was still a seven mile queue of pilgrims waiting to lay wreaths at the Cenotaph and the number of pilgrims from the provinces were causing 'abnormal rail traffic'.[78] Prior to the interment the *Daily Herald* had been hostile:

Who have organised the pageant?
Politicians press and pulpit. The people who helped make the war, who prolonged the war, who grew rich out of the war. The Man who Won the War. These men have by a supreme piece of impudence, issued special tickets to themselves to view the obsequies of their victim.

While the great pageant is thus used for the emotional doping of the people, other and named victims, hundreds and thousands of them, plead in vain for even what they had before the war. They are workless, they beg in the streets.

I understand all the big restaurants are providing as the second part of the days festivities, elaborate dinners with special increased prices.[79]

The rhetoric of this criticism was to re-emerge stronger still within the next few years (see Chapter 2), but in 1920 the *Daily Herald* was forced to take note of the genuine symbolic power of the Tomb of the Unknown Warrior and the strength of the popular reaction to it.

'As we stood there in silence while the muffled drums began to whisper, as it were a million miles away and grew and grew into the sound of a rushing wind, the stone atrocities faded, the vulgarity and bad taste were forgotten, the pomp and circumstance forgiven.'[80]

One hundred thousand wreaths were laid at the newly unveiled Cenotaph by those who had visited the grave of the Unknown Warrior:

> For by now the monument is a mighty bed of blossoms. There are wonderful woven wreaths of exotic blooms, shining waxen against the rich darkness of evergreens; and there are countless humble sheaves of chrysanthemums bought from the hawkers in the roadway. There are glorious crimson roses, roses of love which will always endure; and there are sprays of violets... There was a very small boy stopping to lay a tiny plant among the flowers last night, who brought tears to the eyes even of policemen standing by and who caused a woman who heard him to burst out in sobs" Oh Mummy" he cried, "What a lovely garden my Daddy's got." [81]

Despite the mass of floral tributes, the Cenotaph was the subsidiary monument in that week. It was the tomb of the Unknown Warrior that fulfilled a need that the Cenotaph, which is literally translated from Greek as 'empty tomb'[82], could not fulfil. The need to have some contact with what could at least be imagined to be the real body of the lost son or husband was a terrible necessity for so many of those who knew nothing of the fate of those they had lost. For example: 'There was a woman carrying a great bunch of white heather tied with a tartan knot who had been journeying since the early hours of the morning from a homestead on the slopes of Pentlands. Her man was one of the "missing" and in her heart was the thought that he might be the "unknown" '.[83]

An even more explicit identification was reported in 1921. An elderly lady brought a wreath of chrysanthemums to the Cenotaph after having been informed by a clairvoyant that 'the bones of her son lay under the tomb of the Unknown Warrior in the Abbey'.[84]

It was the civilian bereaved who felt these emotions towards the 'Tomb of the Unknown Warrior', particularly women.[85] By contrast ex-servicemen, both in 1920 and in subsequent years, seem to have felt little towards the Unknown Warrior. The sheer quantity of unknown and unknowable dead bodies that littered the battlefields of the war was well known to the ex-servicemen, the statistical improbability of the Unknown Warrior being anyone known to them would be all too evident. It would be difficult to achieve the necessary suspension of disbelief to relate emotionally to an unmarked corpse.

The power and effect of the Tomb of the Unknown Warrior was based on the lack of a name. While the warrior was nameless, he could act as a surrogate body for the mourning of thousands. Yet the second requirement of coming to terms with grief was the naming of the dead. The year after the entombment of the Unknown Warrior there was a smaller service in a lesser cathedral which can stand as representative of many such events in the early 1920s. On 11 November 1921, the Lord Lieutenant of Cornwall presented a Book of Remembrance, containing the names of 5,003 Cornishmen, to the dean and chapter of Truro Cathedral. 'The function was one of Diocesan and County importance and was attended by representatives of all parts of the County. The cathedral was filled and seats were reserved for those who had lost relatives. A pathetic sight was the number of schoolchildren, many of them quite tiny tots, whose fathers had made the great sacrifice'.[86]

Such local rituals were the supplement and counterpart to the great national rituals at Westminster Abbey and the Cenotaph. In the early part of the inter-war period, before the integrating effects of radio were widely felt, they may well have been the most significant component of Armistice Day.[87]

The creation of permanent war memorials, a process that went on through the early 1920s, provided a local focus. Surprisingly few appear to have actually been unveiled on 11 November.[88] It seems likely that the need for a local site at which the bereaved could pay homage and the urgent need for naming the dead (most small memorials consist of a list of names) meant that war memorials were brought into use as soon as they could be built. (The larger provincial city memorials, which usually did not carry lists of names, could be constructed more slowly because the sub-localities in cities, such as parishes, would already have catered for that need.)

On 11 November 1920, the war memorial was unveiled in the village church of Ilfracombe, Devon. The service was held in the evening:

> The service which was of a very impressive character was attended by members and officials of the Urban Council, Territorials, Comrades of the Great War, VAD nurses, coastguards, Church Lads Brigade and Freechurch ministers, headed by the band of the comrades of the Great

War. The service opened with Kipling's recessional and the hymn "The son of God goes forth to war" was sung immediately before the unveiling ceremony.[89]

On the same evening in Leeds, 'the Lord Mayor of Leeds and the Lady Mayoress were present at the unveiling of war memorials at Christ Church, Hunslet, Leeds, the dedication being performed by the Bishop of Richmond'.[90]

Sheffield unveiled its war memorial on 11 November 1925. The City Council assembled at 10.40 a.m. and processed to the new memorial. At 11.00 a.m. the Silence was observed, followed by the hymn, 'O God our help in ages past'. The first wreath was placed on the memorial by the Lady Mayoress. This was followed by the first verse of the National Anthem. Buglers from the Hallamshire Battalion of the York and Lancashire Regiment sounded the Last Post and Reveille.[91] All of the standard elements of the Armistice Day ceremonial were incorporated in the proceedings.

At Llandudno the dedication service was longer. It began with the hymn 'O God, our help in ages past' and was followed by a prayer by the Rector. The monument was unveiled and dedicated by the Bishop of Bangor and the ex-moderator of the Presbyterian assembly. The two minutes' Silence was then observed. After the Silence wreaths were placed on the memorial by relatives of the 'Fallen' and others. The second hymn was 'Iesu Cyffail f'enaid cu' and this was followed by 'Hen Wlad fy Nhadau'. Finally the first verse of the National Anthem was sung.[92]

Once war memorials were in place they acted as the natural focus in smaller communities, for example in Norfolk:

> Armistice Day was observed at Holt with the two minutes silence at 11 a.m. immediately after which a short service was taken by the rector, the Rev H.A. King, near the war memorial in the market place at which several of the members of the British Legion were in the congregation. Beautiful wreaths adorned the war memorial, one bearing a card inscribed '1914–1919, Holt and District Branch of the British Legion, Lest we forget!'... Wreaths were also placed on the memorial by relatives of the deceased.[93]

In an even smaller community in Cornwall, 'The war memorial was the scene of a service at Fowey... The hymn "O God our help in Ages past" was sung impressively by the large number present. A maroon was fired at eleven and intense silence was kept for two minutes. Mr Stern offered prayers and the service concluded with the singing of the National Anthem.'[94]

The village of Warcop in Westmoreland had sent sixty four men to war, one in ten of the population; its memorial bore eleven names. Sixty years later, Edward Short remembered the annual services of his boyhood in the 1920s. The children were marched from school by their schoolmaster, an ex-sergeant major, and lined up, 'by the memorial with military precision'. The ritual was a, 'great occasion with the gentry and most of the village folk huddled around looking very sad and shivering in the early cold'. He felt that the dead were, 'still part of our little community'.[95]

One possible act of local commemoration was the laying of wreaths by the local veterans organisations, the National Federation of Discharged and Demobilised Sailors and Soldiers, the National Association of Discharged Sailors and Soldiers, and the Comrades of the Great War. After the amalgamation of these bodies in 1921, this was done by the British Legion.[96] In communities large enough to have any form of civic structure at all, local civic representatives paid tribute on Armistice Day. In some communities, schools or youth organisations participated prominently in the ceremonies. In 1921, at Nanpean in Cornwall , 'A white wreath was laid by staff and children of Foxhole school before the silent period and afterwards a wreath of red, white and blue flowers from the children and staff of Nanpean schools was laid by little Gertrude Moses, she being the eldest girl in attendance whose father had made the supreme sacrifice for his country.' The children then passed the memorial and laid bunches of flowers at its base.[97] At St Mary's Church of England Infant School, at Tetbury in Gloucestershire, the usual morning assembly in 1921 was replaced by a visit to the memorial service at the local church by all but the smallest children, they, 'had a little talk and a prayer with Miss Dance'.[98] The gathering in Tetbury was at the memorial tablet in the church because the major civic memorial was a recreation ground.[99]

Clare College at Cambridge University had also taken a pragmatic approach to the subject of memorialisation by building much needed additional accommodation as a 'memorial court'. Yet one of the subscribers to the memorial fund, Lt. Col. Barham, ensured that this pragmatic memorial would function as a sacred space once a year by making it a condition of his donation that at 11 a.m. on 11 November the college would hold a religious memorial service, 'centred upon the placing of a poppy wreath beneath the bronze plaque of the names of the fallen underneath the arch'.[100]

In larger communities, Armistice Day was less focussed. In part this was due to the later construction of memorials. It also was connected with the obvious point that urban populations were naturally dispersed over a wider area at work and at home. Richard Garret has described the first two minutes' silence that he can remember from his childhood as a domestic observance: 'As the hands of the grandfather clock in the hall approached eleven, the household seemed to slow down. When it struck the hour, there were two bangs from far away. Everyone stood silent with their heads bowed... Two minutes passed. My parents and the servants frozen in absorbed immobility, stirred.'[101]

In as far as provincial urban commemoration had a focus, it was the civic centre with its business and administrative surroundings. It seems probable that white collar workers and shop assistants could take a five or ten-minute break in the working day and assemble in the centre on 11 November. In Manchester in 1925, 400 individual employees from the CWS Headquarters 'swelled the assembly' in front of Manchester Town Hall and the next year 'for this purpose only, a short leave of absence with pay was granted to the ex-servicemen in Manchester'. In 1927 leave was also granted in the same way to employees in Newcastle.[102]

The city centre would generally act as a focus regardless of whether the memorial was in the centre or not.[103] In Birmingham the 'Hall of Memory' was opened in 1925, approximately 300 yards from the Town Hall in Victoria Square. In previous years the central meeting place for the two minutes' silence had been the square, and this was incorporated into the 11 November ceremonial in 1925. The civic procession arrived at the town hall at 10.45 a.m. while the police band played solemn music. At 10.55 a.m. maroons signalled the approach of the silence which was signalled by the playing of the Last Post at the Town Hall. The end of the silence was signalled by the same bugler playing Reveille. The band then played 'O God our help in ages past' and the Bishop of Birmingham led the crowd in the Lord's prayer. The National Anthem was then sung. It was only after this, at 11.15 a.m., that the civic procession moved on to the Hall of Memory to lay wreaths. The Lord Mayor placed the first wreath at 11.20 a.m. followed by relatives of the deceased and finally the police laid wreaths on behalf of 'representative bodies'.[104]

This elaboration of ritual was still more marked in Belfast, where the Cenotaph was located on the City Hall grounds. By 1926, Armistice Day in that city required a four-page programme to list the thirty-nine various representative bodies laying wreaths at the

Cenotaph before 11.00 a.m. The list began with the Governor of Northern Ireland, the Lord Mayor of the City and the Prime Minister of Northern Ireland. They were followed by representatives of the forces, by ex-service associations, by the police, civil servants, youth organisations and a whole variety of voluntary organisations. Included in this tribute were organisations as diverse as the Rising Sons of India (an Orange Lodge), The Salvation Army and the Italian Fascists.[105]

In Norwich, 'the difficulty of making a signal which should be heard instantly in every part of the city accounts for the fact that observance tends more and more to concentrate itself on the market place'.[106] By contrast, on 'Remembrance Sunday', the Sunday preceding Armistice Day, the focus in Norwich was the city cemetery and in particular the tomb of Edith Cavell.[107] In 1923, when Armistice Day was on a Sunday, the Salvation Army held a remembrance service at the cemetery which drew a crowd estimated at 30,000.[108]

This pattern of having separate focal points for Armistice Day, on those occasions when it was also a working day as opposed to Remembrance Sunday, was not unique to Norwich. In Plymouth, the city had two impressive war memorials on the 'Hoe' by 11 November 1924, the city memorial, unveiled in May 1923 and the nearby Royal Naval Memorial unveiled in July 1924.[109] Despite this, the focus of Armistice Day remained in the civic centre. The 'Hoe' is perhaps half a mile or more from the true centre of Plymouth and it is horrendously exposed to the weather in November.[110] By contrast the Guildhall square was convenient and sheltered. 'A crowd of many thousands concentrated in the Guildhall Square, Plymouth. Others went to various churches where commemorative services were held, but it was in the Square, where the two minutes' silence gained greater profundity through its contrast with the noises of the traffic that the largest assembly gathered'.[111]

The war memorials in Plymouth were not neglected during November but it was Remembrance Sunday which saw the public gather at the war memorials. When 11 November fell on a Sunday, as it did in 1923, the main gathering took place at the War Memorial rather than in Guildhall Square.[112]

In 1927 it was observed that the number of ex-servicemen present in the gathering in the Guildhall Square was limited and that by far the greater number present were women. Gatherings in public places and in churches were dependent on the ability to move away from the place of work.[113] Women engaged in housework and shopping had a certain degree of control over their time and shop assistants and clerical workers would be more likely to be able to take a break from work in order to gather. As a result, the public face of crowds on Armistice Day was often predominantly female. This in turn helped shape the picture of the bereaved as primarily women. Sometimes this was implicit as in this description of Armistice Day in Penzance:

> It was an impressive sight to watch the faces of that expectant crowd of people with the brilliant sunshine radiating upon their faces, though doubtless many of their hearts were sad at the thought of those dear ones they had once loved and now lost. Fond memories must have stirred of former days when hand clasped the hand it would clasp no more...[114]

This description of those who visited the Tomb of the Unknown Warrior on Armistice Day 1927 made the point more explicitly:

> There were many mothers in that long file; some gripped at the wooden rail a little as they half turned to look at the tomb. Some bent and laid wreaths or bunches of flowers. One woman with a sad suffused face drew from her bosom a single white rose and laid it at the tomb; another placed three bunches of violets. Occasionally a woman knelt and said a short prayer.[115]

Although there were undoubtedly men present at the Abbey, the newspaper item was titled 'Mothers' prayers at warrior's tomb'. In 1922 the *Methodist Recorder* went as far as to say that, 'Remembrance Day is only a national spirit because it is first and foremost a family spirit... The mother and the sister at home will not forget – they above all others.'[116]

By the late 1920s perception was being channelled through rhetorical constructions, one of which was the association of the bereaved with women. Men seem to have accepted this. A poem by S.H. Morris who identified himself (or possibly *herself*, see footnote) as, 'Honorary Secretary of the NAFDS, Wood Green', was anonymously printed for circulation on 14 November 1920. The piece took the female voice as the appropriate one:

> Shrine of Stone in Grandeur stern
> What can thy message be
> So many things I wish to learn
> Of one so dear to me

Does he know from Heaven above
Of grieving Hearts forlorn
And does he know of an endless love
Far greater now he's gone

It seems to answer Sacred Stone
That my dear one is near
It would seem that I am not alone
In spirit he is here[117]

A language had grown up around Armistice Day, for which the bereaved, usually pictured as women, were the main subjects.

The Language of Consolation

For looking back on the history of our nation, there was every reason to believe that God really had a destiny for England and that with all our faults and shortcomings, he had used us to fulfil that destiny in the world... These moments of silence might well be devoted to thoughts of thanksgiving, not only for the great victory vouchsafed us, but in that He had used us as his instruments in achieving that victory. The suspense would, also of course be an occasion for thoughts of appreciation towards those gallant men who fought for us and particularly those who laid down their lives – "the glorious dead" whom the King especially asked us to remember. We should bear in remembrance too, the parents who freely gave up their sons... and in whose home was left an empty chair.[118]

The Bishop of Ripon, addressing a congregation in Leeds on the Sunday before the first two minutes' silence, unashamedly used the traditional rhetoric of patriotism, blending it with a providential view of the national destiny. The connection between the rhetoric of patriotism, the 'high diction', the traditional justifications of war which were condemned in the preface to Wilfred Owen's poetry,[119] and the plight of the bereaved is made obvious by the frequent juxtaposition of the two. Laurinda Stryker has shown that the contemporary response to the war contained far more continuities with pre-war perceptions than has usually been accepted. Even amongst the most 'radical' war poets the ability to transmute suffering into 'sacrifice' was largely unimpaired.[120] Yet it was only in relation to the civilian bereaved that this concept was taken a stage further. The wartime chaplains studied by Stryker did not on the whole see the 'sacrifices' of the soldiers as redemptive.[121] They were too orthodox in their theodicy and too close to the realities of the war. Yet 'patripassionism' was a strong theme in the immediate post war years, reflecting perhaps the belief that England could be brought to moral redemption by contemplation of the sacrifices of the dead.[122] It was a convenient means of justifying the ways of divine providence, even if it was theologically lazy to the point of heresy.

In this context of simplified establishment Christianity the role of sacrifice could be invested with great ideal force. For example, at the service for receiving the Book of Remembrance in Truro Cathedral, the Bishop addressed the congregation as follows:

> Our first thought goes out today to those whose loved ones made the sacrifice. We stand awed in the presence of their sorrow. We thank them for their dear ones lives and we pray that the God of all comfort may touch them with His compassion and that He may teach them the gift of those 5,000 lives is a gift well worth making and never in vain. What is the great message today for them... It was a war to crush once and for all the foul spirit that is rending the world with all its horrors, a spirit of self interest an ogre of contentiousness. It was crushed and bleeding on the day that Armistice came. It is our business to see that it is wholly killed... [123]

Christian idealism was part of the language used to console the bereaved.[124] In his Armistice Day sermon in 1923, the Archbishop of Canterbury spoke of looking back in 'proud bereavement' at those who, 'went forth at their country's call just because it was their country's call'.[125] As these examples indicate the language of consolation generalised the sacrifice of the dead to incorporate the sacrifice of the bereaved. The grief and pain of the parents was also a suffering for the redemption of the country every bit as valid as the 'supreme sacrifice'. The pride that they could feel removed any shame that might be implied by non-combatant status. At the dedication of the Magdalene College (Cambridge) war memorial, the Bishop of Ely linked the dead and bereaved with the victorious outcome:

> ... on the part of those left behind, long days and nights of never ceasing anxiety, ending in irreversible tidings of bereavement and sorrow; and all these details of College and family and personal life, so intimate and so sacred, linked with events the most momentous and far reaching in their effect on the history of the human race.
>
> This service is the Amen of this college to its commemoration of its sons and to its Thanksgiving to Almighty God who (if we are faithful now) gave victory to that cause of liberty and justice and truth to which these men dedicated themselves and died.[126]

The Bishop of Bradford combined the rhetoric of Christian sacrifice with that of imperial destiny in a quite remarkable, providential, interpretation of the war:

> The Bishop asked what was England's highest title to immortality? It was not her wealth, he said, not the vast extent of her Empire and not even her constitution and wonderful democratic form of government. It was the measure of her service to humanity. Not always had she realised the high destiny to which God had called her. There were blots on her escutcheon and dark pages in her history. But increasingly of late years, this had been her ideal, if slowly and somewhat hesitantly pursued. On this Day of Remembrance we thanked God that England's sons were true to this ideal and that He called us, as we believed to serve humanity and save the world from tyranny and domination of material force. We mourned the dead but it was with hearts aflame with thankfulness and pride, and not despairingly we mourned.[127]

The distinction between this rhetoric and the interpretation of the war which came into vogue later is quite subtle, but nonetheless real. During the early twenties there is frequent reference to the Great War as having destroyed militarism, but such references are still couched in a patriotic idiom. Militarism is an external enemy characterised as the Prussian state. It is defeated on the battlefield by the Christian valour of British soldiers. That a world without war is sincerely desired is a constant theme. Yet there is no sustained critique of military or patriotic values as a way of achieving this. The main distinction between the earlier and the later interpretations of the war is that in the former analysis peace is an achievement of heroism and victory, whereas from the late twenties it is a lesson to be learnt from suffering and disillusion. In the immediate post-war period it was believed that the British soldier had established peace principally by winning.

If a sermon departed substantially from this line, it was liable to be criticised. A 'church layman' wrote to an Anglican newspaper in 1923 complaining that at the armistice service that he had attended, 'was essentially a memorial service for the fallen' and that 'there was not one single reference to the deliverance they, by the grace of God accomplished, nor of praise to Him who alone gave us victory.'[128] At Westminster Hall on Armistice Night 1921, G.A. Studdert Kennedy, the wartime padre known to the troops as 'Woodbine Willie', attacked the prevailing consensus by claiming that the war had been futile and that 'we had lied as a nation and besmirched our honour'. On the same platform was another wartime padre destined for even greater prominence. Canon H.R.L. Sheppard took issue with Kennedy. He 'expressed the hope that no mother who had lost a son or wife her husband would go home with the impression as he feared they might that those lives had been given in vain'. Sheppard stated that he could think of at least fifty reasons why the sacrifice was worthwhile. This is a clear example of the conscious use of the rhetoric of consolation. Sheppard was to change his views on the war in the future, but he would always try to validate the sacrifice.[129]

More secular voices concentrated simply on national pride, although strong ethical overtones were present throughout the language of patriotism.[130] The line between secular and religious was frequently blurred. Horatio Bottomley claimed prophetic inspiration for an article in the *Daily Mirror.* 'I heard a voice from Heaven saying unto me, write'. He went on to describe his 'feelings' at the burial of the Unknown Warrior: 'I gaze at the Immortals and see that they are satisfied, "It is as well we had the war," I think I hear them say and again the voice says write.'[131] Robert Kee, who was born in 1919, recalled his earliest impressions of the war in a review for the *Spectator* in 1962. He remembered the 'glare of national self-congratulation and piety in which the War was officially bathed'. A school Armistice Day had a 'compelling air of tribal solidarity'. The fundamental facts were breathtakingly simple for the schoolboys, 'We had beaten the Germans. The retreat from Mons had been a wonderful thing. Angels had appeared for us there. We had won the Battle of the Somme. Sir Douglas Haig was a great hero'.[132] The front page of the *Eton College Chronicle* on 11 November 1920 carried epigrams from the *Greek Anthology* extolling heroic death, including the following translation from Simonides speaking for the dead of the Persian war:

> If death with glory be the crowning test
> Of perfect life, we most of all are blest
> Hellas is free, and this was all our aim
> And here we lie, our shroud unaging fame.[133]

In the years immediately following the war the word 'triumph' could be used in an unembarrassed fashion, for example by the *Daily Express* in 1919:

> To-day, at the eleventh hour will strike the anniversary of a great triumph and a great deliverance – how great will only be realised in days to come... Though our hearts may swell with the legitimate pride of victory,

our minds should dwell on the sacrifices of success and on the burdens it has laid upon our shoulders...[134]

In the *Daily Mirror* the next year, Mrs Lloyd George wrote, 'had we lost the war we would have lost most of the things that make life worth living. But they did not lose. They won for us a complete and lasting victory.'[135] Seven years later the *Daily Mail* was still striking the note of national pride, extolling the British role in the final victory and affirming the worthiness of the struggle:

Once more the nation celebrates Armistice Day and returns to the grave memories of the war and the commemoration of its dead who gave up their lives in the struggle for human freedom... There is no sacrifice from which the British people shrank. It believed then and still believes that the war was waged to re-establish right in the world and to bring enduring peace to man... In every element and on every front its sons had a leading part in the final victory and in this respect its record of achievement was not equalled, still less surpassed by any other combatant power. This truth requires to be stated in justice to our dead...Was it all worth while ? Cynics may ask as they look back on those years of suffering and bereavement and contemplating a million British graves. But it was worth while. By standing firm against brute force the British nation set a great example of faith and devotion.[136]

How effective was the traditional rhetoric of sacrifice and service to the country in reconciling the bereaved with their loss? It is difficult to say with any certainty. In a poem written for Armistice Day in 1923, Rudyard Kipling suggested that his own pain was beyond consolation:

When you come to London stone
    (Grieving – grieving!)
Bow your head and mourn your own
With the others grieving.

For the minutes let it wake –
    (Grieving – grieving!)
All the empty-heart and ache
That isn't cured by grieving

Where's our help from Earth or Heaven
    (Grieving – grieving!)
To comfort us for what we've given
And only gained by grieving[137]

If the man who is seen as the embodiment of Edwardian patriotism at its most extreme was not comforted by the rhetoric of

God, King and Empire, it might be thought that it was not effective.[138] Nonetheless, there is evidence to suggest that traditional values and symbols could give comfort. In the *Eastern Daily Press* in 1923 it was stated that, 'it is comforting to know that others recall their losses and the sacrifices of those who yielded up their lives, and the knowledge of this sympathy helps assuage the pain of the bereaved'.[139] A practical example of this was shown at the dedication of the Edinburgh city Cenotaph in 1927, 'Mrs Fraser of Holyrood Terrace, who had five sons killed in the war was presented to Prince Henry... [she] mentioned that this was the first Armistice anniversary on which she had left the house. The Prince expressed his deepest sympathy with Mrs Fraser, and at the close of the conversation stepped back and saluted her.'[140]

A story of similar significance appears in the *Daily Mail* the same year. Kate Shallis of Harlesden, NW, who lost four sons in the war, described her impressions on being present for the first time at the Cenotaph service:

> The celebration at the Cenotaph was too wonderful to be real – so it seemed to me... To-day looking down upon it all from a high window in Whitehall, I had thoughts such as no one has been able to express to me... the King came and placed his wreath at the foot of the Cenotaph while the Queen at her window facing mine stood straight and still watching him – then I felt that the King and Queen and I and the masses of people were just one big family, thinking together the same dear thoughts of our million sons who died for us. I could see the Queen's face quite clearly and it seemed to me to be pale with the sorrow which she was feeling for all the mothers whose sons never came back home. I felt she was proud of my four boys who gave their lives for King and Country and that she was sorry or me... I felt proud of my sons and of their courage; I felt proud that I was their mother.
>
> The ceremony at the Cenotaph must have been, I think some little satisfaction to all the mothers whose sons died. It must have made them feel that their boys' sacrifice and their own had not been forgotten.[141]

That this woman at least had been comforted by the idea of her sons dying for 'King and Country and the idea that the Royal Family were aware of the fact is quite evident. The same issue carried a description of a torchlight procession in the the heart of the poorest area of the East End which had taken place on the evening of Armistice Day. Women, mothers in particular, were seen at the centre of that ceremony: 'the very heart of the procession, a group of poor women – typical housewives of the district – women who had wept and suffered, whose anguish from the war was to last much longer than that of their sons who had died.'[142] According to the *Scotsman*, many of the women at the London Cenotaph on 11 November 1927 were still wearing 'deep mourning'.[143]

One expression of popular sympathy with the bereaved, particularly women, occurred in the medals controversy of 1926. In 1924, King George V had expressed his hope that the relatives of those killed in the war would wear the medals awarded to those who had died for the cause. This pronouncement had irritated the service chiefs who were sensitive on the question of the unauthorised wearing of medals by those who had not won them personally. In particular the War Office claimed that nurses and other women who had been awarded medals personally had complained to them about relatives wearing medals in memory of relatives on 11 November.[144] At a Home Office conference on Armistice Day on 7 October 1926 it was decided to remove the request from the communiqué of that year. An inquiry from a bereaved father[145] to the King was forwarded to the Home Office and when he was told that the Home Office did not intend to encourage relatives to wear medals, the letter and reply were forwarded to the *Daily Express* appearing on 6 November 1926.

The civil servant principally involved, H.R. Boyd, attempted to limit damage by briefing 'the responsible press', but, in his own words, 'by accident or carelessness a lady was enabled to overhear practically the whole of the conversation. It turned out that she was a Daily Express reporter. The result in the next day's *Sunday Express* was a highly coloured report. The story was headed with two quotations. One purported to be from Boyd: 'The War has been over for eight years. It is time that sentiment gave way to common sense... we would rather relatives did not wear war medals'. The other quotation was from a woman interviewed at the Cenotaph: 'I lost two sons in the war. I will wear the DCM and the MC they won whether the Home Office forbids me or permits me.'[146] Naturally Boyd was horrified at the way he had been presented in the press: 'In particular there was not one word... of what was repeatedly dinned into her, that there was no ban on the wearing of medals.'[147] A hurried press statement clarified the issue and in effect represented a climb-down in the face of popular indignation stirred up by the Beaverbrook press. Nothing could show more clearly that the bereaved mother was the pre-eminent subject of Armistice Day in the United Kingdom.[148] The *Westminster Gazette*, in one of the least hysterical press reports editorialised that, 'so long as there are mothers to mourn, the wearing of these decorations must meet a human instinct deep in the heart of women of all classes'.[149]

The back page of the 1927 Armistice Day edition of the *Daily Mail* carried the headline 'The men who won, and the women who lost.' It is a neat expression of the dichotomy between the two groups seen as being at the heart of what Armistice Day was about, the bereaved, identified as women, and the ex-servicemen. But ex-servicemen were not simply identified purely as victors; they also had a place as *victims* of the war. It will subsequently be necessary to consider the origins of the Haig Poppy appeal in order to explore this image.

Notes to Chapter 1

1. P. Berton, *Vimy*, Toronto, 1986, p. 307.

2. For discussion of the history of the Cenotaph, see, E. Homberger, 'The Story of the Cenotaph', *Times Literary Supplement*, 12 Nov. 1976, pp. 1429–30. The Cenotaph was constructed to represent the war dead of the British Empire at the celebrations for 'Victory Day' on 19 July 1919.

3. Alfred Mond, 15 Oct. 1919: Public Record Office, PRO CAB 24/GT 8335.

4. Sir Percy Fitzpatrick, memorandum submitted to Lord Milner for the attention of the War Cabinet: PRO CAB 24/CP45 (4 Nov. 1919).

5. Although a certain Patrick O' Neill claimed in November 1919 that he had put forward the idea in a letter to his local paper and that this was clear evidence that 'His Majesty's advisers read the "Evening Mail" of Birmingham.' This seems improbable. Letter, *Birmingham Evening Mail*, 10 Nov. 1919, p. 4.

6. PRO. CAB 24/CP45. It is interesting that these arguments were put forward by someone with a South African background. South Africa was notoriously the most divided of the Dominions. Not only did it have the basic racial divisions that it retains to this day, but additionally it had a bitter division between the English and Afrikaans-speaking communities which were less than a generation removed from the Boer War. Overlaying both of these divisions and reflecting them was one of the most bitter class struggles in any dominion, the extremely tense situation in the Transvaal gold fields. During the early 1920s this struggle transformed into armed insurgency, which was suppressed with military force. As a society, the Union of South Africa was in desperate need for unifying symbols. See Bill Nasson, 'The Great Divide: Popular Responses to the Great War in South Africa', (unpublished Faculty seminar paper, University of Capetown). Cited with the author's permission and with thanks for discussion of this point.

7. Hobsbawm and Ranger, *The Invention of Tradition*, Cambridge, 1983, particularly the introduction by Hobsbawm, pp. 1–14.

8. There were precedents for a regular and indefinite commemoration of historical events for legitimating purposes. During the sixteenth and seventeenth centuries the

anniversaries of Elizabeth I's coronation, the defeat of the Armada and, best known of all, the failure of the Gunpowder Plot had been regularly celebrated. These events had real ideological significance in re-ordering the calendar to fit the Protestant view of providential history. See D. Cressy, *Bonfires and Bells; National Memory and the Protestant Calendar in Elizabethan and Stuart England,* London, 1989.

9. PRO CAB 24/CP 45.

10. PRO CAB 23/18, p. 12, 5 Nov. 1919.

11. See for example *Daily Express,* 7 Nov. 1919, p. 1.

12. *Daily Express,* 11 Nov. 1919, p. 6.

13. *Daily Herald,* 11 Nov. 1919, p. 1.

14. The *Catholic Herald* made this particular point in 1920. Two cartoons published either side of Armistice Day were particularly barbed. One showed a rampaging ape-like British soldier with rifle, bayonet and firebrand threatening a 'celtic' woman and her child. The caption read:

YOUNG IRELAND: Will the brute never stop, mother?

MOTHER: Yes, my son, he will stop for two minutes on Armistice Day.

The second cartoon showed the ghost of the Unknown Warrior looking at the grave of 'An Irish Child Killed by the Military' and exclaiming, 'Was it for this we died!'. See *Catholic Herald,* 6 Nov. 1920, p. 7; 20 Nov 1920, p. 7. See also *The Nation,* 13 Nov. 1920, p. 219.

15. See H.N. Brailsford,' After the Silence', *Daily Herald,* 12 Nov. 1919, p. 4.

16. *Western Morning News and Mercury,* 12 Nov. 1919, p. 5.

17. *Daily Express,* 11 Nov. 1919, p. 6.

18. *Belfast Telegraph,* 12 Nov. 1919, p. 3.

19. The difficulties of accurately coordinating the firing of maroons in the London area to avoid the maroons of one district being fired during the silence in another led to the abandonment of maroons in 1924, but there was no adequate alternative and they were restored the following year. See letter from Sir Rowland Blanes to Rt Hon Edward Short 13 Oct. 1922 in PRO: HO 45/11557/392664/23. Also, minute in HO 45/392664/89 and Report in HO 45/12329/481781/48.

20. See: *Daily Herald,* 12 Nov. 1919, p. 1; *Yorkshire Post,* 10 Nov. 1919, p. 8; *Scotsman,* 12 Nov. 1919, p. 9; *Birmingham Evening Mail,* 10 Nov. 1919, p. 4; *Eastern Daily Press,* 12 Nov. 1919, p. 8; *Western Morning News and Mercury,* 12 Nov. 1919, p. 5; *Royal Cornwall Gazette and Cornwall County News ,* 12 Nov. 1919, p. 4; *Newcastle Daily Journal,* 10 Nov. 1919, p. 5; *Western Mail ,* 12 Nov. 1919, p. 3; *Yorkshire Post,* 12 Nov. 1919, p. 8; *Glasgow Herald,* 10 Nov. 1919, p. 10; *Daily Express,* 12 Nov. 1919, p. 1; *Eastern Daily Press,* 12 Nov. 1919, p. 5. Factory hooters signalled the silence in some mill towns, for example in Bury. See G. Moorhouse, *Hells Foundations: A Town, its Myths and Gallipoli,* London, 1992, p. 155.

21. *Yorkshire Post,* 12 Nov. 1919, p. 8. The permanent memorial in Bradford was unveiled officially on 1 July 1922, the sixth anniversary of the first day of the battle of the Somme, in which the 'Bradford Pals' battalion had been slaughtered. In several areas in the industrial north 1 July was a day of mourning to equal 11 November and it has remained a significant date amongst Ulster Unionists to this day. See D. Boorman, *At the Going Down of the Sun,* York, 1988, p. 128. Another date of localised significance was 25 April in Bury, Lancashire. This was the garrison town of the Lancashire Fusiliers who distinguished themselves during the Gallipoli landings. The war memorial in Bury, designed by Lutyens, was unveiled on 25 April 1925. See Moorhouse, *Hell's Foundations,* p. 181.

22. Birmingham erected a 'pedestal' between 1921 and 1924. See *Birmingham Evening Mail,* 11 Nov. 1921, p. 6.

23. *Yorkshire Post,* 12 Nov. 1919, p. 8.

24. *Western Morning News,* 12 Nov. 1919, p. 5.

25. *Daily Express,* 12 Nov. 1919, p. 1.

26. *Birmingham Evening Mail,* Editorial, 11 Nov. 1919, p. 2.

27. *Daily Express,* 12 Nov. 1919, p. 1.

28. Letter from W. Grant to his family, in the possession of his great nephew, Rev. Colin Holden. Photocopy courtesy of Prof. K. S. Inglis.

29. J. Gore, *King George V: A Personal Memoir,* London, 1941, p. 318.

30. Extracts from the Diaries of H. Wilson and H.A.L. Fisher for 11 Nov. 1919, in M. Gilbert, *Winston Churchill, Volume 4 , 1917–1922,* Companion Volume 2, London, 1977, p. 953.

31. *Scotsman,* 12 Nov. 1921, p. 11.

32. *The Nation,* 15 Nov. 1919, p. 230.

33. *Yorkshire Post,* 12 Nov. 1919, p. 8.

34. J. Thomas, *The North British Railway,* vol. 2, London, 1975, p. 202. See also, *Glasgow Herald,* 10 Nov. 1919, p. 10; *Scotsman,* 10 Nov. 1919, p. 7.

35. *Glasgow Herald,* 10 Nov. 1919, p. 10. Also see photograph of 'the scene at Gerard Telephone Exchange...the first voluntary cessation of work in the history of the telephone exchange.' *Daily Mirror,* 12 Nov. 1919, p. 8.

36. The failure of Rochdale mill owners to stop the machinery during the two minutes' silence in 1921 caused a walk out during the afternoon by the work force. *Manchester Guardian,* 12 Nov. 1921, p. 9.

37. *Yorkshire Post,* 12 Nov. 1919, p. 8.

38. *Nottinghamshire Free Press and Derbyshire Chronicle,* 14 Nov. 1919, p. 5.

39. *The Times,* 12 Nov. 1919, p. 16.

40. *Daily Express,* 12 Nov. 1919, p. 6; *Daily Mirror,* 12 Nov. 1919, p. 5. There were some dissenters from this view, Mr Alexander Cameron in a letter stated that, 'It is axiomatic that really great things cannot be repeated. Yesterday's tribute was simple solemn, spontaneous and (in the restricted sense) universal. Let it also be unique. This would give it true distinction, and make it (as it deserves to be made) in the highest degree historic and memorable.' *Scotsman,* 13 Nov. 1919, p. 10.

41. For example, see, *Methodist Recorder,* 11 Nov. 1920, p. 3, 'When all the land in quietness attempts its sacramental offering before God'. The tradition of silence as a way of mourning in prelude to resurrection may in fact go very deep in the traditions of the English church. In the Anglo-Saxon period a *SWIG DAEG* was a day on which silence was meant to be observed during the every day business of life. These days were the final three days of the Passion week a period of mourning for the death of Christ before the resurrection on Easter Monday. See T. Northcote Toller, *An Anglo Saxon Dictionary,* Oxford, 1972, p. 955. In more modern times silent prayer was reintroduced into the church via Quakerism and had permeated into first the more mainstream Nonconformist churches and then the Church of England, although it was not part of the liturgy as such. A strain of Anglo-Catholic pietism also contributed to the new stress on silent prayer, particularly in private. See D.L. Edwards, *Christian England,* vol. 3, London, 1984, p. 350.

42. *Birmingham Evening Mail,* 11 Nov. 1919, p. 2. The local influence of prominent Quaker families, particularly the Cadbury family, may be the reason for this statement.

43. Emile Durkheim, *The Elementary Forms of Religious Life,* London, 1915, 1984 edition, pp. 399–400.

44. From the poem 'Lamplight' by May Wedderburn Cannan. She served as a VAD. Her fiancé died in 1918. C. Reilly, *Scars Upon my Heart: Womens Poetry and Verse of the First World War,* London, 1981, p. 16.

45. The debt the subsequent argument owes to David Cannadine's essay on this subject is enormous. Cannadine deals with these subjects on a much broader canvass than I can do here. See D. Cannadine, 'War and Death, Grief and Mourning in Modern Britain', in J. Whaley (ed.), *Mirrors of Mortality: Studies in the Social History of Death,* London, 1981, pp. 187–252.

46. To provide a more accurate figure would involve an enormous amount of work and would probably be misleading in any case. This figure is based on the following propositions:

a. The British death toll was 722,785.

b. The age structure of the combatants compared to the life expectancy of their parent's generation, suggests that most of the men killed would have been survived by both parents and that the overwhelming majority would have been survived by at least one. At least one million parents could be expected to have survived their children.

c. 344,606 pensions were granted to orphans and 192,678 to widows; these two categories total about 550,000 if it is assumed that a percentage of those entitled may not have claimed.

d. Average family size for the 'war generation' suggests two siblings for each casualty. This produces almost one and a half million bereaved siblings.

The obvious objection to these figures is that a substantial number of the bereaved would have been bereaved more than once. Many would have lost two children or a husband and a brother for example. Against this, allowance ought to be made for the large numbers of 'Canadians' and 'Australians' killed in the war, who, when closely examined can be seen to have been very recent immigrants to those countries from the United Kingdom. The relatives of these men (numbering perhaps 50,000 of the combined Australian–Canadian death toll of 120,000) would generally have remained in Britain. See J.M. Winter, *The Great War and the British People,* Cambridge, 1985, for statistics used here. See P. Berton, *Vimy,* for numerous examples of recent immigrants in the Canadian Army.

47. The first hundred individual obituaries to the war dead in a Welsh newspaper published on 11 November 1930 provide an interesting profile of bereavement in the middle of the period under consideration. They are submitted, as far as can be identified by the following relatives:

12 mothers. 2 fathers. 13 both parents. 3 single parent unspecified.

2 father and siblings. 6 mother and siblings. 9 both parents and siblings

10 siblings alone

6 wives and 1 or more children. 6 wives (no children mentioned).

1 cousin. 1 aunt and siblings. 1 fiancé. 1 colleague.

1 mother, wife and child.

The rest of the dedications are unidentifiable. Overall roughly 60% of the obituaries are from individual family members, the balance are from regimental associations, veterans groups and work places. See, *Western Mail,* 11 Nov. 1930, pp. 1–2.

48. The success of the BBC television dramatisation of *Testament of Youth* in 1978 and the enduring popularity of the film *The Prime of Miss Jean Brodie* in 1969 are evidence of the sustained power of the image of the bereaved fiancé. Statistically the image of a generation of spinsters is a myth; even Vera Brittain was married by 1925.

49. This is not to underestimate the potential trauma involved for survivors of such events as the Gallipoli landings, the death march that followed the surrender at Kut or the many ships torpedoed in the North Atlantic. It may still be argued that the Western Front, with its promiscuous destruction of men and landscape, had a peculiar quality of its own.

50. L.M. Capps, 'The Memorial as Symbol and Agent of Healing ', in W. Capps, *The Vietnam Reader,* London and New York, 1991, pp. 272–289. Conclusion based on interviews with visitors to the Vietnam memorial.

51. C. Geertz, 'The Way We Think Now: Ethnography of Modern Thought' in C. Geertz, *Local Knowledge,* New York, 1983, pp. 147–163, 151.

52. See W. Stroebe and M. Stroebe, *Bereavement and Health,* Cambridge, 1987, pp. 25–26. and particularly pp. 30–31.

53. The Navajo are preoccupied by death, while attempting desperately to deny it. For a discussion of the Navajo see S.I. Miller and L. Schoenfield 'Grief in the Navajo: Psycho Dynamics and Culture', *International Journal of Social Psychiatry,* 19, 1973, pp. 187–91. For Japan see J. Yamamoto 'Cultural Factors in Loneliness, Death and Separation', *Medical Times,* 98, 1970, pp. 177–83. These cases have been deliberately chosen for their extreme nature.

54. For admiration and emulation of Victoria see L. Taylor, *Mourning Dress, A Costume and Social History*, London, 1983, pp. 154–160. Pat Jalland has taken issue with this interpretation of Victorian mores and by implication reasserts the purely psychological causality of grief. In an article on death, grief and mourning amongst upper class Victorian families, she suggests that Queen Victoria was seen as excessively depressed over the loss of Albert by contemporaries. Jalland considers Victoria to have been a classic case of excessive grief similar to cases described by Gorer and Parkes and showing the same psychological profile, based on childhood bereavement.Whilst it is true that her mourning was widely condemned in the late 1860s, Jalland fails to point out that this condemnation was politically motivated by Republican sentiment generated at the time of the 2nd Reform Act. One of Victoria's principal critics was Joseph Chamberlain, who, as Jalland points out, demonstrated almost comparable grief over the loss of his wife during the same period. To address Jalland's argument further, the four cases of 'excessive grief' which she identifies, Victoria, Ramsay Macdonald, Joseph Chamberlain and Lord Aberdeen, were all prominent figures. Jalland suggests that the additional pressures of public prominence played a part in their intense emotional reaction. Yet one might equally suppose that the quantity of documentation regarding such figures gives a stronger insight into the affective state of these people, than is the case of the 'counter examples' cited, many of which seem to be based on more casual and ambiguous evidence. Jalland may be right, but the case is not yet proved. After all, if Victorian elites had considered Victoria's grief truly excessive, one can easily imagine a range of actions which could have been taken (medical treatment, regency or enforced abdication), measures which might have been taken a century earlier or a century later. See, P. Jalland, 'Death, Grief and Mourning in the Upper Class Family 1860–1914', in R. Houlbrooke, *Death, Ritual and Bereavement*, London, 1989, pp. 171–187.

55. See Stroebe and Stroebe, *Bereavement*, p. 19.

56. Taylor, *Mourning Dress*, p. 267. As early as August 1914 there had been public appeals that mourning dress should not been worn for those who had been killed in action. See editorial in the *Pall Mall Gazette*, 1 Sept. 1914, p. 3.

57. G. Gorer, *Death, Grief and Mourning in Contemporary Britain*, London, 1965; E. Kübler-Ross, *On Death and Dying*, London, 1970; R. J. Lifton and E. Olson, *Living and Dying*, London, 1974.

58. Most notably, P. Aries, *Western Attitudes towards Death from the Middle Ages to the Present*, London, 1976.

59. 'The more egalitarian relationships of 'self-care' and 'self-management' have also created higher expectations; increased critical reactions to any attempt at imposing constraints, supernatural or otherwise, induced a higher degree of mutually expected self restraint... During this period conjuring with death (anxieties) had lost its compulsive force for growing numbers of people...' C. Wouters, 'Changing Regimes of Power and Emotions at the End of Life: The Netherlands 1930–1990'. Unpublished paper, cited with permission. From a different perspective, Wouters is as sceptical as Cannadine about the romanticisation of death in the Victorian period which has been a feature of many works on the subject.

60. R.C. Solomon, 'Getting Angry: The Jamesian theory of Emotion in Anthropology' in R.A. Shweder and R.A. LeVine (eds.), *Culture Theory; Essays on Mind Self and Emotion*, Cambridge, 1984, pp. 238–254, 249.

61. See Cannadine, 'War and Death', p. 217.

62. Earl of Oxford, *Memoirs and Reflections, 1852–1927*, London, 1928, vol. 2, p. 159.

63. R. Blake, *The Unknown Prime Minister*, London, 1955, p. 355.

64. C.F.G. Masterman, *England After the War*, London, 1922, p. 79.

65. H. Lauder, *Roamin' in the Gloamin'*, London, 1928, p. 184. It is instructive to compare these parental reactions with the response of a mother to the loss of her son on the Scott Polar expedition in 1912. 'For Caroline Oates the blow of her son's death

was perhaps the bitterest experience of her life. Every night she slept in the bedroom he had used. In her handbag she kept one of his regimental epaulettes, and there were always fresh flowers under his portrait.' P. Cordingley and S. Limb, *Captain Oates; Soldier and Explorer*, London, 1982. Many mothers may have responded in a similar fashion in the next few years.

66. For further examples see D. Winter, *Death's Men*, London, 1978, pp. 276–278.

67. See E. Kübler-Ross, *Living with Death and Dying*, London, 1982, pp. 175–178, for discussion of the need to relate to the dead body. For being able to mention the name of the dead family member, see Gorer, *Grief and Mourning*, pp. 25–29 and particularly pp. 69–77.

68. Silence was the appropriate behaviour during the solemnity of funerals for those who had come to pay their respects. It could be extended to an entire community's solidarity. After the 1901 disaster, the first of the two appalling explosions at the Senghennydd pit, as the bodies of the men were retrieved, the local community refrained from hymns: 'Once again there was an absence of singing. Instead there was the moving, silent and solemn respect of a mining community which stood silent to watch them pass.' J.H. Brown, *The Valley of the Shadow: An Account of Britain's Worst Mining Disaster: The Senghenydd Explosion*, Port Talbot, 1981, p. 42.

69. Alfred Noyes, 'The passing of the Unknown Warrior', *Daily Mirror*, 12 Nov. 1920, p. 5.

70. A.L. Borden, 'The Cenotaph: Armistice Day', *Liverpool Review*, December 1930, facing p. 483. The Cenotaph referred to is the Liverpool civic memorial.

71. R. Blythe, *The Age of Illusion*, London, 1963, pp. 1–14. The account is a little unreliable in places, but not substantively different from the version of events outlined in the Public Record file on the activity of the Memorial Committee. PRO CAB 27/99.

72. Lord Stamfordham to Dean Ryle, cited in Blythe, *Illusion*, p. 8. This correspondence is in the Royal Archive at Windsor, to which doctoral students are denied access.

73. PRO CAB 27/99, p. 4.

74. There is some question about this. Press reports indicate six bodies were exhumed, but the initial plan of the Committee mentions four. These were selected from the Somme, Ypres, Arras and the Aisne. See PRO CAB 27/99. Minutes of Memorial Committee 19 Oct 1920, p.26, p.35. The whole question is somewhat open, but it is clear that the secret intention of the committee was to exhume a 1914 corpse i.e. probably a regular army member. The original suggestion from the Army was that the body should be taken from a site where the Royal Naval Division had fought, but this Division was not in France or Southern Belgium in 1914. The Navy waived any claim on Committee, agreeing with a general view that a 1914 body was preferable for practical reasons. The implications of this action would have been substantial if known. Contrary to public rhetoric, the Unknown Warrior was not Navy, Airforce, Colonial or Dominion. He was also not a Kitchener volunteer or a conscript and was very unlikely to have been a territorial or an Indian. The representative nature of the body would have been seriously undermined had this been known at the time and the truth could still be sensitive today.

75. Initially it was intended to accomodate the fighting services at the Ceremony in the Abbey. The committee service representatives and Dean Ryle pressed this view. They were overruled by the Cabinet. Curzon informed the committee that 'the bereaved were more deserving of consideration'. Minutes of Memorial Services Committee, 1 Nov. 1920, 3 Nov. 1920, PRO: CAB 27/99, pp. 45, 48. Priority was given at the service in the Abbey: (a) to women who had lost a husband *and* a son (b) women who had lost only sons (c) other widows. The ordering of priorities is suggestive. It is noteworthy that fathers do not get any priority at all. Bereaved members of parliament were the only fathers invited. The identification of the

bereaved with women was already becoming conventional. Committee conclusions, 5 Nov. 1920, PRO: CAB 27 / 99, p. 22. See also India Office, Curzon Papers, MSS. Eur. F112/318. (Thanks to Patrick McGinn for pointing this out.)

76. R. Huntington and P. Metcalfe (eds) *Celebrations of Death: The Anthropology of Mortuary Ritual,* Cambridge, 1991, pp. 33–34.

77. *Daily Mirror,* 13 Nov. 1920, p. 3.

78. *Daily Mirror,* 15 Nov. 1920, pp. 1–3.

79. Francis Meynell, 'The Unknown Warrior', *Daily Herald ,* 11 Nov. 1920, p. 4.

80. *Daily Herald,* 12 Nov. 1920, p. 1.

81. *Daily Herald,* 13 Nov. 1920, p. 1.

82. It is worth considering the implications of this. The description 'empty tomb' inevitably brings to mind the empty tomb of Christ after the resurrection. In this sense, far from being a centre point for a cult of the dead, the Cenotaph was a denial of death in a theological sense. Arguments about whether the cenotaph should be surmounted by a Christian symbol or inscription were missing the point; the Cenotaph carried a coded Christian message in its very name.

83. *Daily Herald,* 13 Nov. 1920, p. 1. The outpouring of real emotion towards the Tomb of the Unknown Warrior was less *consistent* than the respect paid to the Cenotaph. I agree with David Lloyd that the Cenotaph was ultimately the more significant monument because it was directly relevant to all the families, not just the families of the missing. But the funeral nature of the 1921 ceremony was vital because of the provision of a real body.

84. *Birmingham Evening Mail,* 12 Nov 1921, p. 5. For the importance of spiritual messages see, J.M. Winter, 'Spiritualism and the First World War' (unpublished paper delivered to Cambridge Social History Seminar, 1992), and J.M. Winter, *Sites of Memory* (forthcoming). For pilgrimages to the Tomb of the Unknown Warrior see David Lloyd's forthcoming doctoral thesis.

85. It was suggested by contemporaries that strong feelings towards the unknown warrior were limited to families who had a relative missing. *Manchester Guardian,* 14 Nov. 1921, p. 6.

86. *Royal Cornish Gazette and Cornwall County News,* 16 Nov. 1921, p. 6.

87. The Home Office allowed total latitude to local authorities to organise Armistice Day as they saw fit. After the Second World War a number of local councils wrote to the Home Office requesting instructions. In reply one was told that, 'It was never the practice between the wars to circulate local authorities about Armistice Day celebrations.' Reply from H.A. Strutt to Town Clerk of Llangollen Urban District Council, 20 Oct. 1945. PRO HO 45/20277/891772/19.

88. The Imperial War Museum is currently engaged in a survey of British War Memorials which should yield a more definite quantative picture. Of the approximately 180 programmes for war memorial dedications at the IWM, only six were unveiled on 11 November; Llandudno, Colwyn Bay, Bognor, Greenwich, Kenfig Hill (and Sheffield? According to other sources the unveiling was 28 October but there is some ambiguity here between unveiling and dedication). Eight more were unveiled on the nearest Sunday. Memorials not included in the IWM file which are known to have been unveiled on 11 November include Liverpool (1930), Belfast (1929), Derby (1924), Bolton (1932), Nottingham(1927). See, Boorman, *At the Going Down Of the Sun.* A general rule appears to be that the bigger and later the memorial, the greater probability of it being dedicated on 11 November.

89. *Western Morning News,* 12 Nov. 1920, p.5.

90. *Yorkshire Post,* 12 Nov. 1920, p. 5.

91. *City of Sheffield; Programme of Proceedings, Armistice Day 1925,* IWM /K3981

92. *Dedication of Llandudno War Memorial; Order of Ceremony,* 11 Nov. 1922.

93. *Eastern Daily Press,* 14 Nov. 1921, p. 9.

94. *Royal Cornwall Gazette and Cornwall County News,* 16 Nov. 1921, p. 6.

95. E. Short, *I Knew My Place,* London, 1983, pp. 119–120.

96. See account of Armistice day in Redruth, *Royal Cornwall Gazette*, 17 Nov. 1920, p. 4. In the same year, at Tregoney, a service for ex-servicemen was held at the memorial on the Sunday preceding 11 November, but is described in the newspaper as an Armistice Day service. This raises problems since it appears that Armistice Day was being used loosely in Cornwall to describe events on 11 November and also on the Sunday preceding. It is therefore difficult to state with absolute confidence that the Redruth service was on 11 November. As a general rule, ex-servicemen's commemorations were more often on the Sunday than 11 November. For Tregoney see, *Royal Cornwall Gazette*, 10 Nov. 1920, p. 4. Ex-servicemen may have been more prominent in Scotland on 11 November. For examples see the accounts of local ceremonies, *Scotsman*, 12 Nov. 1927, p. 12.

97. *Royal Cornwall Gazette*, 16 Nov. 1921, p. 7. See also the account of the ceremony in Newton Stewart where, 'the school children marched to the memorial where they placed a wreath', *Scotsman*, 12 Nov. 1921, p. 11.

98. St Mary's Infant School, Tetbury, Log Book 1920–21, pp. 141–142. Photocopy courtesy of Mrs Christine Gregory.

99. Personal knowledge.

100. H. Godwin, *Cambridge and Clare*, Cambridge, 1985, pp. 80–81.

101. R. Garrett, *The Final Betrayal; Armistice 1918...And Afterwards*, Southampton, 1989, p. 1.

102. P. Redfern, *The New History of the C.W.S*, London, 1938, p. 212. For an account of a service in the CWS hall in Newcastle see, *Newcastle Daily Journal*, 12 Nov. 1936, p. 9.

103. This was still true in Nottingham as late as 1933. Despite the well established nature of the memorial on the banks of the Trent and the fact that 11 November was a Saturday, the service in the old market square attracted more people than the civic service at the memorial. *Nottingham Guardian*, 13 Nov. 1933, p. 5.

104. *Birmingham Evening Mail*, 10 Nov. 1925, p. 4. See also, 11 Nov. 1925, p. 4.

105. *A Day of Remembrance; Belfast's Tribute to the Memory of the Glorious Dead, 11th November , 1926 – ' Armistice Day'*. Included in PRO HO 45/12840/511682. The whole programme is a none too subtle display of the machinery of Protestant rule, Orange Lodges, 'B' specials, Protestant clergy, etc.

106. *Eastern Daily Press*, 12 Nov. 1921, p. 4.

107. *Eastern Daily Press*, 13 Nov. 1922, p. 5.

108. *Eastern Daily Press*, 12 Nov. 1923, p. 5.

109. See D. Boorman, *At the Going Down of the Sun: British First World War Memorials*, York, 1988, p. 42, pp. 135–6. With the Armada memorial and the Royal Marines memorial also within a few hundred yards, this is one of the most concentrated areas for war memorials in the country.

110. Personal observation.

111. *Western Morning News and Mercury*, 12 Nov. 1924, p. 3. See also *Western Morning News*, 12 Nov. 1927, p. 6.

112. *Western Morning News*, 12 Nov. 1923, p. 3.

113. In Kings Lynn in 1921, 'many of the shops and business premises were closed for an hour to enable their staffs to attend the remembrance services that were being held in the various churches and chapels of the town.' *Eastern Daily Press*, 12 Nov. 1921. This appears to have been very unusual, if not unique.

114. *Royal Cornwall Gazette*, 17 Nov. 1920, p. 7.

115. *Daily Mail*, 12 Nov. 1927, p. 4. See also, 'The War the Women Knew', *Evening Standard*, 10 Nov. 1928, p. 14.

116. *Methodist Recorder*, 9 Nov. 1922, p. 12.

117. This piece survives by chance. It was sent by 'Mr S.H. Morris 10 Oct. 1945, with the suggestion that it be used at the 'Cenotaph ceremony' according to the Home Office official who had to read it and who appended the comment, 'of no great merit'. In fact the card enclosed is not specific as to gender and the letter

accompanying it is signed S.H. Morris. A woman might have been 'honorary secretary' to a veterans organisation. The language of the poem suggests a female author, even so the fact that it was apparently sponsored by a male veterans organisation supports the point: PRO HO 45/20277/891772/14.

118. *Yorkshire Post,* 10 Nov. 1919, p. 8.

119. See discussion in Hynes, *A War Imagined,* pp. 182–183.

120. L. Styrker, 'Languages of Sacrifice and Suffering in England during the First World War'. Unpublished PhD, Cambridge, 1992. See also T. Bocacz, 'A Tyranny of Words; Language, Poetry and Anti-Modernism in England during the First World War.' *Journal of Modern History,* 3, September 1986, pp. 643–668.

121. Stryker, 'Sacrifice and Suffering', p. 78.

122. In one important respect this language was established before the war. The rhetorical response to the disastrous Scott expedition to the South Pole centred on the moral lesson of the heroic Captain Oates, which deflected attention from the amateurish incompetence which had caused the tragedy. One historian has pointed out in a massively documented work that, 'nowhere in the records of the Polar party is Oates explicitly said to have given up his life out of heroic self-sacrifice. The tale depends on the hint in Scott's account.' R. Huntford, *Scott and Amundsen,* London, 1979, p. 560.

From this hint a massive legend was constructed. Oates became the pre-eminent hero of pre-war Britain, a moral exemplar of the highest order. There are a number of direct connections between the story and the methods and rhetoric of war commemoration. For example, a film of the expedition, *90 Degrees South,* was released in 1915 and was seen as an explicit message about the validity of sacrifice, so much so that the Chaplain General recommended that it be shown to the troops in France. (Cordingley and Limb, *Oates,* p. 168.). The Admiralty officially listed Scott as 'Killed in Action' (Huntford, *Scott and Amundsen,* p. 559.). Most intriguing of all is a comment by 'Teddy Evans' who led the expedition that recovered the bodies. On discovering the bodies there was, 'a moment of hush and overwhelming sorrow – a great stillness ran through the ship's little company.' In the book he wrote years later, Evans was still haunted by that suspension, 'I have been reminded of it particularly on the anniversaries of Armistice Day.' D. Thomson, *Scott's Men,* London, 1977, p. 295. For contemporary reports and the elaboration of the Oates story, see various articles, poems, letters and editorials in *Daily Mail,* 11 Feb.–15 Feb. 1913.

123. *Royal Cornwall Gazette,* 16 No. 1921, p. 6.

124. See the sensitive discussion of traditionalist conventions in S. Sillars, *Art and Survival in First World War Britain,* New York, 1987, pp. 137–138, 161–162. Although Sillars, like a number of other writers, overstates the significance of public school and sporting metaphors in the description of the war, he is more aware than most of the vital psychological function of 'high diction' in making grief bearable. For some examinations of the roots of the connection between patriotic rhetoric and Christianity see, A. Summers, 'Militarism in Britain before the Great War', *History Workshop Journal* , Autumn 1976, pp. 104–124, and also O. Anderson, 'The Growth of Christian Militarism in Mid Victorian Britain', *English Historical Review* , January, 1971, pp. 46–72.

125. *The Guardian,* 16 Nov. 1923, p. 1052.

126. *Magdalene College War Memorial; Dedication by the Bishop of Ely, November 11th 1923,* Cambridge, 1923, p. 3.

127. *Yorkshire Post,* 12 Nov. 1921, p. 10. See also the address by Rev. L.E. Baumer to the 'Boys Model School ', Norwich, reported in *Eastern Daily Press,* 12 Nov. 1919, p. 8.

128. *The Guardian,* 16 Nov. 1923, p. 1047. As this was prior to the revisionism of John Terraine and others it may be safely assumed that the capitalised entity was God rather than Sir Douglas Haig.

129. *Morning Post,* 12 Nov. 1921, p. 8. For an account of Studdert-Kennedy and his relationship with Sheppard, see W. Purcell, *Woodbine Willie,* London, 1962.

130. Roland Stromberg has noted that in 1914, 'religion or at any rate morality had grown secular... ideas were holistic, cutting across boundaries of thought... This Quasi-Christian language of sacrifice and redemption became common political coinage throughout the war (and suffered a considerable debasement).' R. Stromberg, *Redemption By War: The Intellectuals and 1914*, Lawrence, Kansas, 1982, pp. 55–56. Where I would differ from Stromberg's analysis is that the stress he places on communitarianism overcoming anomie as the reason for a 'Christian revival' was principally a concern of limited group of intellectuals. I believe this language was more important as a consolation for the family and the individual.

131. *Daily Mirror*, 12 Nov. 1920, p. 3.

132. Quoted in, B. Bond (ed.),*The First World War and British Military History*, Oxford, 1991, p. 274. However, René Cutforth, later a war correspondent, remembered from the mid-1920s, 'the embarassing sight of masters in tears on Armistice Day.' R. Cutforth, *Later Than We Thought; A portrait of the Thirties*, London, 1976, p. 10.

133. *Eton College Chronicle*, 11 Nov. 1920, p. 913. For classical models of patriotism in public schools, see, P. Parker, *The Old Lie; The Great War and the Public School Ethos*, London, 1987, pp. 84–98. For further examples of poetry relating to early Armistice Days, see, 'Remembrance' by "Tempus" in *The Student* (University of Edinburgh), 19 Nov. 1919, p. 2; 'November the Eleventh' by "H st G", in *Durham University Journal*, 21, No.7, December 1920, p. 228 and ' The Eleventh Hour' by Evelyn Grant Duff in *The National Review*, December 1920, pp. 490–491. All of these poems express sentiments of elevated patriotism and use the highest of 'High Diction'. For revealing examples of the persistence of 'High Diction', see the poems,'Remembrance' and 'The Poppy' in the *Scotsman*, 11 Nov. 1927, p. 8.

134. *Daily Express*, 11 Nov. 1919, p. 6. Also see, *Daily Mirror*, 12 Nov. 1919, p. 1.

135. *Daily Mirror*, 12 Nov. 1920, p. 7.

136. *Daily Mail*, 11 Nov. 1927, p. 10.

137. *The Times*, 10 Nov. 1923, p. 10.

138. However, Kipling strongly deprecated the attempts to demilitarise and de-emphasise Armistice Day which were made in the late 1920s.

139. *Eastern Daily Press*, 12 Nov. 1923, p. 4.

140. *Scotsman*, 12. Nov. 1927, p. 11.

141. *Daily Mail*, 12 Nov. 1927, p.12.

142. *Daily Mail*, 12 Nov. 1927, p. 8. See also, *Manchester Guardian*, 12 Nov. 1928, p. 8, for description of women at the Cenotaph and Westminster Abbey.

143. *Scotsman*, 12 Nov. 1927, p. 11.

144. PRO HO 45/12840/511682/9, Armistice Day Conference Minutes, 28 Sept. 1927. Also HO 45/124688/495788/38: 'Report on the wearing of medals on Armistice Day. Undated (Nov. 1926).

145. It had been assumed by the Home Office that the enquiry had come from a woman, an interesting mistake.

146. *Sunday Express*, 7 Nov. 1926, p. 1. For mothers wearing medals, see report on a mother 'with two Victoria crosses, pinned to her breast', who, 'stood among the crowd around the War Memorial at Folkestone yesterday during the Silence'. *Daily News*, 12 Nov. 1928, p. 9.

147. HO 45/124688/495788/38: 'Report on the wearing of medals on Armistice Day'.

148. The congregation at Westminster Abbey in 1926 were described as, 'Mostly women and mostly women with the medals of the beloved dead – medals of the known warriors on their breasts.' *Westminster Gazette*, 12 Nov. 1926, p. 1. The same issue noted that Princess Beatrice had worn the medals of her son, Prince Maurice, who had been killed in action.

149. *Westminster Gazette*, 11 Nov. 1926, p. 6.

2

Unknown Soldiers:
The Marginality of Veterans
on 11 November

Soldiers from the Wars Returning

If ex-servicemen retained a place in the popular perception of what 11 November was about, it must be remembered that it was a subordinate place. The civilian bereaved always came first in any clash of interests.[1] This chapter will explore how it was that the British ex-servicemen, unlike their American or French counterparts, came to have so little control over the development of public commemoration. The first significant point to be made is that, unlike the French and American veterans' organisations, the British Legion had insufficient power as a lobby to have 11 November declared a public holiday. From its foundation, the British Legion's 'policy in regard to the day on which the signing of the Armistice' was, 'that the day should be adopted as a National Holiday'.[2] The response to an enquiry directed to the Home Office in 1922 shows that the objective was unlikely to be obtained, 'The Home Secretary's view is that it would probably be a mistake to make this day a national holiday. November is not a suitable time of year for it nor would a national holiday seem to be consistent with the spirit of Remembrance which is the chief note of Armistice day.'[3] Unlike the French veterans, who were able to force a government to institute a public holiday on 11 November 1922, British veterans were too little organised and too heterogeneous in their attitudes.[4]

How British veterans remembered the war would clearly influence their attitude to commemorative rituals. Their memory of the war would be determined to an important extent by their experience of the peace. The vast majority were reintegrated into

Notes for Chapter 2 can be found on page 86.

civil society surprisingly well. The threads of home life, jobs and relationships were picked up once more and the return to civilian life and civilian identities began. At certain times and in certain company their identity as war veterans would return. Mental and physical scars would occasionally be felt. Yet most of the time civil roles were resumed, as husbands, fathers and sons, as miners, dockers and clerks, as trade unionists and members of friendly societies; a whole host of definitions essentially unrelated to the years spent in the services. Sometimes the buried past would emerge in unlikely places. Don Howarth remembered how on holiday in Blackpool, his father, 'would be seized by strangers, men who had served with him in the trenches and who now identified themselves by recalling the names of places in Flanders.' On such occasions his chidren, 'caught a glimpse of a different world in which he was a different man, unknown to us.'[5] Yet normally Howarth was scarcely aware of the war or his father's part in it.[6]

However, a substantial minority were unable to shed the identity acquired during the war so lightly. Most obvious were those, numbering perhaps 500,000, who had been seriously maimed during the war. The variety of wounds inflicted by the technology of modern warfare was immense. High explosive and high velocity small arms, combined with infection and frostbite, produced over 240,000 major amputees in the United Kingdom.[7] Approximately 10,000 veterans were blinded. 55,000 veterans suffered from severe respiratory diseases, many of which were associated with the long term effects of chemical warfare. 13,000 veterans suffered from war-related psychoses, nearly 60,000 from 'neurasthenia'. Skin diseases, recurrent malaria, chronic rheumatism, tuberculosis, terminal syphilis; the list of war-related disabilities was endless. Sometimes the legacy of the war bordered on the bizarre:

> Trooper Samuel Rolfe, known all over the world as 'the man who lived in a hot bath' has died... He suffered from an illness caused by mustard gas in the war which removed all the skin from his body...The doctors finally devised the treatment of a perpetual bath after it was found that he could not even bear to rest in pyjamas which had been thickly covered in vaseline.[8]

For the maimed, the memory of the war was focused by a continual physical reminder, something present for 365 days in the year, not simply at regimental reunion, encounters with old comrades and on Armistice Day. Armistice Day from the start, but more particularly after the innauguration of the Haig Poppy appeal, was to focus attention on their sufferings. When the tomb of the Unknown Warrior was inaugurated in 1920, three blinded veterans from St Dunstan's represented the 170 inmates at the ceremony. Herbert Thompson, one of the three chosen, described his feelings:

> The ceremony at the Abbey left an indelible impression on my mind – a feeling of ineffable sadness and melancholy, yet there was a message of inspiration and hope. I felt as if the spirit of the Unknown Soldier had whispered in my ear, 'Courage brother; hope on'... I understood all, even though every step and every movement had to be explained to me by an accompanying guide. The atmosphere was impregnated with meaning. The Great Alchemist by some miracle vouchsafed to me a more powerful vision than those who had eyes to see. Clear cut pictures of France and Flanders rose up before me. The dread solemnity of the occasion stirred the most poignant memories. I felt with my comrades almost ashamed that I had given so little, while he who was sleeping by us had given all... I came to the Abbey glad that I had been chosen from among so many, I went away sorrowing, but with the message of hope locked in my heart.[9]

It is unlikely that many of those severely wounded would have echoed the view that they had given little, but the attention bestowed on the maimed and the appeals for public support and attention, that accompanied Armistice Day may indeed have provided a message of hope. The tribute of the community might be small compensation for a life spent in a wheelchair, but it was important that the debt owed to the mutilated was acknowledged and seen to be acknowledged.

That the debt was acknowledged did not neccessarily mean that it was paid. Although the majority of disabled veterans found employment 100,000 disabled ex-servicemen were unemployed in 1920. The government relied on voluntary action on the part of employers, under the King's National Roll scheme to encourage the employment of disabled ex-servicemen, but it refused to institute any measure of compulsion.[10] The idea that those who had been disabled by the war were automatically entitled to full public support was a minority opinion. George Bernard Shaw voiced this opinion in reply to a letter from the Editor of the British Legion Journal, 'Disabled men drag down wages and the standard of work. They should not be employed at all industrially. The duty of the country is perfectly clear. These men were disabled in its service, and should be supported unconditionally.'[11] Shaw held views that most would have considered extreme; even the British Legion, tireless in its campaigns for pensions and compulsory employment, was unprepared to associate itself with that position, believing that it was an impractical policy aim. Instead it campaigned for preferential treatment: 'to secure the removal of the severely incapacitated or disabled ex-servicemen and women from the ordinary competitive market by the scientific and compulsory distribution of the severely incapacitated or disabled ex-servicemen and women amongst the industries of this country.'[12]

This aim was not achieved until after the Second World War. Instead the British Legion was forced to resort to the semi-charitable approach of supporting disabled servicemen through protected Legion managed industry, most notably the Poppy Factory (see Chapter 3). Such measures could not possibly cope with a problem of the scale described.

It was not only disabled ex-servicemen who faced unemployment once the post-war boom was played out and the slump began. Indeed the majority of those unemployed during the early years of the 1920s had been in the armed forces during the war.

There are many obvious reasons why this should have been the case. Young men predominated amongst both the volunteers of the early war years and the conscripts of the later years. These men had not established themselves in trades, nor had they completed apprenticeships or other forms of training. Some had enlisted in the first place due to unemployment caused by slumps in the building trade. Others had been 'combed out' by conscription on the grounds that they were not essential personnel in their industries. Few would have been trade union members of longstanding. Unskilled and inexperienced, these men were vulnerable to redundancy in the face of recession. Furthermore the principle of 'last in, first out' obviously disadvantaged servicemen against those who had remained in industry during the war and almost 125,000 men had not been demobilised by February 1920.

It should not, therefore, be surprising that in the immediate post-war period 'unemployed man' and 'unemployed ex-serviceman' were close to synonymous. Only approximately one in nine ex-servicemen were unemployed, but in early 1922 approximately 600,000 of the 1,000,000 registered unemployed were ex-servicemen, representing over two-thirds of the male unemployed.[13]

That so many of the unemployed were ex-servicemen would prove to be a fundamental challenge to government. There was a general feeling that these men had a claim on the resources of the community, a right earned by their willingness to serve in wartime. As early as 25 November 1918, the government passed a bill extending the payment of unemployment benefit to the uninsured, because few ex-servicemen would have paid sufficient under the 1911 Act to qualify for relief. Twenty-nine shillings per week would be paid to unemployed ex-servicemen until March 1921.[14] The idea of non-contributory unemployment benefit was a major breakthrough on the path to full social security and was directly attributable to the war.

In part the motivation for this measure was a genuine sense of gratitude and the feeling that driving unemployed veterans to seek assistance from the poor law would be deeply embarrassing. There was also an element of fear. It was believed that unemployed ex-servicemen might easily become radicalised or possibly even insurrectionary.[15] The spate of mutinies which occurred during the process of demobilisation cannot have improved the government's confidence. It was alarming that some veterans joined the extremely radical National Union of Ex-servicemen (NUX). Wal Hannington points out that a substantial number of veterans had returned home with their rifles, such was the rapidity of demobilisation in the latter half of 1919. [16] In such circumstances a policy of concession seemed sensible.

If the reassessment of unemployment benefit averted disaster, it did not prevent discontent. Ex-sevicemen wanted reasonably paid employment rather than marginally bearable unemployment. Most of them found it, but large numbers suffered temporary unemployment and in the areas where the recession began to bite earliest (Scotland, Wales, Northern England) some began to see that their prospect of ever finding secure employment was doubtful. The result was understandable bitterness amongst veterans: 'Of course, I have been angry and bitter concerning the betrayal of promises made to the men of the 1914–18 war, a land fit for heroes etcetera. Many of my miner friends suffered long periods of unemployment and poverty. The greatest of all indignities was having to watch their children line up at soup kitchens.'[17]

The appearance that the state was prepared to undergo an enormous financial burden in war, yet was unwilling to provide proper support to those who had risked their lives and given their time and blood, seemed ironic:

One universal question that I have never seen answered: two or three million pounds a day for the 1914–1918 war, yet no monies were forthcoming to put industry on its feet on our return from the war. Many's the time I've gone to bed, after a day of "tramp, tramp" looking for work, on a cup of cocoa and a pennyworth of chips between us; I would lay puzzling, why, why, after all we had gone through in the service of our country, we have to suffer such poverty, willing to work at anything but no work to be had.[18]

Some individuals found it impossible to contain their anger:

When I was out of work I had to go before a means test panel. There was a very fat lady on the panel cuddling a Pekinese in her lap. She said "We've all got to pull in our belts a hole or two these days." I was fed up and told her, "Your words belie your appearance. That bloody dog has had more to eat today than I've had". There was a lot of argument and it ended in a row... I was charged with common assault and got three months in Wormwood Scrubs.[19]

More normally the reaction was resignation tempered by a black humour which barely hid the despair: 'I signed on for twelve months at the Labour exchange. They used to call us the 29th Division because we got 29s a week.'[20]

The first collective responses came in the winter of 1920, as unemployed ex-servicemen began to band together to form local associations. According to Wal Hannington, these early associations were essentially leagues of beggars. They applied to the police for permits to take collections in the streets in affluent areas. Hannington states that such permits were readily granted in order to defuse the possibility of the men becoming politically radicalised.[21]

Such radicalisation was exactly what Hannington wanted. In his view the turning point came with the brutal suppression by the police of an unemployed meeting in Whitehall in October 1920. According to Hannington many of the unemployed at the demonstration were wearing their medals. The choice of Whitehall as the focus for the march is interesting. Was it connected with the newly completed permanent Cenotaph?

According to Hannington the police baton charge to clear Whitehall came as a shock to the protesters:

who hesitated to believe that such treatment would be meted out to men who had only recently returned from the battlefields after four years of warfare in which they had been made to believe "that their grateful country would never forget them". The comradeship of the trenches was over. Ex-soldiers in blue were now ready to club down ex-soldiers in rags at the bidding of the only class that had profited from the war.[22]

Making due allowance for Hannington's Communist Party politics and also his non-combatant status, it is still probably an accurate description of a turning point in the attitudes of many unemployed ex-servicemen. Inevitably Armistice Day provided a focus for this feeling of betrayal. Even as early as 1919 unemployed soldiers had approached the Lord Mayor of Manchester, when he appeared for the first two minutes' silence, to ask for 'work not doles'.[23] In 1921 there are reports of public protest on Armistice Day in provincial cities. For example:

> The observance of Armistice Day in Liverpool was marred by a regrettable scene in one of the principal thoroughfares. A body of men, numbering 200, purporting to represent the unemployed of the city, chose the hour of eleven for demonstrating their grievances...This scandalous procedure lasted for nearly a minute and such cries as "Anyone want a medal" and "What we need is food not prayers", were heard. A portion of the demonstrating unemployed forced their way through the dense crowd of people who were standing silently still, but the unruly ones were eventually held up by mounted police and compelled to remain standing for the remainder of the two minutes.[24]

According to the organisers of the Liverpool demonstration they were 'tired of the hypocrisy and inhumanity exhibited' in the ceremony because for some of the unemployed the silence would soon be 'the silence of the grave'.[25]

In Dundee a similar protest led to mob violence: 'The disturbers were the Communist crew, who have labelled themselves, on what justification they would find it hard to explain, the "organised unemployed" and the song they sang during the two minutes of the year dedicated to the dead was the anthem of the revolutionists, the "Red Flag".' According to the *Dundee Advertiser*, 'the demonstrators did their best to rob the dignified ceremonial of all its solemnity and grandeur. It was a striking tribute to the vast throng of Dundee manhood who stood bare headed during the two minutes of what should have been a solemn silence that they kept their seething indignation under control.' The paper believed, 'It was the tears of women that alike inflamed and subdued the fierce blaze of angry passion'.[26] The passion did not remain subdued for long:

> Immediately after the sounding of the "Last Post", the crowd, who were at boiling point, made for the demonstrators. Red banners were still flourishing, whilst the "Red Flag" was in full blast, when the crowd broke in upon the procession and wild melee followed. The red flags and banners were seized from the grasp of the bearers and the flags were

torn to shreds, while the poles were smashed to pieces. Several of the processionists were seated off lorries and their chairs were pulled from beneath them and hurled down into the street. The crowd mounted the vehicles and tore down the banners that were still displayed there, the pieces of the poles being used to belabour the processionists. The police were unable for a time to keep the angry people from attacking the red flaggers and it was only with the greatest difficulty that they separated the combatants.[27]

The incident, resembling a Fascist 'action', is described with gruesome relish. That there was some genuine popular indignation involved is unquestionable, but the actions of the police in allowing the procession and the reaction that followed to take place appear distinctly suspicious.[28] The description of the protesters as 'communists who labelled themselves as the organised unemployed, identifies them as an early branch of the National Unemployed Workers Movement. According to Hannington the Scottish branch of the movement was intensely militant in 1921: 'Riots broke out in many towns and much damage was done before the authorities would make concessions.'[29] In Dundee in particular the latter half of 1921 appears to have been tense and 'a public building was burnt to the ground'.[30] This may suggest that by allowing the NUWM to disrupt Armistice Day the local authorities hoped to manipulate a backlash against the movement. This may have been successful; a correspondent claiming to be an, 'Ex-unemployed, Ex-Soldiers wife' wrote to the *Advertiser* that, 'until now I have done all I can to help the processionists...I shall never again put my hand in my pocket...Perhaps if the powers that be could administer a few strokes of the cat-o-nine tails it might dampen their ardour a bit.'[31]

It is noteworthy that all of the arrests for breach of the peace were made from the leadership of the protesters. James Thomson, a forty-six year old labourer, who was identified as an agitator, was sentenced to sixty days imprisonment and Mary Soutar, a mill worker, received forty days.[32] One other female mill worker, three male mill workers and a labourer had been arrested.[33] Two of the male mill workers and James Douglas, the other labourer, would have been of military age during the war. They may well have been ex-servicemen, a letter from 'Red Heckle' to the *Advertiser* stated that, 'Some of them that I have actually seen in the ranks of "Red" demonstrations, it was my misfortune to have had dealings with in France... If so "ex-conscripts" would be their proper designation. They were dragged into the army by the conscription net, and their names are writ large in the "crime sheets" and sick lists of the unfortunate units to which they were drafted.'[34]

Clearly the popular response to this kind of protest was liable to be negative. In London the protest was more orderly. It was decided by the London District Council of the Unemployed that a march to the Cenotaph by unemployed ex-servicemen would be a particularly powerful image. The police were informed of the intention to march and although the marchers were not allowed to join the main procession they were granted permission to march past the cenotaph at the end of the ceremony. The handbills distributed by the organisers urged the participants to, 'revere the memory of our class who fought, bled and died, BUT DON'T FORGET THE UNKNOWN WARRIORS LIVING'.[35]

According to Hannington, twenty-five thousand of the London area unemployed[36] marched to the cenotaph to lay a wreath:

> Whitehall and the streets surrounding it were densely packed with mourners and sight seers. This time they saw a sight that they had never seen before. As the banners of the various contingents were raised ready for the march, it was seen that each banner had hundreds of thousands of ex-service men's medals pinned on to it. Thousands of ex-servicemen took pawn tickets from their pockets and pinned them on the lapels of their coats. The bands of the unemployed movement were draped in red and black, and at the head of our procession was carried a large wreath with an inscription that read: "From the living victims – the unemployed – to our dead comrades who died in vain."[37]

There was irony and parody in this procession, but also solemnity and respect for the dead. The authorities had anticipated trouble, perhaps even hoped for it, but the large bodies of police present proved almost unnecessary. The Camberwell contingent were persuaded to delete the part of the inscription on their wreath which claimed that the dead had died in vain, to avoid giving offence.[38] In Hannington's opinion the majority of those gathered at the cenotaph were sympathetic to the marchers: 'On they came, steady and inevitable. Be-medalled and bearing obvious signs of poverty they stirred the dense throng of sightseers to a sense of deep emotion and a realisation of the injustice which was being meted out from man to man.'[39]

The respectful nature of the protest impressed the bystanders. Even the Conservative popular press was sympathetic rather than hostile.[40] Hannington 'reports' a conversation amongst those watching. (Almost certainly invented, if Hannington was in the procession how could he have heard this exchange?)

"Who are those people?" asked one young woman to another on the sidewalk. "Why – they're the unemployed." "Then good luck to them." said the first girl bitterly, almost savagely.

"Disgraceful," snorted a red-faced old man, with a fur clad young thing on his arm. "These men are Bolsheviks," he said. "But look at their medals," said the girl. A woman in a black shawl turned on the old man. "Shut your bloody gap! If you had been out of work as long as my old man, you'd be a Bolshevik." A murmur of approval went through the crowd.[41]

It is not the factuality of this account but the style that is of interest. The older man with the young 'fur clad' girl on his arm is clearly a non-combatant. The implication is that he has money and therefore that he did well out of the war. In other words, a profiteer. If this interpretation is correct, it is in line with an important left-wing rhetorical opposition. The left identified those who fought with the unemployed and those who did not fight with the rich. The moral worth of the unemployed was enhanced by their association with war service and the moral worthlessness of the rich was emphasised by their link with profiteering. Eric Leed states that the encounter with the profiteer by the frontline soldier is often a key moment in the memoirs of combatants. It was the moment which undermined the 'economy of sacrifice'. As the soldiers gave their blood, the profiteer engrossed that medium of exchange, for private gain.[42] There was no more emotive symbol in the immediate post war years.

On 11 November 1922, the *Daily Herald* had an editorial supporting the unemployed:

> What will you be thinking of while silence falls upon the country for two minutes at eleven o'clock today. Perhaps of a son or a husband, of a brother or a close friend who died in the belief that the war was to make a better world. Four years since the war officially ended and we have nearly a million and a half unemployed on the registers (which by no means includes all)...[43]

The editorial went on to call for the 'conscription of capital', an idea which was seen as appropriate to raise on the day when 'our minds turn to the victims of the conscription of manhood'. In support of this point an implicit contrast was made, between the unemployed and the wealthy and by implication the veteran and the profiteer: 'Of course the 'two minutes' great silence will be generally observed, but for the evening, particularly in London, many hotels and restaurants announce dances from one guinea to five guineas.'[44]

Accompanying this item was a poem by Alfred Noyes, 'The Victory Ball'. It is worth quoting at some length:

> The cymbals crash
> And the dancers walk
> With long silk stockings
> And arms of chalk
> Butterfly skirts
> And white breasts bare
> And shadows of dead men
> Watching 'em there
>
> Shadows of dead men
> Stand by the wall
> watching the fun
> Of the Victory Ball
> They do not reproach
> Because they know
> If they're forgotten
> It's better so...
>
> "Pish!" said a statesman
> Standing there
> "I'm glad they can busy
> Their thoughts elsewhere
> We musn't reproach 'em
> They're young you see"
> "Ah" said the dead men
> "So were we!"[45]

Apart from the poem's objectionable misogyny,[46] the other structural contrast is between fat, sleek non-combatants, profiteers and 'statesmen' and the betrayed combatant. In the case of the poem the soldiers are dead, but in the context of its reprinting in the *Herald* they stand symbolic of the unemployed, the maimed and the homeless ex-servicemen as well. The division between home and front during the war had become equated with the division between classes after it.

A Time to Mourn and a Time to Dance[47]

On 10 November 1921, a group of disaffected ex-servicemen, along with their sympathisers, launched a daring raid to steal a field artillery piece. The authorities might have been more alarmed were it not for the fact that the raiders belonged to Caius College, Cambridge and the gun to Jesus College.

The Cambridge Regiment had presented a German gun to every (male?) college in the University. Caius undergraduates were greatly annoyed to see that their college had been awarded a trench mortar whereas Jesus had been given a field gun. They swopped the destination labels and appropriated the larger piece.

The subterfuge was discovered and the trophy committee intervened to restore the original decision, moving the field gun back to Jesus and the mortar to Caius. Caius students refused to accept this decision as final. They set up a secret committee to plan the recapture of the gun. For several weeks beforehand, Caius undergraduates cleaned and oiled the Jesus gun secretly at night and sawed a gap in the railings surrounding Jesus. On 10 November they struck.

150 Caius men infiltrated the Jesus college grounds late at night. Working silently, less than 15 yards from occupied rooms, they cut the field gun free from its concrete base without being heard by anyone. Then, using sandbags and matting, they hauled the gun, which had had all of its working parts carefully oiled to prevent noise, out of Jesus College. They escaped undetected, having left a six penny toy gun in the place of their trophy.[48] On the morning of Armistice Day, the field gun was discovered outside the Master's lodge in Caius.

A trivial incident? In some respects certainly, but what remains fascinating is the form in which the prank was conducted. This is not a case of a rugby club bursting into a college and dragging away a trophy by brute force. What it resembles is a perfectly conducted trench raid. Meticulous reconnaissance, careful cold-blooded preparation, absolute secrecy, detailed planning and the exploitation of surprise, these were skills learnt by junior officers in the most deadly of schools. Skills that were still in demand in many areas of Europe in 1921, amongst Freikorps, Fascisti and Black and Tans, organisations that blended veterans and those who narrowly missed the fighting, for altogether more sinister purposes. A benign and amusing example of the trench-fighter spirit, but one that illustrates that it was not only the unemployed marchers who were having difficulty in blending back into the normative behaviour of civilian life, there were others who were not yet ready to forget where they had been.

Readjustment to civilian life, in the midst of the social tensions of defeated Germany and ambiguously victorious Italy, produced a distinctive, violent culture amongst ex-servicemen. In France, ex-servicemen were reintegrated by means of clear public recognition of their achievement. In Britain, ex-servicemen, as a group, were both omnipresent and generally invisible. But occasionally they emerge from the shadows in the early 1920s, sometimes as the angry figures of the disillusioned unemployed, but at least as often as boisterous young men celebrating friendship and survival.

That exuberant high spirits might be a feature of 'soldiers from the war returning' is a suggestion that seems almost heretical. The picture of a twentieth-century war veteran is a picture of a scarred, disillusioned man, angry at society, haunted and solitary. It is a picture most familiar to us today from numerous films and books on Vietnam. It is a picture which was created in the aftermath of the First World War. The classic, almost paradigmatic account of the mood of the war veteran comes from *Goodbye to All That*. Here, Robert Graves describes his reaction to the news of the Armistice:

> In November came the Armistice. I heard at the same time of the deaths of Frank Jones-Bateman, who had gone back again just before the end, and Wilfred Owen, who often used to send me poems from France. Armistice-night hysteria did not touch our camp much, though some of the Canadians stationed there were sent down to Rhyll to celebrate in true overseas style. The news sent me out walking alone above the marshes of Rhuddlan (an ancient battlefield, the Flodden of Wales), cursing and sobbing and thinking of the dead. [49]

The perfect picture of the melancholic veteran, walking alone with thoughts of dead comrades, leaving celebration to civilians and crass colonials. It is also a retrospective invention. Graves' reaction to the Armistice at the time, was nothing of the sort:

> Things were very quiet up here on the 11th. London was full of buck of course, but in North Wales a foreign war or a victory more or less are not considered much. Little boys banged biscuit tins and a Verey light or two went up at the camp but for the rest not much. A perfunctory thanksgiving service with nothing more cheerful in it than a Last Post for the dead; and then grouses about demobilization. Funny people les anglais. [50]

The Graves of 1918 is the real ex-servicemen, with a tough, cynical posture and a suggestion of regret that things had not been a little more rowdy and celebratory. The author of *Goodbye to All That* reinvents the character to produce a much more noble and moving figure.

Examining Armistice night 1918 is a good approach to assessing the ex-serviceman's mood. For a long time due to descriptions such as the one in *Goodbye to All That,* there has been an image of Armistice night as being essentially a display of civilian hedonism, whilst the soldiers met the Armistice news numb and bitter. Arthur Marwick states bluntly, 'For that society of men in the front line there was only numb relief, no jubilation.'[51] An examination of what happened on 11 November 1918 produces a much more complex picture.

The first thing that should be pointed out is that the requirements of continued military discipline in the front lines made an unrestrained celebration impossible in many places. Equally, it should be pointed out that Belgium and Northern France had few resources to allow a wild party at the frontline in November 1918: few women, little alcohol, not even much food. Within these limitations it is quite clear that there was a degree of jubilation and high spirits that greeted the Armistice at the front line. Colonel Richard Meinertzhagen, a British officer, stated that on the Armistice night, moving between the French and British zones was to go from Frenchmen 'yelling with delight and all displaying small tricolour flags' to 'unrestricted licence'.[52] Corporal Stanley Butcher wrote, 'I think the Army is going mad. There is one huge Brock's benefit in coloured signals, flares and very lights...what I would give to be home tonight.'[53] The second comment is revealing, it was not melancholic memories of dead comrades, although doubtless many veterans had these memories, but lack of resources, which was preventing the frontline soldiers from ostentatiously celebrating survival. Fireworks, in the form of flares, were almost all that they had readily available. Corporal O.W. Flowers describes the use to which those were put: 'When we heard that the Armistice was signed, we thought we would have a bit of fun. There were a lot of small dumps about, ammunition and verey lights, so we set them alight – firing shots into them and then of course you only wanted one to go up and all the rest went. We had a real Guy Fawkes. The officers never interfered...'[54]

In the rear echelons in France the possibilities were somewhat greater and were exploited accordingly. In Dieppe, according to a French witness: 'Tommies, their foreheads wreathed in green sat astride barrels of beer, drunk and babbling, whilst lorries decked out with the Union Jack, the Belgian and Italian colours, drove through the town.'[55] With the cruelty and misogyny that demonstrates much of the pent up tensions of the frontline, Australian convalescents marked the Armistice by raping the women in a Boulogne brothel and burning its furniture.[56] In Paris, British soldiers on leave joined in the festivities. Several dozen British soldiers joined the American actress Shirley Kellogg on stage at the Casino de Paris, when she sang 'Scotland the Brave.'[57]

The festivities in London took on a distinct military look as well:

> There was a wild conglomeration of Tommies, Jocks, Australians, Yanks, sailors, wounded men, Italians, Belgians, Indians, French, Portugese, Land-girls, 'Waacs', 'Wrens', Munition girls and everyone else in uniform parading and howling and hooting and dancing through the streets and breaking things and hurting each other.[58]

Nelson's column still bears the scars of the bonfire lit by Canadian and Australian troops at its base on Armistice night. In many accounts the riotous behaviour of Dominion troops is stressed. This is almost certainly based on fact; Australians in particular revelled in their reputation for indiscipline. But a degree of caution should be used in assuming that the worst excesses of Armistice night were a manifestation of colonial wildness. It is clear from the description above and from others that many British troops were mingled in with the rioters.[59]

The purpose of this digression into the events of the day of the Armistice is to show that there was another side to the reaction of servicemen to the end of the war which has not been sufficiently stressed.[60] This is directly relevant because it set the tone for many ex-servicemens' attitudes towards the correct style of commemorating the *anniversary* of the Armistice. Many wanted to replay the bacchanalia of Armistice Day 1918, others wanted to experience the party that, by virtue of being in the frontline, they had missed. Years later, Charles Carrington described the development of Armistice Day from a perspective that is very different from our usual suppositions about First World War veterans, but which probably reflects the attitude of many:

> The first Armistice Day had been a carnival, the second Armistice Day, after its solemn pause for the Two Minutes' Silence which George V was believed to have initiated, was a day of festivity again. For some years I was one of a group of friends who met, every Armistice Day at the Cafe Royal for no end of a party, until we found ourselves out of key with the new age. Imperceptibly, the Feast-Day became a Fast Day and one could hardly go brawling on the Sabbath. The do-gooders captured the Armistice and the British Legion seemed to make its principal outing a

day of mourning. To march to the Cenotaph was too much like attending
one's own funeral, and I know many old soldiers who found it
increasingly discomforting, year by year. We preferred our reunions in
private with no pacifist propaganda.[61]

The process by which exuberant celebration of Armistice Day
became equivalent to brawling on the Sabbath is more complex
than Carrington suggests, but the analysis is an interesting one
which provides a useful point of departure. There is interesting
evidence from the first few years of Armistice Day that a substantial
number of ex-servicemen did indeed treat it as a day of festivity.[62]
For example, in Leeds the ex-servicemen at the University had a
riotous evening on 11 November 1919:

> In the absence of what, from their point of view might be regarded as a
> fitting and authorised celebration of Armistice day, the ex-service men
> among the students at Leeds University decided to mark the occasion in
> characteristic fashion. They celebrated as only students can. Good
> fellows all, they set out in force to have a jolly time, and they had it
> without a doubt.
>
> About 120 strong they marched in procession from the University at
> 6pm to the centre of the city. The original intention was to have a torch
> light procession, but the torches were not available. Instead they had the
> band of the Leeds Rifles to show them the way and their progress was
> illuminated by fireworks of all kinds... Large crowds who became infected
> with their radiant good humour, watched the procession...It was indeed a
> merry throng which sat down to dinner at Messrs Powolnys'... To the
> accompaniment of a cornet and various weird instruments such as
> tommy talkers...the company marched to the Empire music hall where
> they occupied the first five rows... It is hoped to make the celebrations,
> which was universally voted a great success, an annual event.[63]

Such behaviour appears to be commonplace amongst the more
economically secure and privileged veterans in the first five years
after the war. In Oxford on Armistice evening in 1920 most of the
student revellers, 'wore service medals on their tunics and their faces
almost gave audible expression to the words "have a good time
gentlemen: we've all been through a lot together, only don't do too
much damage".'[64] As one Oxford veteran put it, 'Why should we be
sombre and subdued on the anniversary of the greatest day of our
lives?'[65] Younger students were drawn into these festivities. As an
undergraduate at Oxford in 1922, the youthful Graham Greene
managed to injure himself during an Armistice Day 'rag'.[66]
Restaurants, hotels and dance halls responded to this demand for

Armistice Day celebrations by laying on entertainments for 11 November.[67]

At first sight such behaviour appears to be a classic case of trivialisation of the memory of the war, a process described by George Mosse.[68] Such an assessment is an oversimplification of the veterans' feelings on Armistice Day.[69] But from two contemporary viewpoints the Armistice night revels were abhorrent. For unemployed ex-servicemen, they were an offence in class terms, a mockery of their poverty. For the civilian bereaved, they were unseemly behaviour on a day that should be marked by reverence. Through the early 1920s a body of opinion developed which sought an end to anything that could be construed as detracting from the solemnity of 11 November.[70] These feelings came to a climax in an intense public debate, conducted through the newspapers, in October and November 1925.

There was a subdued debate in *The Times* throughout October 1925 in which various opinions on the correct tone for the evening of Armistice Day were expressed.[71] Then the debate gathered pace. On 20 October 1925, Canon H.R.L Sheppard, an ex-army padre and Vicar of St Martins-in-the-Field, already established as something of a celebrity as a radio broadcaster, wrote to the *Times* :

> Is it dreadfully old fashioned to be shocked at the announcement again this year, that a great Victory Ball is to be held on Armistice night? If so I confess that I should wish to be counted amongst the backnumbers on this occasion. Dancing is frequently the obvious and fitting form of gratefully commemorating a glad event, but a fancy dress ball on a grand scale as tribute to the Great Deliverance which followed on the unspeakable agony of 1914–18 seems to me not so much irreligious as indecent...
>
> The situation is complicated but scarcely relieved by the fact that the proceeds of the ball will go towards relieving the financial anxieties of a wholly deserving hospital...
>
> Is it too late to obtain for the hospital the assistance that it is now naturally looking for and yet to beg that Victory Balls of magnificence and their equivalent in thoughtless and ill-timed Armistice commemorations at hotels and restaurants should not be encouraged at least while this generation retains the heart-ache of a tender and thankful remembrance.[72]

This personal complaint triggered a remarkable quantity of response in correspondence to various newspapers. Two responses the following day in *The Times* illustrate an essential feature of the debate which followed:

Mr Sheppard's letter in the *Times* to-day will give great pleasure to the relatives of those who made the "great sacrifice". Many of them have long wished for someone to interpret their feelings in as lucid and powerful a manner as Mr Sheppard has done in your issue to-day.

If Mr Sheppard's letter succeeds in evoking "the frown of public opinion" against this fancy dress ball, I shall be glad to contribute £ 50 towards making up any deficit.[73]

Speaking in the name of the relatives of the dead against celebrations on Armistice Day was the normal rhetorical approach, although veterans were also to be invoked. But celebration also had its defenders:

As one who has attended a dance upon every anniversary of Armistice day, may I protest against the implication of callousness and lack of feeling which several of your recent correspondents would appear to make? Each one of us who were alive during the war, has several anniversaries in the course of the year upon which he cannot fail to remember his own dead and all who died: and for a day of universal remembrance, Armistice day has been set aside. There is however, no day in the year which has been appropriated to the commemoration of the nation's thankfulness that a term was put to the war, that so many who might have died did not die, that victory crowned our arms...we who rejoice in the pleasures of Armistice Night next month shall have taken our part as sincerely as your correspondents in the solemn silence and the services in our churches. The change from prayer to thanksgiving is incongruous only to those who are conscious of incongruity.[74]

The defenders of celebrations generally made these arguments. They argued that it was right to celebrate the relief with which the end of the war had been greeted as an end to bloodshed and a promise of prolonged survival to the soldiers in the frontline. They also argued that it was right to celebrate the achievement of the war, the victory won. Finally, they argued that there was nothing incongruous about the juxtaposition of mourning and dancing; the second was a counterpart to the first, a feeling of celebration that life goes on and one that the dead themselves would have understood. In fact, such celebrations with their attendant cameraderie were seen in a peculiar way as incorporating dead comrades. These arguments clearly meant more to veterans than to civilians. One such veteran gave his opinion to the *Times*:

As one who is the only survivor of four brothers may I be allowed to say in regard to the Victory Ball that I have the feeling that the last thing that they would wish is that they should stand in the way of our enjoying ourselves. Personally I shall not choose November 11 for holding my revels: but I realize that what would not be possible for me may be perfectly possible for others. Armistice Day has a double significance; it is a day of commemoration for the dead; but it was also a day of deliverance for the living. I do not see why both celebrations should not take place on the same day. The first Armistice Day was a day of rejoicing. But, the morning has now become, by usage, a time of remembrance. Why must that prevent the evening from being given over to the other aspect without any thought of disloyalty to the dead?

For November 11 was for all survivors quite tremendously *the* day of victory and deliverance. The enemy of those long and dreary years, who had seemed invincible, threw up the sponge at last. The case of right, as we saw it, had triumphed; and to each individual soldier came the irrepressible feeling that with ordinary luck he had once more the prospect of long years of life...Sorrow was turned into joy. Let the sorrow and the joy both be celebrated; let us look forward as well as back.[75]

The letter is doubly fascinating. As one of those who had lost close relatives, this officer could not himself celebrate on 11 November; it would be unseemly and emotionally impossible. However, as a veteran, he was prepared to write in defence of his comrades who chose to do so. It was in controversies of this sort that identities became sharpened, those who belonged to both categories being forced to choose between differing opinions. Those who wished to end celebrations on Armistice Day were not prepared to accept celebration of survival as a worthy motive; quite the contrary, as one correspondent to the *Daily Mail* wrote: 'To go to a ball on Armistice Night is as indecent as though, after having attended the funeral of father, mother, brother or sister, one should rejoice that one was still alive.'[76] This letter demonstrates how the debate had spread from the rarefied letters pages of *The Times* to the popular press. The *Daily Mail* had begun to campaign for an end to celebrations on Armistice Night:

As once more the anniversary of Armistice Day approaches, there are clear signs of public debate about the manner in which that date should be observed. A custom is growing up of keeping the day with junketing and feasting – with expensive dinners and dances.

Of all the days in the calendar, excepting Good Friday, it has the most solemn associations...

The British people have never shown themselves lacking in either taste or judgement on the great issues, and they are right in feeling that it is better to keep Armistice Night in the home than in the dancing hall.

On 23 October the paper printed a 'poem' supporting this position:

When England bows her head
And silent stands.
Mourning her million dead
In distant lands,
What other thoughts are in her heart beside
Sorrow and love and pride?

You who would make the night
Of that great day
All merriment and light
And careless play,
Remember those wounds, though unrevealed
To sight, are yet unhealed.

Be happy if you will:
But leave each heart
That mourns its dearest still
This day apart
Untouched by thoughts that bring the soul to earth
Or loud and thoughtless mirth.

The shout exultant dies; But yet we keep
Hearts that must ache and eyes
That still must weep
Shall not you too, by whom no tears are shed
Pay reverence to our dead?[77]

The newspaper claimed an overwhelming popular response to its campaign:

Letters are reaching the *Daily Mail* from all parts of the country written by men and women of all classes, conveying conclusive proof of the existence of a general and profound conviction that Armistice day is essentially a day for solemn remembrance and that indulgence in revelry then is unseemly. Many of the most vigorous responses are from men who experienced the horrors of the Great War, and very touching is the plea for reverent observance of women who had lost their nearest and dearest.[78]

Although the support of veterans was claimed, the letters actually printed seem to have more often spoken on behalf of the women who lost their 'nearest and dearest'. A Mrs Hamilton wrote that: 'The day will bring back sad memories and many a burning tear will rise to the eyes of fathers, mothers and widows who lost their dear ones in the war. The right way to honour the Glorious Dead is to observe

Armistice Day reverently.'[79] Similarly, a letter of support to Sheppard from Lady Astor stressed the importance of considering the bereaved, 'I am with you all the way about Armistice. I have been hurt and cried inside, on Armistice Day, and I am just an ordinary creature who lost friends. What must mothers and wives feel?'[80]

As early as 20 October, the accusation had been made in *The Times* that those who were celebrating on 11 November were those with the least right to do so: 'We stand before the Cenotaph at 11 a.m and eat drink and dance at 11 p.m. Armistice Day was, I believe, intended to be a holy day for the observance of ceremonies connected with the end of hostilities, not a half-holiday for *war profiteers and heedless non-combatants*.'[81] (My italics.)

The accusation implicit in the *Daily Herald* in 1922 was made explicitly in *The Times* in 1925. Those who attacked festivities on Armistice Day could not believe that veterans would want to celebrate. After two weeks of heated attacks in the *Daily Mail,* the *Daily Express* decided to respond by defending what it believed was the veteran's view. On 6 November it solicited an opinion from no less a personage than Earl Haig, former commander of the B.E.F. and head of the British Legion: 'I recommend that Armistice Day be observed throughout the Empire as a day of remembrance. In the forenoon all ages should attend a thanksgiving service with a parade of veterans at the local war memorial. In the afternoon games suited to the climate should be played, in the evening people should rejoice according to taste.'[82]

It could hardly be claimed that Haig did not have an interest in seeing victory celebrations occur on 11 November; after all in the eyes of the public it was his victory. The fall in his reputation would only come after his death. However, as head of the British Legion he was reasonably sensitive to ex-servicemen's opinions. (He retained respect in the Legion long after his public reputation elsewhere had declined for his surprising sensitivity as a leader of that organisation.) A more extreme view was voiced by another senior officer:

"I am entirely in favour of Armistice Day being regarded as an occasion for rejoicing," said General Sir Herbert Belfield to a Daily Express representative yesterday. "The solemn remembrance of the dead, should, of course, find a place in the day's celebrations, but I regard Armistice Day as a day for rejoicing over the victorious ending of the country's four year ordeal. Possibly the services in memory of the dead should be held, not on Armistice Day at all, but on, say, All Souls' Day.[83]

It is interesting to speculate whether the General was aware of the importance of All Saints' Day as a day for remembering the war dead in France.

Such views could be dismissed as no more than would be expected from the High Command who had experienced the war in an existence remote from the dreadful realities of the frontline. But less exalted voices expressed similar opinions:

> My friends may be odd, but they have without exception decided not to alter their plans for Armistice Day. By reason of their generation they are all ex-army men, and the majority of them have arranged either to give or to be present at dinner parties and dances.
>
> They if anyone, have surely the right to decide what is the most fitting way to spend the day.
>
> I have respect for Mr Sheppard and others who think pleasure out of place on that evening but I cannot agree with them.[84]

Some were much less willing to see that the critics had any case:

> Sir – The thanks of a large number of people will be accorded to the 'Daily Express' for its attitude over Armistice Day, for publishing Earl Haig's manly message and generally discountenancing the injustice of the eleventh hour attack on those who have associated themselves with celebrations, many of them concerned with charity...
>
> As for this club (whose members cease work to observe the Silence while one of their number places a wreath on the Cenotaph), owing to the disturbance caused in peoples minds, it is to be deprived of any profits to be handed over to naval charities, their guarantor is to be mulcted into needless loss, and its members with their women folk who meet to celebrate the Peace are to be branded outcasts![85]

The *Daily Express* even joined in the poetic polemic, with a contribution from Mrs Louisa Baldwin, mother of the Prime Minister:

ARMISTICE DAY 1924
Now shall our dead keep festival with us to-day
Our happy dead, for radiant, strong and young are they
Who look with wonder on us that we should be sad
When they in their far abode are glad.[86]

Both sides in the polemical struggle trumpeted their victories. On 6 November the *Daily Mail* announced that Liverpool, Bath, Birkenhead, Oldham, Rochdale, Lowestoft and Stoke-on-Trent had refused dance licenses for 11 November.[87] On 4 November it publicised a protest meeting to be held at Rochford, Essex against 'dancing and other unnecessary forms of entertainment on the afternoon of 11 November'.[88] It waxed indignant at the decision of the London County Council Highways department to grant an extension of drinking hours to the Council's Old Comrades Association.[89]

On 6 November, the *Daily Express* triumphantly printed a list of all the London Hotels and restaurants that had refused to be intimidated and which were holding Armistice Night parties:

> Carlton and Ritz – Gala dinner, supper and dance. The restaurant of the two hotels will be decorated for the occasion and a feature will be made of the flags of Allies festooned on the tables of the Carlton restaurant.
>
> Savoy – More than a thousand visitors have been booked for the night's dinner and dance. Music and dancing until 2 a.m.[90]

Interestingly, commercial establishments stood up to public pressure against celebrations on Armistice Day much better than charity balls:

> The position with regard to Armistice night in London hotels and restaurants was explained on Thursday by the general secretary of the Incorporated Association of Hotels and Restaurants. The business of these establishments next Wednesday evening would be no different he said, from that usually carried out on other nights of the week, except that Flanders Poppies would be sold on behalf of the British Legion. The business of hotels and restaurants was to cater for the public, and they had to meet public demand on Armistice night as on other nights.[91]

By way of contrast, the Albert Hall 'Victory Ball' which had started the whole argument was cancelled, and the Hall was made over for that night to H.R.L. Sheppard to hold a service of remembrance. The reason given by the committee was that in view of the appeal made by the Archbishops of Canterbury and York and the Moderator of the Free Churches Council it was felt inappropriate to go ahead.[92] (That appeal will be dealt with below.) Instead the charity ball was rescheduled for 12 November, the Prince of Wales agreeing to attend.

Sheppard was gracious in victory, appealing to people to attend the charity ball on 12 November in large numbers so that the hospital would not lose its charitable support. His plans for the replacement event in the Albert Hall were much more solemn:

> Even at this very short notice it would doubtless have been possible to provide for this occasion a wealth of oratory and music, but, if I know anything of the minds of the men who gave their lives in the war, they would be honoured most by the spontaneous tribute of a simple commemoration, unadorned by elaboration of any kind, in which all

who bear them in memory could take part. The service at 8.30pm (which will last only three-quarters of an hour) will be of the simplest character and the singing entirely in the hands of the audience.[93]

The prolonged public argument over whether or not it was permissible to dance on the evening of 11 November is difficult for a modern observer to understand. It would be easy to regard the whole debate as trivial were it not for the total earnestness with which it appears to be conducted, the sheer scale of correspondence and newsprint expended on it and the fact that some reasonably major public figures become drawn into the argument. The *Nation* described the success of Canon Sheppard's campaign 'as one of the most surprising events in recent memory', apparently without considering the statement a little hyperbolic.[94] Before proceeding further an attempt should be made to analyse what it was all about.

Analysis of an Odd Controversy

The role of the press in the controversy was paramount. It was incautiously suggested in *The Nation* that because a minor editorial in the *St Martin's Review* had wrought such huge controversy, it demonstrated the weakness of the 'million power press' by comparison.[95] The editor of the *Daily News* responded by pointing out that 'nobody would have heard of the gentle editorial in "St Martin's Review" if the million-power press of all grades had not given it enormous publicity and opened their columns to the wide range of public opinion.'[96]

The controversy over the correct tone to be adopted on Armistice Day 1925 drew in many divergent strands of thought. The dispute between the *Daily Mail* and the *Daily Express* shows these two newspapers taking two quite distinct, but recognisably 'conservative' populist lines in dealing with the question.

The *Daily Mail* took a position which stressed domestic and family virtues, it centred its arguments on respect for family grief. Unsurprisingly, women were given emphasis.[97] In a broad sense, it was also a religious argument, treating Armistice Day as a 'Holy' festival, analogous with Good Friday. The view point could be described as 'moral conservatism'.

The *Daily Express* took a notably different view. It defended the right of people to choose their activities on the evening of 11

November against the public pressure of a 'religious' group of busybodies intent on enforcing a moral norm. Its standpoint could be described as 'libertarian conservatism'.

Both view points had a long history in the development of conservative populism.[98] The view that an Englishman had the right to enjoy his free time as he chose had been a mainstay of the urban Conservative appeal against the perceived encroachment of the Liberal 'Nonconformist State' in the latter years of the 19th century. The aftermath of the war gave a new life to this; the restrictions of the Defence of the Realm Act (DORA) on shop, restaurant and most particularly pub opening hours was a continual target for the anger of the *Daily Express* in the 1920s. Its defence of dancing on 11 November was a logical extension of this position.

By contrast the *Daily Mail* was more puritanical and censorious on the subject of public morals, supporting the puritanical Home Secretary, Sir William Joynson-Hicks (labelled Jix by his many critics)in his campaigns to reimpose 'Victorian' morality. In this respect it is important to note that one of the first letters of support received by the *Daily Mail* was from Lady Joynson-Hicks:

> Personally, I would much sooner not have any sort of festivity on Armistice Day, for I think that the day should be kept quietly... I much dislike the kind of rejoicing which has gone on in hotels and other places on previous Armistice Nights: It seems to me that even more of that sort of thing is being arranged this year than hitherto.[99]

Both the *Daily Express* and *Daily Mail* (and their supporters) phrased their arguments in terms of patriotism. Neither showed the slightest tendency to criticise the conduct of the war or the consequences of the peace. They were prepared to criticise their opponents for an unnatural and unpatriotic attitude to the commemoration of the war:

> From the earliest times – until this year, when an unwholesome and unnatural change is sought to be made – mankind has signalled its gratitude and joy for its success in war, and its release from the travails that war brings, by prayer and by merry making. The two courses are not inconsistent.[100]

If these two viewpoints had been the only ones brought to bear on the question of Armistice celebrations then it is possible that the argument would have been deadlocked. However, there was a second argument that could be brought to bear against Armistice celebrations; social justice.

The organisers of the Albert Hall Victory Ball stated that it was the appeal of the church leaders which caused them to cancel the planned celebration. Yet an examination of that appeal makes it quite clear that there is in fact no *direct* mention of the controversy in that appeal. What, therefore, caused the organisers to read it as an appeal to them to cancel? To quote the appeal may be enlightening:

> ARMISTICE DAY – AN APPEAL TO THE NATION
> *Armisticetide , 1925*
> The observance of Armisticetide this year offers us as a nation an opportunity, which we desire, God helping us, to use aright.
> Locarno as our clearest thinkers assure us, means the opening of a new and brighter chapter in the tangled story of European relationships. Let the thought spur us to face with redoubled courage and new confidence the problems which are confronting us at home...
> Our supreme need is a clearer atmosphere – an atmosphere in which men will hate to be at variance and will long to understand. Try to understand how acute is the distress among us. Try to understand how life must feel to those who are the actual sufferers – those in whose homes unemployment works havoc of heart and mind... Callousness to the anxieties of others is a menace to peace...We suggest, where possible, the note of remembrance, of reflection, of expectant prayer should be kept from the Sunday before Armistice Day until the day itself...
> Randall CANTAUR: Cosmo EBOR: David Brook, Moderator of the Federal Council.[101]

What was it in this letter which was taken as criticism? It must have been the phrase about 'callousness to the anxiety of others',[102] which in turn was definitely and clearly linked to the unemployed. It is the inclusion of the unemployed (including, of course, many unemployed ex-servicemen), which tipped the balance of the argument.[103] As early as 1921, Hugh Edwards M.P. had written to the Prime Minister to condemn the gala dinners at London Hotels on the grounds that 'widespread unemployment and consequent destitution' made such festivities 'unseemly' and 'unwarrantably extravagant'.[104]

The combined stigma of offending the bereaved and a segment of the ex-service community, particularly at a time when the tension in the coalfields was seen as leading to a general sharpening of class antagonism was too much for the organisers of 'charitable' functions in 1925. Indeed the aftermath of the miners' strike in South Wales would see a brief re-emergence of protests of a similar nature to those in 1921. Neath ex-servicemen organised a protest movement which disrupted the annual memorial service at Briton Ferry.[105] Extravagant charity events in a time of hardship threatened to exacerbate class conflict. Such conflict was damaging to the ex-service ethos and may have caused even the most frivolous ex-servicemen to modify their support for festivity on 11 November. The commercial establishments were more hard nosed, probably because no one suggested compensating them for the loss of very lucrative business, but by 11 November 1926 they had also bowed to the pressure and stopped victory celebrations.

To demonstrate that all such arguments about identification with interest groups have their limitations, the final word should be given to one particular bereaved mother, who was very much an individual in her attitudes. Margot Asquith had lost her step-son, Raymond, on the Somme in 1916, but she nonetheless remained Margot Asquith, ever suspicious of puritanical moralising:

> I think in the interests of well wishers it should be clearly understood that in the future Armistice Day should be kept as a day of mourning and reflection.
>
> I hope that the aftermath of this religious revival will not prevent people attending the balls which in deference to public opinion, have been postponed from the 11th to the 12th.[106]

A Festival of Remembrance

One interesting suggestion made during the controversy of 1925, was that there should be a more egalitarian alternative to celebrations which were mostly for the wealthy:

> I have read with great interest the letters in *The Times* in regard to Armistice Day. Instead of the banquets and dances given to those who enjoy that sort of thing all the year round, would it not be possible to raise a fund and with the help of all the large hotels and fashionable restaurants, to entertain all those who fought in the Great War bringing them together on Armistice Day to enjoy an evening of good cheer and music, with a warm welcome from friends who remember with gratitude what they went through in those dark days.[107]

Although nothing came of this particular proposal, it demonstrated that there was a way of circumventing part of the criticism of festivities on Armistice Day. By limiting the celebrations to veterans and at the same time incorporating *all* veterans, not just a privileged minority, celebrations would avoid two criticisms. First, there could not be an accusation that it was a 'half holiday for profiteers' and additionally, it could not be suggested that they would be offensive to those too poor to take part.

As mentioned above, Armistice Day changed profoundly in 1926:

> The really astonishing feature of Armistice Day this year was its pronounced seriousness. As time passes, the sense of jubilation on this day of memory decreases. There was a marked difference even from last year...There were many dances then, and the restaurants and night clubs were full to overflowing. Many people who danced last Armistice Day felt that they could not do so last night [108]

It is not entirely fanciful to suggest a note of regret in this report in the *Daily Express* society column, given the defence of dancing that had been made there the previous year. Equally, it is not implausible to suggest that it was the sense of a void on Armistice evening, the awareness of the lack of an outlet for the camaraderie that had accompanied the dinner dances and parties, that led to the *Daily Express* sponsoring the first 'British Legion' Festival of Remembrance at the Albert Hall on 11 November 1927.[109] The initiative appears to have been taken by a Mr Mike Wardell of that newspaper.[110]

The festival was partly a newspaper 'stunt' of the variety that had been first initiated by Northcliffe with the *Daily Mail* and had been picked up by Beaverbrook at the *Daily Express*, but it was consistent with the line that the paper had taken two years before. Various features of the event are worth noting. The festival was billed as a festival of 'remembrance', therefore avoiding any charge that it was unseemly as a celebration.[111] Although not religious in nature the festival would include hymns. Its principal feature, in fact, was to be community singing, an activity that the *Daily Express* was already involved in popularising.[112] This was clearly a more acceptable form of celebration than dancing. Attendance was to be open to any serviceman or woman who had served overseas during the war; the 10,000 places at the Albert Hall were to be allocated by a committee of the British Legion. It was specified that 'uniform or day dress' was to be worn, an implicit prohibition of evening dress which distanced the festival from the celebrations of a few years earlier. The festival was also to be free of charge. The cumulative result of these measures was to avoid any charge of exclusivity or elitism. Any funds raised would be used for charitable purposes by the British Legion.[113]

Because this was a Beaverbrook sponsored enterprise there was bound to be an Imperial dimension. The festival at the Albert Hall was officially described as the 'Empire Festival of Remembrance' and was to be the first programme simultaneously broadcast by the BBC to all parts of the Empire:

> The object in holding the festival, which the *Daily Express* is proud to have organised in conjunction with the British Legion, is to impress on all who can take part in it and also the millions who will listen in all over the world – the necessity for renewing that comradeship that existed during the war and to remind the British Empire of the unpaid debt to those men still unplaced in civil life who served their country.[114]

According to Stuart Hibberd, the BBC announcer who opened the broadcast, the success of the Festival broadcast led directly 'to the eventual formation of the Empire Service' in 1932, and therefore marks the ultimate origin of the BBC World Service.[115]

The participation of the Prince of Wales guaranteed interest in the broadcast. Nor was he the only prominent celebrity who would be attending. Winston Churchill, Lord Allenby and Sir Ian Hamilton, as well as numerous lesser known military figures would attend. The hall was decorated with the ensigns of the battleships at Jutland and the British standard from Ypres, borrowed for the evening from the Imperial War Museum.[116]

The response was overwhelming. 50,000 applied for the 10,000 tickets causing the *Daily Express* to organise a second, outdoor festival in Hyde Park to cope with the overflow.[117] Although the nature of the venues naturally biased attendance towards those living in the London area,[118] who could obviously get to the Albert Hall or Hyde Park more easily, the fact that it was a Saturday evening made it more plausible for veterans from further afield to attend.

What did the festival mean? In an article published in the *Daily Express* on 10 November, the editor of the *Sunday Express* saw its significance as being an acknowledgement of the 'glorious living', particularly those 'still unplaced in civil life':

> The Remembrance Festival in the Albert Hall on Armistice Night is a fit and due sequel and supplement to the hallowed rites of the Cenotaph silence...No future generation can charge us with having been neglectful of "Our Glorious Dead". When time has hallowed our monuments, when our little stones and our little crosses are softened by the weathering centuries, men will be touched by the agony of our world wide mourning... But the Cenotaph symphony as it soars above Whitehall does

not completely assuage our sense of duty and our pang of obligation. Our Glorious Dead if they could speak, would call upon us to remember Our Glorious Living. Their thoughts are with the men and the women they left behind them. Their spectral fingers would point to their comrades in a gesture of comradeship. They would appeal to us to unite in devotion and loyalty to the victims of the great victory and the great peace...

This is the true meaning of the Remembrance Festival. This is the high mission and message of those marching songs that ten thousand soldiers will sing in the Albert Hall to-morrow night. For nine years Field-Marshal Earl Haig has tirelessly toiled to keep alive in us a sense of obligatio "to all those gallant fellows to whom we all owe more than any of us can ever repay.". . .

Cenotaphery is not enough. Prayers and hymns are not enough. Brass bands and pipes are not enough. Episcopal benedictions are not enough... Our Glorious Living do not ask of us any sacrifice comparable with theirs. They do not beg for alms. They only demand a little share of the heritage which they and their dead comrades won for us and our children.[119]

The article goes on to give case studies of ex-servicemen whom the peace had not treated kindly. It describes the homeless, the unemployed, the crippled and the neglected. Part of the meaning of the Festival of Remembrance would be to publicise the fate of such men.

At last it seemed the circle would be squared. The desire of large number of veterans to get together to enjoy themselves and celebrate their camaraderie had been given official sanction. Yet as a festival of 'remembrance' it would be acceptable to the families of those who had died, it would not look like an indecent celebration of survival. It would also be a festival to publicise the fate of the least fortunate veterans and to try to remind the public of a debt of honour, rather than appearing as an insulting celebration whilst some veterans struggled with poverty, illness and despair.

'Remembering we forget much that was monstrous'[120]

An anonymous columnist in the *Daily Express* wrote of the men who were to attend the Albert Hall festival:

[They] form willy-nilly a class apart from mankind – they have been "under fire". Their distinction is not of bravery but of knowledge. They have breathed the air that buzzes, screams and thunders with death...

Every war is followed by a period of unrest, for the minds of men who have been under fire are no longer the fallow fields of civilian thought: they have been hallowed to brutality. Strange things sprout in them along with the seeds sown by solicitous politicians. The men who have been under fire have been tortured into acid thinking...There is an instinctive loyalty to "his pals" and an occasional flicker of genuine hatred roused by opposition.[121]

This is an almost perfect example of what George Mosse describes as 'the myth of war experience'.[122] The concept of knowledge being the distinction between combatant and non-combatant is central. It is what the soldier has seen, sensed and felt that marks him out. He has passed through a liminal state in a strange landscape and become initiated in esoteric mysteries.[123] This could be perceived as a *Rite de Passage*.[124] Groups undergoing such a process, according to Victor Turner, undergo an experience of *Communitas*, an undermining of every day hierarchies and an intense feeling of mutual closeness.[125] *Communitas* in its origins strains towards openness and universality, but over time tends towards closure and in-group solidarity (although retaining the potential to open out once again). It is clear that the intense feelings of comradeship experienced during the war were something similar to this experience of *Communitas* and it is also clear that it was exactly this sensation that the gathering at the Albert Hall in 1927 recreated. The medium by which it was expressed and transmitted was the singing:

> The climax was reached last night in the "Daily Express" Remembrance Festival at the Albert Hall where 10,000 men and women who served overseas gathered to sing the old Army songs and hear the Prince of Wales.
>
> It was indeed a historic festival. Not only the 10,000 participated. A vast invisible audience throughout Great Britain joined in the songs and listened to the Prince. Beyond them a still vaster audience of countless millions in every quarter of the earth heard the singing and the Prince's words.
>
> For the first time the miracle of an Empire broadcast was accomplished. For the first time one man spoke to the whole world. For the first time the Empire thought and felt and sang in unison.[126]

The technical possibilities inherent in radio helped foster the sense of openness which Turner describes as the 'anti-structure' inherent in *Communitas*. The solidarity and unity extends beyond the 10,000 at the Albert Hall to all veterans, to all inhabitants of the United Kingdom, to all inhabitants of the Empire and logically, ultimately to 'the whole world'.

H.V. Morton was present at the Albert Hall and gave an account of his emotional reaction to the songs:

> We did not realise until last night that the songs we sang in the Army were bits of history. In them is embalmed the comic fatalism which carried us through four years of hell. How easily we slipped back into it! Cynicism was blown clean out of us. We were young once more as we can never be again and we went deeper into our memories...Thirteen years fell from us. We ceased to see the Albert Hall and the thousands of faces white in the arc lights; we looked into an abyss of memories where long columns passed and repassed over the dusty roads of France, where grotesque, unthinkable, things happened day and night – the brief joys, the sharp sorrows of those days, the insane injustices of fate, and above it all the memory of the men we knew so well...It seemed to me that we had caught the only decent thing in the war – the spirit of comradeship. We had come to the hall as individuals; we were now once more an army marching in our imagination to the old music.
>
> We laughed because tears were in our heart. We shouted for old songs not on the programme. We encored ourselves. We stamped and shouted our delight...[127]

The sense of reconnection with the dead, with comrades scattered in civilian life, even with his own youth is very apparent in Morton's description. The breaking down of hierarchy is apparent in his description of the reaction to the Prince of Wales:

> "Old comrades and friends," he said, "will you please all sit down". They cheered him and sat down... More cheers swept the hall as he walked through the hall to his box *raising his hand in salute*. He walked the length of the Albert Hall unattended through a cheering mob of men. Grizzled Old Bills turned towards him with something like worship. He was the Prince. He had served in France.[128] (My italics.)

The Prince saluted the ordinary soldier. Like them he has served in France. Yet ultimately anti-structure is just a temporary release from structural hierarchy. When the moment is over they are commoners again and he is the Prince, the hierarchy highlighted and strengthened by the temporary release from it.

The songs which were sung that night at the Albert Hall encompassed the whole range of soldiers' songs short of the most ribald and frankly obscene. The festival began with 'Pack up your troubles' and ended with ' Abide with me'. It encompassed the sentimental, 'The long, long trail' and 'A perfect day', the strident, 'Soldiers of the King', the patriotic, 'Keep the home fires burning', the humorous 'K-K-Katy' and 'Sister Susie'; and even the cynical.

Two songs that came into the last category ought to be quoted to indicate that the festival was not as reverent as its title suggested. The first is, 'And when I die':

And when I die
Don't bury me at all,
Just pickle my bones
In alcohol.
Put a bottle of booze
At my head and feet,
And then I know
my bones will keep.

There is something deeply incongruous about this song at a festival of 'remembrance', even though it was a good representation of the attitude of frontline soldiers towards death, which was expressed even more blatantly in a song such as 'The bells of hell'; with its brutally cynical refrain, 'The bells of hell go ding a ling a ling, For you but not for me.' That song was emphatically *not* sung at the festival, despite its well attested popularity during the war. Another cynical song that *was* sung at the festival was 'I want to go home':

I want to go home.
I don't want to go to the trenches no more,
Where the guns and the whizzbangs and the cannon do roar,
I want to go home,
Where the Germans can't get at me.
Oh my, I don't want to die,
I want to go home.

The unheroic view of the war was represented by such songs at the festival, along with the patriotic, sentimental and religious.[129] All were sung with gusto in a celebration of comradeship. This was the unifying factor; in other respects the attitudes of the veterans to the war was complex and ambiguous. It was a memory of both pain and fortitude in the face of pain; of cruelty and of self-sacrifice; of disaster and mismanagement, but also a memory of the final triumph. It encompassed fear, laughter and sorrow. The myriad faces of war were filtered through the myriad faces of peacetime experience. In Britain, comradeship was something intermittent, it lacked the unifying 'veterans' political language of Germany or Italy and, in a different way, France.[130] The British veterans had a complex attitude to their experience, one which defied simplification. Compared with the insistent force behind the need to create a simple meaning to the war for the sake of the bereaved, it was too disparate.

The festival of remembrance at last created an outlet for this through a celebration of comradeship, but only in a tamed and toned down manner. The songs were those that would be at least minimally acceptable to the bereaved; the whole festival was hedged round with a semi-religious aura. The spontaneous 'carnivalesque'[131] celebrations of veterans in the early 1920s had been channelled into respectability. In 1937, the 'London Correspondent' of the *Manchester Guardian* reminisced that, 'once it was impossible to get a room in the big restaurants on Armistice Night. Now there are many empty rooms. The big gathering at the Albert Hall now includes what is left of a score of other gatherings'.[132]

Provincial festivals followed the pattern of the Albert Hall festival. By 1936 there were 'Festivals of Remembrance' in all parts of the country, in Scotland, South Wales, Jersey and West Somerset, at High Wycombe, Aylesbury, Milburn upon Tyne and Exeter.[133] These were often timed so as not to coincide with the BBC broadcast from the Albert Hall.[134]

But the incorporation of veterans into Armistice Day was also a process of marginalisation. The BBC might broadcast the 'Festival of Remembrance' every year after 1927, but by 1936 a BBC internal memorandum was describing it as 'the British Legion sing-song at the Albert Hall' and calling for it to be followed by a suitably elegiac piece of music (and precede three bible readings) which would, 'wash out the taste of the super-sentimental orgy from the Albert Hall and reset the frame for these readings.'[135]

Ten Years On

An exchange of letters in the *Harrovian* in 1928 on the subject of the tenth anniversary of the Armistice indicates that there was a developing dissatisfaction about the way in which the war was commemorated. A letter dated 11 November from 'VOX CLAMANTAS' made the usual request that Armistice Day be used as a day of idealistic commitment to a more unified nation.[136] The letter was entirely unremarkable, but it provoked a vigorous response from C.W. Carrington in the next edition. Carrington attacked those people who wished 'to tell us what we ought to learn from

Armistice Day. That day commemorates the Million Dead who fell doing their duty; our duty is to be ready to die in the same way if the call comes "That is all ye know on earth, and all ye need to know." ' He proceeds to question all of the idealistic rhetoric that had developed around the ritual: 'No doubt, it is right at other times to speak of building a New Jerusalem, of making an England fit for heroes. Perhaps, even, though I am not sure on this point, we need to be reminded of the blood and horror of war, so that we may work to create a world where there is no more war.' But for Carrington this rhetoric was inappropriate on 11 November. On Armistice Day the less said the better, and he called for the 'stern reticence' of the best war poetry to be applied to the day.[137] Assuming that this is the same Charles Carrington quoted earlier, this is the voice of an outspoken veteran at odds with the solemn platitudes which marked the tenth anniversary.[138]

In the same year, the *Oxford Magazine* carried an editorial by an anonymous veteran. He expressed the attitude of many ex-servicemen to Armistice Day:

> The ceremony of Armistice day, in England, at any rate, is essentially a civilian ceremony; it expresses in the main the non-combatant attitude towards the war. No soldier could have invented it, unless, indeed at a considerable interval of time; for him, it is far too spectacular and emotional, and remote from the real issues of the battlefield.
>
> Most soldiers have a fairly clear idea of what used to be meant by a hero, and must for that reason deprecate the loss of all meaning which that word has suffered. They know, too, the process of growth and change, which, as the war dragged on, made itself felt, often with devastating effect, in minds which at the beginning of things, had not been clouded by a doubt...
>
> How hard it is to give divine honours to the dead, and at the same time to understand that the cause for which they died, however urgent for support at the moment when it could no longer be ignored, was yet the outcome of centuries of folly and falsehood (theirs as much as ours) which we are pledging ourselves to repent of and amend. Though the 'cause' was great it was caused by much that was not great at all.[139]

Amongst some of the more articulate veterans, the memory of the war was being reconstructed. An attempt was being made to come to terms with the complex reality of the experience, seen with the perspective of the peace that followed. The simplicities of August 1914 had been undermined by the publication of diplomatic papers of various nations which shed doubt on the easy interpretation of the war as 'German aggression'. Some of the machinations of the allied propaganda machine had been revealed. Memoirs of politicians and generals revealed petty clashes of personality, ruthless ambition, dishonesty and incompetence. The men who had laboured and suffered in the mud of Picardy and Flanders read these books, or at least extracts from them in newspapers. They reflected on the peace that had not created 'a land fit for heroes'. Some took note and some of the more literary veterans began to write. It is not necessary to postulate a 'repression of war experience' to explain why there was an outburst of writing on the war in the late 1920s and early 1930s. It took time to pull together the disparate elements of memory into the necessary coherence of fiction, to identify the heroes and, much more important, the villains, and to turn history into a coherent narrative. When this was done, the memory of the war and with it, Armistice Day, the repeated public expression of that memory, would be transformed.

Notes to Chapter 2

1. This has already been demonstrated in the medals issue; see chapter 1. For the marginalisation of veterans generally see, Winter, *Death's Men*, pp. 246–48.

2. *British Legion Annual Report and Accounts for 1921*, London, 1922, p. 22.

3. PRO: HO 45/11557/392664/32. Marginal comments on letter from Miss E.M. Watson CBE, 14 Dec. 1922.

4. See A. Prost, *In the Wake of War*, Oxford and Providence, 1992, pp. 59–60.

5. D. Haworth, *Bright Morning; Images of a Lancashire Boyhood*, London, 1990, p. 43.

6. Ibid., p. 84.

7. Winter, *The Great War and the British People*, p. 275.

8. *Sunday Express*, 25 Jan. 1925; quoted in J. McMillan, *The Way it Was: 1914–34*, London, 1979, p. 106.

9. McMillan, *The Way it Was*, p. 108.

10. G.Wootton, *The Official History of the British Legion*, London, 1956, p. 48.

11. Quoted, Ibid., p. 50. See also the contribution of George Bernard Shaw to a British Legion charity album of facsimiles:

> Justinian in History's view
> Your fame's not worth half a snowball
> Because ungrateful monarch you
> Begrudged Belisarius his obol
>
> Again the veteran begs his bread
> From you, who swore he should not rue it
> For shame! It was for you he bled
> It is for you to see him through it.

Belisarius was the Byzantine general who was imprisoned and blinded by his Emperor. Begging in streets, he was showered with coins by his grateful countrymen. See, *The British Legion Album In Aid of Field Marshall Haig's Appeal for Ex-servicemen of All Ranks*, London, no date, 1923? Pages not numbered.

12. Wooton, *Official History*, appendix 2, p. 202.

13. British Legion estimate. See Wootton, *Official History*, p. 31. The opinion of Wal Hannington of the NUWM was similar. See W. Hannington, *Unemployed Struggles*, London, 1936, p. 12.

14. For a full discussion of this see T. Wilson, *The Myriad Faces of War* , Oxford, 1986, pp. 822–825.

15. See S.Ward, 'Intelligence surveillance of British Ex-servicemen 1918–1920', *Historical Journal*, 16 (1973), pp. 179–189.

16. Hannington, *Unemployed*, p.13.

17. L/Cpl Evans quoted in M.Middlebrook, *The First Day on the Somme*, London, 1971, p. 309.

18. Pte Turner, Ibid., p. 309.

19. Pte Kidd, Ibid., p. 309.

20. L/Cpl Law, Ibid., p. 309.

21. Hannington, *Struggles*, pp. 13–14.

22. Hannington, *Struggles*, p. 17.

23. *Daily Herald*, 12 Nov. 1919, p. 1.

24. *Yorkshire Post*, 12 Nov 1921, p. 10. Also *Liverpool Weekly Post*, 12 Nov. 1921, p. 10; *Liverpool Courier*, 12 Nov. 1921, p. 5. See also 'Directorate of Intelligence, Special Report No. 131: Report on Revolutionary Organisations in the United Kingdom, 17 Nov. 1921,' p. 14. For convenience I have viewed this report in the papers of Archbishop Davidson who, interestingly, received a copy; Lambeth Palace Library, Davidson Papers, vol. 200, ff. 31–41.

25. *Eastern Daily Press*, 12 Nov. 1921, p. 6.

26. *Dundee Advertiser*, 12 Nov. 1921, p. 1.

27. *Yorkshire Post*, 12 Nov. 1921, p. 10.

28. Processions of all kinds were banned after the riot, see *Dundee Advertiser*, 15 Nov. 1921, p. 1.

29. Hannington, *Struggles*, p. 40.

30. Hannington, *Struggles*, p. 40. The *Dundee Advertiser*, 14 Oct. 1921, p. 1 reports an earlier incident of violence involving the same 'organised unemployed', but no arson. The reporting of most of the local papers was bitterly hostile to the protesters. The local trade union paper described the *Advertiser* as openly antagonistic to the working classes; see *Dundee Jute and Flax Workers Guide*, December 1921, p. 5. This moderate paper does not mention any of the 'organised unemployed' rioting, but provides ample evidence of the severe class tensions in the town which had followed the end of the wartime jute boom. According to the leader of the Union, 'The great body of the workers in this industry are either unemployed or on short time.' This was combined with an attack on the owners for not using their wartime profits to cushion the blow of recession. See *Dundee Jute and Flax Workers Guide*, August 1921, p. 8.

31. *Dundee Advertiser*, 12 Nov. 1921, p. 1.

32. *Dundee Advertiser*, 24 Nov. 1921, p. 4.

33. *Dundee Advertiser*, 14 Nov. 1921, p. 3.

34. *Dundee Advertiser*, 12 Nov. 1921, p. 2.

35. *Liverpool Weekly Post*, London Correpondent, 12 Nov. 1921, p. 10.

36. Estimates in press sources range from 5,000 to 20,000. See *The Times*, 12 Nov. 1921, p. 5 and *Daily Telegraph*, 12 Nov. 1921, p. 8. Hannington dates the protest as occurring in 1922, but he is clearly mistaken.

37. Hannington, *Struggles*, p. 77. According to the *Daily Telegraph*, one ex-serviceman wore pawn tickets instead of medals; according to the *Times*, 'several' did

so. The *Daily Telegraph* states that many women and children were part of the unemployed march, whilst the *Daily Mail* implied that the marchers were all male.

38. *Daily Mail*, 12 Nov. 1921, p. 5; *Eastern Daily Press*, 12 Nov. 1921, p. 6.

39. Hannington, *Struggles*, p. 78.

40. *Daily Express*, 12 Nov. 1921, p. 5 and *Daily Mail*, 12 Nov. 1921, p. 8. The exception to press sympathy was, predictably, the *Morning Post* which seemed more concerned with the plight of a Mrs Ramsay, who had been thrown from her 'brougham' when the horses took fright at the demonstration, than sympathetic to the plight of the demonstrators; *Morning Post*, 12 Nov. 1921, p. 8.

41. Hannington, *Struggles*, p. 78.

42. E. Leed, *No Mans Land: Combat and Identity in World War 1*, Cambridge, 1979, pp. 204–207.

43. *Daily Herald*, 11 Nov. 1922, p. 1.

44. *Daily Herald*, 11 Nov. 1922, p. 5.

45. Alfred Noyes, 'Victory Ball' reprinted in *Daily Herald*, 11 Nov. 1922, p. 5. The images of this poem bear a striking resemblance to the climactic scene of Wilfred Ewart's novel, *The Way of Revelation*. In turn it is clear that the final section of that novel, in which an unfaithful woman dies of a drug overdose in the arms of her soldier lover, is an almost exact fictional rendering of an incident which occurred after the Albert Hall victory ball on 11 November 1919. Mrs Alma Steans, a society beauty died in the arms of her ex-soldier husband after taking poison that evening. See the lurid account of the coroner's inquest in the *Daily Mirror*, 15 Nov. 1919, p. 3. These three images of the victory ball, taken together, produce a remarkable image of decadence.

46. More apparent in the full version.

47. Ecclesiastes, 4:5.

48. The most substantial account of the incident is in the Caius college magazine, which describes the raid in a parody of an official military history. The raid was planned by ex-Lieut. G.F. Hopkinson, North Staffordshire Regt (attached R.E), MC, BA 1919. The terminology of the raid is pure western front; 'Gap party' for removing railings, 'Covering party and fighting patrols' for dealing with police and proctors. See *The Caian*, XXX, 1 (Michaelmas term, 1921), pp. 30–40. I would like to thank C.M. Jamet for bringing this document to my attention. A less organised 'gun raid' was carried out on Armistice Day 1919 by students of St Bartholomew's Hospital on the gun belonging to University College London. See, *Daily Mirror*, 13 Nov. 1919, p. 2.

49. R. Graves, *Goodbye To All That* , London, 1929, p. 246.

50. Letter, Graves to Nichols, quoted in Hynes, *A War Imagined*, p. 255.

51. A. Marwick *Britain in the Century of Total War 1900–1967*, London, 1968, p. 61. Marwick's evidence for this statement is a single quote from a novel by Richard Aldington from 1930. As such, it says more about the 'myth of the war' than the reaction to Armistice.

52. Quoted in S.Weintraub, *A Stillness Heard Around the World*, Oxford, 1985, p.328.

53. Ibid., p. 328.

54. L. Macdonald, *Voices and Images of the Great War*, London, 1988, p. 316. See also Private Frank Dunk who managed to find some alcohol 'When the French folks heard, out came the flags and wine, beer, all sorts, and everyone got totally pickled', p. 309.

55. Weintraub, *Stillness*, p. 243.

56. Ibid., p. 243.

57. Ibid., p. 236.

58. Robert Sherwood, Canadian Black Watch, quoted Ibid., p. 265.

59. Ibid., pp. 270–271.

60. Armistice Day was not an isolated case of high spirits. The partying continued on Victory Day; at the Berkeley Hotel officers of the 19th Hussars attending a victory

party stood on the tables and sang 'John Peel'. See R. Graves and A. Hodge, *The Long Weekend*, London, 1941, pp. 30–31.

61. C. Carrington, *Soldier from the Wars Returning*, London, 1965, p. 258.

62. Examples include the description of the Unionist Association First Annual ball in Newcastle where amongst the '400 ladies and gentlemen' there were many wearing Khaki and service dress, *(Newcastle Journal,* 12 Nov. 1919, p. 9). At the first Armistice Ball in 1919 at the Albert Hall, 'many wounded men were on the floor and their feet seemed to have lost none of their cunning.' *(Daily Mirror,* 12 Nov. 1919.) At Maxines in Edinburgh in 1921, 'an appropriate note for the occasion was seen in the naval and military uniforms of the male dancers.' *(Scotsman,* 12 Nov. 1921, p.10.)

63. *Yorkshire Post*, 12 Nov. 1919, p. 8.

64. *Isis*, 570, 17 Nov. 1920, p. 1.

65. *Isis*, 546, 19 Nov. 1919, p. 5. See also, *The Serpent: Official Organ of the Manchester University Student Unions,* 8 Dec. 1919, pp. 56–57 and 7 Dec. 1920, p. 31, for accounts of Armistice 'rags'. The attitude could be summed up by the comment in *The Serpent,* 7 Dec. 1920, p. 37: 'Another Armistice Day has passed! And it was a good Dance too!'

66. N. Sherry, *Life of Graham Greene,* London, 1991, p. 120.

67. See for examples, the advertisements for a 'Grand Armistice Fancy Dress Ball' at the Hyde Park Hotel (Price £1.15.0 for a double ticket) and for an 'Armistice Dinner-Dansant' at the Belgravia Restaurant (Price 10s 6d). *The Times,* 8 Nov. 1922, p. 22. and 9 Nov. 1922, p. 10. The Hyde Park Hotel price was 6s more than the entire weekly allowance for an unemployed ex-serviceman. See also *Manchester Guardian,* 11 Nov. 1921, p. 6, for description of planned festivities.

68. Mosse, *Fallen Soldiers*, pp. 126–156

69. See report on 'rowdiness' of Birmingham University students and subsequent correspondence, *Birmingham Evening Mail,* 11 Nov. 1919, p. 2 and 13 Nov. 1919, p. 5. Whether the students involved in the disturbance during the two minutes silence and those who condemned the disturbance were servicemen is difficult to establish for certain.

70. Particularly marked in the church press; for examples see *The Guardian,* 16 Nov. 1923, p. 1056 and *Church Times,* 9 Nov. 1923, p. 515.

71. See Letters 'Armistice Day' *The Times,* 12 Oct. 1925 p. 12; 15 Oct. 1925, p. 10; 17 Oct. 1925, p. 8.

72. Letter, H.R.L. Sheppard, *The Times,* 20 Oct. 1925, p. 15.

73. Letter, George Sutton, *The Times,* 21 Oct. 1925, p. 17.

74. Letter, C.H.B. Boult, *The Times,* 21 Oct. 1925, p. 17.

75. Letter, 'Company Commander', *The Times,* 21 Oct. 1925, p. 17.

76. Letter, J. Watson, *Daily Mail,* 30 Oct. 1925, p. 7.

77. 'Touchstone', *Daily Mail,* 23 Oct. 1925, p. 8. The amount of 'poetry' and indeed doggerel written on the subject of Armistice Day by contemporaries is initially somewhat surprising. (Not to mention awkward, because poetry is difficult to paraphrase into conventional narrative.) Yet it was a continuation of the tendency prior to the war to commemorate and explain anything and everything in verse. See, Bocacz, 'A Tyranny of Words', pp. 651–652.

78. *Daily Mail,* 24 Oct. 1925, p. 7.

79. Letter, Mrs Hamilton, *Daily Mail,* 30 Oct, 1925, p. 7.

80. C. Scott, *Dick Sheppard,* London, 1977, p. 140.

81. Letter, *The Times,* 20 Oct. 1925, p. 10.

82. Message from Earl Haig, *Daily Express,* 6 Nov. 1925, p. 1.

83. *Daily Express,* 6 Nov. 1925, p. 1.

84. 'Talk of the Town', *Daily Express,* 6 Nov. 1925, p. 4.

85. Letter, Harry Vandervell (President RNVR [Auxillary Patrol] club), *Daily Express,* 10 Nov. 1925, p. 8.

86. *Daily Express,* 7 Nov. 1925, p. 9. The *Daily Express* gave a mercifully edited

version of this elegy. The *Eton College Chronicle*, 5 Nov. 1925, p. 923, subjected its readers to a further two verses, including:

> They hear no more the hideous clash and din of strife
> The victory well won! For us they gave their life
> Their young and joyous life, nor did they count the price
> Be worthy, O be worthy of the sacrifice.

87. *Daily Mail*, 6 Nov. 1925, p. 9. The controversy was reaching many provincial centres. Church leaders appealed for 'an atmosphere where men will hate to be at variance and long to understand' in Bury, Lancashire. See Moorhouse, *Hell's Foundations*, p. 155. This is a direct quote from the Archbishops' appeal on Armisticetide 1925 extracted below.

88. *Daily Mail*, 4 Nov. 1925, p. 7.

89. Ibid., This organisation with 3,000 members might be taken as further evidence of the desire of a certain number of veterans to enjoy Armistice Night, a point not acknowledged by the *Daily Mail*.

90. *Daily Express*, 6 Nov. 1925, p. 1. Also listed: Berkeley, Piccadilly, Princes, Metropole, Cecil, Victoria, Criterion, Trocadero, Palace House, Regent Palace, Belgravia, Coventry Street, Corner House, Embassy Club, Ciro's, Cafe de Paris, and Kit Kat Club.

91. *The Times*, 11 Nov. 1925, p. 9.

92. *The Times*, 5 Nov. 1925, p. 14.

93. Letter, H.R.L. Sheppard, *The Times* , 6 Nov. 1925, p. 15. In 1941, Robert Graves and Alan Hodge claimed that Sheppard held a peace rally that evening. There does not seem to be any evidence for that and it is probable that given Sheppard's later role as a peace activist they projected the image back. It is in fact unclear whether Sheppard held pacifist views at this stage. I suspect that it was meditation on the meaning of Armistice Day in 1925 that was the first stage in Sheppard developing these beliefs. See Graves and Hodge, *Long Weekend*, pp. 328–29. Carolyn Scott claims that Sheppard wrote in hand on his programme for the service at Albert Hall: 'Of course Pacifism must be written into this.' She states that this was written 'years later'. Scott unfortunately gives no precise reference to where this programme is kept. See Scott, *Sheppard*, p. 142.

94. *The Nation*, 7 Nov. 1925, p. 205.

95. Ibid., p. 205.

96. *The Nation*, 14 Nov. 1925, p. 239.

97. Northcliffe was apparently the first press proprietor to take a serious interest in developing a female readership for his paper. Supposedly it was one of Northcliffe's maxims that there should always be one story of interest to women on the front page of the newspaper. See Graves and Hodge, *Long Weekend*, pp. 59–60.

98. See J. Lawrence, 'Class and Gender in the making of Urban Toryism 1880–1914', (unpublished paper, cited with author's permission).

99. Letter, Lady Joynson-Hicks, *Daily Mail*, 24 Oct. 1925, p. 7.

100. Editorial,*Daily Express*, 7 Nov. 1925, p. 8.

101. Appeal by the Archbishops of Canterbury and York and the Moderator of the Council of Free Churches, *The Times*, 3 Nov. 1925, p. 15.

102. In the letter announcing the cancellation the organisers wrote 'all those connected with the Hospital were very averse [sic] to carrying out the project if doing so involved hurting the feelings of others'. Letter, *The Times*, 5 Nov. 1925, p. 14.

103. See letter from Rev. D.C. Tibbenham to *Eastern Daily Press*, 12 Nov. 1925, p. 11.

104. *Manchester Guardian*, 11 Nov. 1921, p. 6.

105. G. Wootton, *The Politics of Influence*, London, 1963, p. 117.

106. Letter, Margot OXFORD, *The Times*, 6 Nov. 1925, p.15. Margot Asquith had been deeply affected by the death of Raymond to whom she had become close.

However, she had hidden her grief in an attempt to maintain a show of normal behaviour, believing that it would be wrong to demonstrate excessive grief, partly in order to support her husband and partly because it would not have been what her intelligent and vivacious step-son would have wanted. Inevitably she was criticised by her many enemies for an apparent callousness. In the political crisis of autumn 1916, judgements on the behaviour of either Asquith were likely to be coloured by the partisan nature of observers. Private letters clearly indicate that the pain she had suffered was real enough even if less than the utter devastation experienced by her husband. See, D. Bennett, *Margot*, London, 1984, p. 271.

107. Letter, Marie Dickens, *The Times*, 20 Oct. 1925.

108. 'Talk of the Town', *Daily Express*, 12 Nov. 1926, p. 4. In 1928 it was reported that, 'neither on Sunday or Monday are there this year to be special Armistice Night celebrations in the great majority of West End Hotels'; *Manchester Guardian*, 10 Nov. 1928, p. 13.

109. In 1926 the Albert Hall was used on 11 November for a charity performance of John Foulds's 'World Requiem' in aid of the Haig Fund, *The Nation*, 6 Nov. 1926, p. 183. This piece was written between 1919 and 1921. It had been performed annually since 1923 for the benefit of the appeal. It was not particularly well received in critical terms, but was protected from the worst criticism by its attachment to a worthy cause. In 1927, Foulds was left with the bill for printing 1,200 handbills and no royalties, having assigned them to the Legion. He emigrated, an 'angry and disappointed man'. The 'World Requiem' has probably not been performed since. See, Hynes, *A War Imagined*, pp. 275–276. Hynes may not have appreciated the significance of the British Legion Festival of Remembrance as a replacement for Foulds's work.

110. Wootton, *Official History*, p. 104.

111. Shortly after Dick Sheppard's death in 1937 it was claimed that the real origin of the festival of remembrance was the service which was held in Albert Hall in 1925. In a sense this is true but in another respect quite misleading. The British Legion Festival differed from the 1925 service in many respects. See, R.J. Northcott, *Dick Sheppard and St Martin's*, London, 1937, p. 11.

112. See reference to Mr Gibson Young, 'who would conduct the festival, having established his reputation in the "Daily Express community singing movement"', in *Daily Express*, 9 Nov. 1927, p. 1.

113. *Daily Express*, 1 Nov. 1927, p. 1; 2 Nov. 1927, p. 11; 5 Nov. 1927, pp. 1–2.

114. *Daily Express*, 1 Nov. 1927, p. 1.

115. See S. Hibberd, *This – Is London...* London, 1950, pp. 32–33, 81.

116. *Daily Express*, 9 Nov. 1927, p. 1.

117. *Daily Express*, 5 Nov. 1927, p. 1.

118. *Daily Express*, 2 Nov. 1927, p. 11.

119. James Douglas, 'To-Morrow', *Daily Express*, 10 Nov. 1927, p. 8.

120. S. Sassoon, 'To One who was with me in the War', Dedicated to Robert Graves, 1927?

121. 'K.S.L.I.', *Daily Express*, 2 Nov. 1927, p. 9.

122. See G. Mosse, *Fallen Soldiers*, Oxford, 1990.

123. See Leed, *No Mans Land*, pp. 12–38.

124. See A.Van Gennep, *Rites of Passage*, Chicago, 1972.

125. Turner's thesis was first stated in V. Turner, *The Forest of Symbols: Aspects of Ndembu Ritual*, Cornell, 1967. The clearest statement of what *Communitas* means is in V. Turner, *Drama, Fields and Metaphors*, Cornell, 1974, pp. 200–204.

126. *Daily Express*, 12 Nov. 1927, p. 1.

127. H.V. Morton, *Daily Express*, 12 Nov. 1927, p. 2.

128. Ibid.

129. Songs listed in songsheet for festival, *Daily Express*, 11 Nov. 1927, p. 10.

130. In Germany the myth of the 'stab in the back' provided a framework for a veteran's politics oppositional to the Weimar Republic. In Italy a similar sense of

betrayal of the Italian war aims by the allies and by 'communists' provided a structure for Fascism. By contrast, in France, the desire for public acknowledgement of the 'Poilu' as saviour of his country from aggression and invasion linked veteran's politics with the culture of 'civism'. There was no such readily available broader political current for British veterans' politics to work through, to turn comradeship into a political force.

131. Using the term to mean the treatment of a serious subject simultaneously seriously and lightheartedly – in this case the memory of the war and the dead.

132. *Manchester Guardian,* 12 Nov. 1937, p. 12.

133. *British Legion Report and Accounts 1936–1937,* London 1937.

134. See report on the Pontypridd Festival, *Western Mail,* 10 Nov. 1930, and the Newcastle and Whitley Bay Festivals, *Newcastle Daily Journal,* 12 Nov. 1936, p. 9.

135. BBC Written Archives Centre, Caversham, Memo: A.D.M to Herbage and Reybould, 21 Aug. 1936, R 34/227/2.

136. *The Harrovian,* 17 Nov. 1928, p. 144. It also called for 'unswerving loyalty to supreme authority', showing that the idealism inspired by Armistice Day could tend towards extremely right wing or even fascist models during this period.

137. *The Harrovian,* 17 Dec. 1928, p. 163.

138. The letter is credited to C.W. Carrington. Charles Carrington was C.E. Carrington, but the tone of the letter is so characteristic as to make it improbable that it could be anyone else.

139. *Oxford Magazine,* 15 Nov. 1928, pp. 1–2. The Tenth anniversary of the Armistice was the occasion for the issuing of a 'medal' by the Royal Mint. It portrayed the Cenotaph on one side and an allegory of peace on the other. The medal was on sale to the general public and was in no way restricted in its circulation. The quality of the production was ironically much better than that for any of the general service medals of the war, a point bound to irritate veterans. See, R. Garrett, *The Final Betrayal...Armistice 1918 and After ,* Southampton, 1989, p. 211.

3

And Men Like Flowers Are Cut: The Haig Poppy Appeal 1919–39

Armistice Day gave rise to one of the most universally respected charity appeals in British history. In order to understand the poppy appeal it is first necessary to discuss two subjects; provision for ex-servicemen prior to the First World War, and the nature of Victorian and Edwardian charities.

The provision of assistance to ex-servicemen had become an issue in the middle of the Victorian period. Prior to the Crimean War, the attitude towards discharged soldiers was a mixture of fear, contempt and neglect. A very small proportion might receive assistance from the Royal Foundation at Chelsea. Others would be reliant on fees paid for service in the militia. The long service system rendered the majority of soldiers unemployable on leaving the colours. In addition to the simple fact of most soldiers being too old to learn a trade, the conditions of service broke the health of the majority. Tuberculosis, malaria, bronchitis, venereal disease and alcoholism were all common place. The inevitable result was that old soldiers made up the hard core of the users of Poor Law casual wards.[1]

Two developments began to change this traditional attitude from the 1850s. The improved image of the 'common soldier', which began with Russell's reporting in Crimea, altered middle-class perceptions of the problem of the ex-serviceman. Literary and artistic representations of veterans became more sympathetic and romantic.[2] Cardwell's army reforms of 1870 also played a key role in that they transformed the nature of the problem. The introduction of 'short service' meant that relatively young and relatively fit men were being discharged from the army.[3]

In 1855, the first employment agency in Britain was brought into being for the benefit of ex-servicemen of 'good character'. Supported by senior officers in the services and the Royal Family, the scheme was developed further in the 1860s by Edward Walter, the brother of the editor of *The Times*. The organisation under his leadership evolved into the 'Corps of Commissionaires'. Initially the Corps gave special emphasis to providing work for the wounded and those of impaired health, but it was found that able-bodied men were more likely to be capable of performing the roles of security guards and messengers that the Corps provided. The ethos of the organisation was evangelical, with a shilling fine for missing church parade. Although 4,000 men had passed through the Corps by 1880, only one man in four lived up to the strict standards required; the majority were dismissed for 'drunkenness'.[4]

After the Cardwell reforms the problems of ex-service welfare became quantitively greater. The requirement to serve in the reserve continued to make ex-servicemen unattractive to employers. The War Office showed crass insensitivity in 1884 by recalling the reserve for the Sudan campaign, a move which convinced many employers that reservists were a bad risk. The response to this problem was the foundation in 1885 of the Association for Promotion of the Employment in Civil Life of Reserve and Discharged Soldiers, under the sponsorship of Lord Wantage. Like the Corps of Commissionaires it was intended primarily as a vehicle for recommending servicemen of good character to employers. By this stage there were voices arguing for a more thorough overhaul of the treatment of ex-servicemen. The Duke of Connaught believed that 'with voluntary enlistment the government are bound either to increase the pay of the soldier or to give him a good pension, or to find him employment... I don't like the government shirking its responsibilities, leaving it to county or private agencies.' The government did in fact provide a modicum of support, in the form of an annual grant of £200 to the association, but on the whole the field of ex-service welfare remained an area of private initiative. The main funding for the association came in fact from serving soldiers and sailors who contributed through the registration of their ships and units with the association.[5]

1885 also saw the foundation of the Soldiers and Sailors Family Association (SSFA). Very few service families were 'on the strength' and therefore entitled to the inadequate shilling per day separation allowance. More importantly, no widows' or orphans' allowance was made for families off the strength and widows pensions were only paid to those 'on the strength' whose husbands had been killed in action (probably still a minority of army deaths at this time).[6]

The SSFA was to become immensely important in dealing with the crisis that further increased concern for servicemen and ex-servicemen at the turn of the century; the South African War. That conflict brought the regular army into close contact with the general public for the first time in almost a century. It was covered in 'human interest' stories by the new mass circulation press and it coincided with the vogue for the poetry of Kipling, in particular the 'barrack room ballads' which were a rehabilitation for the ordinary soldier of the regular army.

Logically, the question of provision for the ex-serviceman and his family became of increased significance. The SSFA raised over £1million during the war, most of which was used to provide separation allowances. More significant as sign-posts to the post-First World War charitable initiatives, were the multiplicity of new schemes for ex-servicemen and bereaved dependants.[7]

In 1899, The Soldiers and Sailors Help Society (SHSS) was founded by Princess Christian with the specific remit of assisting disabled veterans. It founded residential homes at Bisley, maintained workshops in London and provided grants for convalescents. Some 2000 ex-servicemen were assisted in this fashion. In 1900, the *Daily Mail* began its 'Absent Minded Beggars Fund', named after the poem by Kipling. £100,000 was raised and used to fund a hospital at Alton.[8] All of this activity went a certain distance towards solving the perennial problem of the old soldier, but according to the 1909 Royal Commission on the Poor Law, old soldiers were still the largest contingent in the casual wards.[9]

Britain entered the Great War with a tradition that combined minimal state aid for ex-servicemen and their dependants with the action of a range of charitable bodies, some of which had government links. Four features could be said to characterise these charities. First, they came into being in direct response to crises and their financial support tended to decline when the immediate visible crisis had passed. Second, each of the charitable organisations was narrowly focussed, dealing with a specific problem, unemployment, dependants, disablement. Third, each of the organisations held to the assumptions of the charities of their time, distinguishing on moral grounds between the deserving and the undeserving. Fourth, each of the charities was traditional in its methods of fund raising. The Association, as mentioned above, was principally funded by serving members of the forces, a sort of military friendly society. The other organisations were reliant on the traditional resources of Victorian philanthropy, the legacy and the subscription list.

Prior to the First World War, charities were principally reliant on relatively large donations from relatively few people. It is quite probable that fewer than 5,000 people contributed most of the annual finance to the mass of Victorian charities. Attempts to broaden the social base of charitable giving had been made, but they had been more successful in publicity than in financial terms. Saturday funds for hospitals had been instituted in the 1870s, 'but collections taken in factories and other places of employment and amusement never reached the total that the more optimistic supporters of the Fund had predicted. In London in 1890 some £20,500 was contributed in 4300 establishments; ten years later the fund had grown to only £23,000.'[10] One reason for this was that, as Gareth Stedman Jones has pointed out, 'The association of the poor with the collection of charity was not uncontentious, it disrupted the object of the gift relationship as mid-Victorian charity organisers had conceived it.'[11] In 1891 the Royal National Lifeboat Institution instituted 'Lifeboat Saturday', a flag day, but in 1896 the appeal was still only providing 14% of the total income raised.[12] The working-class certainly showed charitable tendencies in an informal sense, in assisting friends and neighbours in dealing with unforeseen and unexpected tragedy such as bereavement and injury, as well as sub-scribing to a multitude of mutual assistance organisations, but donations to organised charities were demanded mostly from the prosperous.

Before discussing the response of charitable organisations to the aftermath of the First World War, it is important to examine the role of the state provision in coping with the problems arising from the conflict. The three main areas for consideration were first, the return of servicemen to the labour force, involving the relief of poverty for those who could not be placed in employment; second, compensation and assistance for those who had been disabled by disease or wounds during their service; and third, support for the dependants of those who had been killed or seriously wounded. It should be stressed that to a very limited degree the state already acknowledged a degree of responsibility in all of these areas prior to the war. The pensioner arrangements of the army and navy, including both institutional and out-relief were a small acknowledgement of the first two points; the third was acknowledged by the limited number of widows' pensions granted, circumscribed by the limits described earlier.

The changed nature and scale of responsibilities created by the war led to a massive expansion in the scope of state support. The huge war-time expansion of the provision of separation allowances, breaking the division between families 'on' and 'off' the strength inevitably set the precedent for a similar redefinition in widows' and orphans' pensions. The sheer numbers of men disabled, perhaps 17% of total enlistments, changed the nature of existing disability allowances irrevocably, leading eventually to the Pensions Act of 1921. The biggest difficulties would be in reintegrating returned servicemen, both able bodied and disabled into the civilian economy. Allowing vast numbers of ex-servicemen to be reduced to pre-war levels of pauperisation was politically unacceptable both on moral grounds and for reasons of social stability. Demobilisation and the inevitable short term unemployment that would be created even if the economy remained buoyant were first met with the unemployed donation. It was soon apparent that some servicemen would not be re-employed before the 'donation' ran out, and this in turn led to the Unemployment Insurance Act of August 1920 which was such a radical departure from the previous principle as to effectively render it a completely new piece of social legislation.

Such legislation represented a huge increase in the breadth of state provision, but the limitations of that provision ought to be kept firmly in mind. Disability pensions were not intended to reach subsistence levels even for the most severely disabled. An interim report in 1923 on the King's Roll employment scheme for the disabled stated that even in the unlikely event of it being possible to provide a full subsistence pension for the severely disabled, it was by no means clear whether this would be in the best interest of the men themselves. It was expected that the pension would be supplemented by earnings or benefits.

For those who could not find work, unemployment benefit of 29 shillings was sufficient to prevent total immiserisation but could scarcely be described as generous. Widows' pensions likewise guaranteed a minimum subsistence but nothing for contingencies such as medical care. The combination of recession and a government committed to retrenchment in the aftermath of the massive expenditure of the war meant that it was politically impossible to sanction the expenditure required to alleviate the hardship suffered by many of those who had made the greatest sacrifices during the war. Yet at the same time expectations had been raised that those who had suffered most for the national cause would be guaranteed more than a minimal level of material security and at least a modicum of dignity.[13]

The principal interest group lobbying for a greater share of resources for those who had suffered for the national cause were the organisations of ex-servicemen. Ex-servicemen's organisations were a new phenomenon, one that had come into existence whilst the war was still in progress. The first such body was the National Association of Discharged Sailors and Soldiers (NADSS) founded in September 1916 under the auspices of the Trade Union movement. In April 1917 the National Federation of Discharged and Demobilised Sailors and Soldiers (NFDDSS) was founded with the encouragement of the National Liberal Club. The Federation soon established a reputation as a radical and partisan body with a strong bias against officers. In reaction to this a third society, the Comrades of the Great War was founded in August 1917, avowedly non-partisan but actually strongly influenced by conservative and coalition politicians. These three groups were joined in 1919 by the National Union of Ex-servicemen (NUX), a left-wing organisation with links with the ILP and more radical organisations. The NUX was openly committed to class politics rather than the more narrowly sectional lobbying of other ex-service organisations.[14]

The unification of the first three bodies into the politically non-aligned British Legion by 1921 has been described in detail by Graham Wootton. It is sufficient to mention here that it was achieved mainly through two incentives. The first was the financial benefits provided by access to the profits of wartime canteens (The United Service Fund). Those who controlled this money decided that unity was the necessary condition of releasing it to ex-service organisations. The second was the immense personal prestige of Douglas Haig who made it clear that he would only agree to lead a unified ex-service organisation.

The significant point is that the lack of unity during the crucial years of demobilisation weakened the ex-service movement as a sectional lobby in Britain. By comparison with, for example, the American Legion, membership was small both in absolute terms and as a proportion of the total number of those who had served. In 1921 membership of the newly created organisation numbered only 18,000. By the end of 1922 this had risen to 117,000. By 1938 it reached a pre-war peak of 400,000 and 100,000 in the Women's Section. Even at its height the British Legion membership represented less than 20% of ex-serviceman and usually less than 10%. This meant that the power of the Legion as a lobby for influencing legislation on ex-service issues was severely circumscribed. Within that limitation it achieved a surprising amount, but it was never in a position to demand any large scale concessions from parliament beyond a more equitable working of the existing legislation on benefits and pensions. What the Legion could achieve, however, was the mobilisation of opinion in favour of remedying at least the most serious cases of hardship through the action of public generosity.

Wear in Honour of Our Dead[15]

Poppy Day was cosmopolitan in origin. It was inspired by the poem 'In Flanders Fields' by the Canadian Medical Officer, John McCrae who was killed in action in 1915.

> In Flanders' fields the poppies blow
> Between the crosses, row on row,
> That mark our place, and in the sky
> The larks, still bravely singing, fly
> Unheard amid the guns below...

Amongst the many who were moved by the poem was an American woman, Miss Moina Michael, who persuaded American ex-servicemen to adopt the poppy as their emblem.[16] Artificial poppies were to be manufactured in the devastated areas of Northern France, by women, for the benefit of children.

In August 1921, Mme Guerin, who was involved with organising the production of poppies in France, contacted Colonel Crosfield of the newly founded British Legion and suggested to him that the British Legion might be interested in using the sale of poppies as a means of fundraising. The idea of the poppy appeal had made a full circle of the allied nations. The British Legion deliberated on the idea for a short time and then agreed to order at least one and a half million poppies for sale on 11 November 1921.[17]

There were doubts as to whether the public would respond favourably to the idea and questions as to whether it would be possible to organise distribution. Certainly the idea got off to a slow start in some areas:

> The appeal made by the Lord Mayor of Leeds ten days ago for volunteers to take collecting boxes and sell poppies on Armistice Day in aid of Earl Haig's Fund for ex-servicemen, has met with an extremely disappointing response, and last night only three or four offers of such help were stated to have been received.[18]

There were also those who were sceptical of the idea that by soliciting voluntary contributions from individuals of all classes it would allow certain groups to evade their responsibilities:

> Perhaps if a little more generosity were shown by the moneyed classes in this country there would be no necessity to appeal to children to contribute their pennies to assist other children left unsupported through the war. This letter may smack rather too much of Socialism for publication in your paper, but nevertheless it is hard facts, and at the present time to appeal to the working class to contribute further funds seems ridiculous.[19]

It is noteworthy that the voluntary principle as such is not criticised in this letter; it is instead a criticism of the wealthy for not pulling their weight in response to voluntary appeals. There is no suggestion that the government should use taxation to remedy this. In practice, the poppy appeal was intended to make allowance for differing abilities to contribute. There was a two-class system of poppies, cotton and silk and it was expected that the better off would buy a silk poppy and pay more accordingly. The donation was expected to be greater than the 1d normal for flag day appeals:

> We have fixed the lowest price – 3d – at which Flanders poppies can be sold, whilst the larger silk Flanders poppies cannot be sold at less than 1s each. In one case we hope that the usual sum given will be 6d, the other 2s 6d. Unless we average 4 1/2d and 1s 9d, the poppy sale will not be a real success. Every penny will go to ex-servicemen through the medium of the British Legion.
>
> Many tell us that in these hard times people can afford no more than 1d. In reply we can only say that we want a sacrifice. We want the nation to know they are honouring the dead and the living and that the poppy is worn as a symbol of "remembrance". On every memorial – city, town or village – a wreath of poppies should be placed. It would be fitting that all the children should gather round these memorials during the two minutes silence wearing the badge of remembrance.[20]

Poppy Day saw some conspicuously extravagant donations from the wealthier members of the community. At Sotheby's a basket of poppies was auctioned. The successful bidder, who remained anonymous in the newspapers, paid £90 and then took a single poppy from the basket, sending the basket up to be reauctioned. The process continued in the same fashion until all the poppies had been individually sold, raising £500.[21] Such reports were commonplaces of subsequent poppy appeals.[22] Their significance was probably more in terms of publicity for the appeal and as an exemplary response than in terms of actual amounts raised as a proportion of the whole.

The public response to the appeal on Armistice Day was overwhelming, for example, in Plymouth:

> Rich and poor, young and old, wore the dainty blooms made by women and children in the devastated areas across the seas. No need for the industrious ladies to seek customers, the latter come to them, proud indeed to support a fund the objects of which appealed with irresistible force to the nation as a whole.[23]

In some areas the principal problem was that supply was inadequate to deal with the demand:

> If only the organisers of Poppy Day in Norwich had had an adequate supply of flowers, they might have made a very much bigger success of their Saturday collection... Efforts were made to procure supplies of poppies supposed to have been left over from sales that had taken place in outlying towns on Armistice Day. But the result was very disappointing, only a few hundreds came to hand... The shortages had been national and the demand everywhere had exceeded supply. Taking account of the urgencies of the situation, Mrs Arnold Miller and Mrs Preston stationed at the Guildhall set to work to make flowers.[24]

Selling poppies was a female prerogative. In Leeds this was done with a certain flair for publicity, 'The hotels, clubs and other public places will be visited by Ladies clad in red poppy costumes, with red cloaks and hoods and black masks, and pistols that are innocent of anything but a little flash of red light'.[25] In Truro in 1922 the local newspaper listed *every* woman involved in poppy selling, street by street, with the total amount raised by each group indicated.[26] The total raised by the first poppy appeal for the Haig Fund was £106,000.[27]

It was immediately obvious that the appeal had shown enormous fundraising potential and had caught the public imagination. For 1922, the British Legion approved the proposal of Major George Howson that, rather than obtaining artificial poppies from France, the British Legion should establish its own factory for the manufacture of poppies, staffed by severely disabled veterans.[28] Initially five badly disabled servicemen were employed and this number grew steadily through the 1920s and 1930s. Funds raised were used to support and finance this factory and to provide support for both ex-servicemen and the families of the bereaved. In the early 1920s the poppy appeal was seen as an efficient method of targeting relief to the genuinely needy, for example, the Mayor of Great Yarmouth stated that, 'what he liked about this fund was that it was properly organised and administered, there were rotters who sang at street corners, but this was to help in the really genuine cases of distress and trouble which had fallen on men through no fault of their own'.[29]

The money collected at a local level was sent to the British Legion headquarters and then redistributed to local branches according to need. In some areas, Norfolk for example, this arrangement was seen as particularly beneficial; the poppy appeal in Norwich raised £448 in 1922, but Norwich received £550 from the central fund.[30] In Dereham at the market stall selling poppies in 1923, the secretary of the local British Legion displayed a statement of accounts demonstrating that the amount received from the headquaters relief fund far exceeded the local contributions.[31]

Nationally, Poppy Day receipts had grown to £503,000 by 1928 and the wearing of poppies on Armistice Day had become a habit that was almost universal, so much so that a central clue in the detective novel, *The Unpleasantness at the Bellona Club,* by Dorothy Sayers was based on the habit. General Fentiman is assumed to have died on 11 November, until Lord Peter Wimsey discovers that no poppy has been found amongst the General's personal effects. Wimsey considers it inconceivable that a 'patriotic military old bird like that' could possibly have been walking the streets as a free agent on 11 November and not have purchased a poppy.[32] Poppy buying was not confined to 'Colonel Blimp' types. In Plymouth, Poppy Day was, 'the one flag day when every man, woman and child with hardly an exception wears an emblem.'[33]

What did the buying and wearing of poppies mean? The *Yorkshire Post* interpreted the meaning of the poppy as being a new element in the general symbolism of Armistice Day: 'This is Armistice Day, the day on which Germany acknowledged the defeat of her great and threatening armies. This is a day therefore of remembrance, gratitude and sympathy, a day on which we should all pay homage to the sign of the Red Poppy in token of our sentiments.'[34]

The symbolism of the poppy as a token of remembrance was something of a paradox, as the connection of poppies with opiates and the oblivion that they induced was well established. It was probably the other aspect of opiates, the alleviation of pain, that appealed most strongly to the popular imagination. With the establishment of the poppy factory, buying a poppy became an act of support for those who were suffering in the aftermath of the war. This, rather than the commemoration of the dead was the principal object, although the two were by no means incompatible:

> In a few days' time the bases of war memorials throughout the country will be hidden in masses of beautiful flowers, the total cost of which I dare not estimate. Is this the tribute those splendid fellows whom we honour would choose if they could speak to us? Would they not rather bid us now, as so many of them did then, in the advanced dressing stations of France and Flanders "See to the other fellow first, he needs it more." Let it then be a point of honour with every one of us, that every wreath, every formal tribute placed on every war memorial shall consist, not of natural flowers at all, but of the Red Flanders poppies which are the emblems of Remembrance Day. By this means every penny spent in tributes to the dead, will through the British Legion find its way to the relief of those broken and destitute men, who in giving their health and their jobs, have made a sacrifice as great in spirit as those who gave their lives.[35]

The use of 'Flanders poppies' for wreaths was already being established by the time this letter was written. A large variety of designs were available by the late 1920s.[36] The origins of poppy wreaths go back to the early years of the Haig Fund. On the second 'poppy day' in Truro, the empty frame of a wreath was placed on the new war memorial by the Lady Mayoress and passers-by were encouraged to fill the frame with the poppies that they had individually purchased.[37] A similar procedure was followed in the Norfolk village of Hoxham the same year.[38]

The use of poppy wreaths for the decoration of war memorials was encouraged by the example of the royal family and other dignitaries at the national Cenotaph service. Indeed, by the late 1920s, London florists were complaining that they were being driven out of the market for wreaths on that occasion, a development which they resented because they had assisted the British Legion with the manufacture of the first wreaths. By 1929, nearly half a million wreath poppies were being manufactured by the poppy factory and the use of Flanders poppy wreaths had become universal.

It was around the Haig poppy appeal that an aspect of Armistice Day which had previously been implicit crystallised. Alongside the language of consolation there was a language of exhortation. 11

November was not simply about commemoration of the dead; it was also about obligation to the living. On Armistice Day, 'those who made peace possible were not forgotten. To the Glorious Dead a silent tribute; to the maimed and the broken the emblem of a poppy, "the sweetest poetry of earth", testifying that those who placed Kings and Empires in their debt shall not lack what generosity can provide.'[39]

Even before the Haig Fund appeal, the question of obligation to the living had surfaced in the press. In discussing the dedication of the Tomb of the Unknown Warrior, the *Cornwall Gazette* had drawn attention to 'the thousands of unknown warriors who have fought and bled to find no other occupation than loitering... These men have suffered untold hardships for their countries sake... now they ask "when is the country going to show its gratitude by deeds".'[40]

The question of obligation to ex-servicemen as victims of the war was one of a whole series of inter-related questions about the identity and nature of the ex-servicemen in British society and about what role they were expected to play on 11 November. As the 1920s progressed the question of ex-servicemen's place on Armistice Day appeared to be settled. They were moved to the margins, as recipients of Haig Fund relief, as celebrants at the British Legion Festival of Remembrance and as a group who laid wreaths on Remembrance Sunday.[41] Yet the veteran's view of the war, complex and ambiguous, resistant to the simplifications required by the language of consolation, would emerge to challenge the established meaning of Armistice Day with tremendous power at the end of the 1920s.

Broadening the Appeal

Poppy Day required organisation. The organisational framework was provided at both national and local levels by the British Legion. Legion headquarters acted as the Haig Fund co-ordinating body, planning distribution and collecting the income. At local level, British Legion branches operated as instigators for the appeal. The role of local branches was to approach the local authorities and co-opt them into setting up an appeal committee. At the Legion summer school at Llandudno in 1926, a class was given by Captain Wilcox on how to organise a poppy appeal. The approved strategy was to approach the Mayor and persuade him to lend his name to the appeal, setting up a committee which he would chair. The pamphlet advised that where possible a local Bank Manager should be brought on to the committee to oversee the accounts and the local newspaper editor to provide publicity.[42] To recruit poppy sellers, it was advised that the Lady Mayoress should be approached. The 'right type' of sellers could be 'Lady friends of members of the committee, members of the women's branch of the British Legion (if there is a women's branch), members of any social or similar clubs in the district, or patrol leaders of Girl Guides.'[43]

The social biases implicit in these instructions are evident. The ideal is clearly a small market town in the south of England. Broadly speaking the Legion was a socially conservative institution which was used to working with existing local power structures. It could also be a flexible organisation and where the local structures were working class in orientation, for example in much of London, the Legion operated with and through these groups.[44] Nonetheless the general trend was for the Legion to reflect the conservative social structure of the regions in which it was strongest, the rural and suburban south.[45]

The strength of Legion organisation in an area may have influenced the ability of the area to raise money for the Haig Fund. A brief examination of some selected results from 1923 and 1924 suggests some relative strengths and weaknesses in regional appeals:

Table 3.1 Haig Fund Collections over two years

	1923 (£)	1924 (£)
Lewisham	917	1146
Cardiff	709	859
Finsbury	480	680
Slough	260	305
Cheltenham	132	221
Ilford	554	720
Wrexham	105	224
Sandwich	35	154
Worthing	220	400
Ipswich	340	450
Derby	281	532

(Source: British Legion General Secretary's Circular, December 1924.)

It is clear from these figures that, relative to population, the Haig Fund was initially more successful in London and the south of England than in the country as a whole.[46] It seems likely that there were two reasons for this. First, British Legion organisation was stronger in the south and the economy was relatively buoyant. No depressed areas were singled out for praise in this source. The availability of disposable income may have conditioned people's willingness to give to the charity. Nonetheless it is probable that the second reason, organisation, was the key factor. The 'Bridgeman Report' on British Legion finance in 1930 underlines the huge relative importance of London to the Haig Appeal at the outset of the appeal:[47]

Table 3.2 Poppy sales for six years

	1923	1924	1925	1926	1927	1928
London (Metropolitan) £:	55,430	54,286	59,967	67,651	77,031	85,971
Provincial (Excluding Scotland) £:	130,090	148,645	183,451	199,697	248,330	289,271

(Source: *Report of the Committee of Investigation of the British Legion, 2nd May 1930.*)

These figures, whilst indicating the continuing disproportionate significance of London, also demonstrate that the differential declined as the appeal became more established. As economic differences between regions remained strong, it seems that popular awareness of the appeal, the efficiency of distribution and the availability of poppy sellers were more important factors than income variation.

Part of the reason that regional variations of income did not seriously affect sales may be the differential 'pricing' of poppies. These 'prices' were the minimum amount that could be donated for each type of poppy. As the appeal increased in sophistication, no less than five varieties of poppy were introduced. They were priced at a penny, threepence, sixpence, a shilling and a half-crown respectively. Penny poppies were aimed at school children and sales in this category increased sharply between 1927 and 1928. They replaced threepenny poppies in schools, the sale of which fell accordingly from over fourteen million to just over eleven million in the same years. This figure remained consistent into 1929. Sixpenny poppies increased from five and one half to six and one half million in the same period and shilling poppies from two million to nearly two and a half million. In 1927, eighty-one thousand half crown poppies were sold by 1929 this had risen by a further fifty thousand.[48]

These figures are useful, as it could be assumed that the four adult types of poppy correlate roughly with social classes, threepenny poppies being the norm for the working class, sixpenny for the lower middle class, shilling for the middle class and half crown for the wealthy. These proportions would seem to fit the general social structure with uncanny precision. If this is true, it would seem probable that all social groups supported the appeal in roughly equal proportions whenever poppies were available to buy. This would back up the qualitative evidence on this point. Local newspapers stress the universality of poppy wearing. An estimate can also be made of how reliant the Haig Fund was on the support of the various social groups. If working class adults were buying eleven million poppies annually and contributing an average four pence each, and their children half of the 1d poppies and contributing one and a half pence each, then the working class as a whole contributed about £ 200,000 in 1929 out of a total of £ 518,489. If it is correct to assume that the lower middle class were the wearers of sixpenny poppies and they bought six and one half million at an average of seven pence each, then including their children proportionately, their contribution was roughly £ 215,000. On a similar basis the middle class proper were contributing most of the rest. If this estimate is accurate (and it probably is reasonably close), the innovative nature of the Haig Fund stands out, as the first charity principally reliant on the financial contributions of those from below the traditional philanthropic classes.[49] A report from Glasgow states that, '£4048 was made up of silver contributions, while there was about four tons of coppers equal to £1,700'.[50] Even the depressed areas of the North East, with heavy unemployment in the 1930s, were capable of substantial contributions, South Shields donated £ 465 in 1936.[51] Given this wide social spread of support, the relative significance of the very wealthy was tiny.

With an appeal on this scale, opportunities for the unscrupulous to take advantage were obvious. Private manufacturers of poppies sprung up during the early 1920s selling similar looking poppies for private profit. The Legion was understandably concerned and issued regular warnings about such profiteers. The most irritating case appears to have been in the late 1920s when poppies were reported which were not only privately manufactured but imported from Germany, adding insult to injury as far as the Legion was concerned.[52]

The Legion was determined if possible to establish a monopoly of commercial Remembrance symbols for its own factory employing disabled ex-servicemen. Initially the Legion was obliged to subcontract to meet demand, but the exposure of the sweated labour used by one of the subcontractors by the *Daily Herald* embarrassed the Legion and genuinely shocked its leadership.[53] Efforts were redoubled to bring all poppy manufacture into the hands of the Legion an aim apparently achieved by the mid-1920s.

Poppy Selling

By the 1930s Armistice Day was the day for the biggest charity appeal of the period. In 1929, gross receipts for Poppy Day were £ 518,489. By 1938 this had risen to £ 578,188. If the average amount donated for a poppy was 1 shilling (By this time poppies were priced at 6d, 1s, and 2s, Poppy Day receipts would also include Car Poppies and Crosses for the Garden Of Remembrance), then it is clear that over 20 million Haig Appeal poppies were sold annually, perhaps as many as 30 million.[54] By the 1930s, the differential pricing of poppies had its critics: 'On Armistice Day when high and low, rich and poor are united in thought, it is preposterous that the outward symbol of their unity should vary.'[55] Poppy selling was concentrated on Armistice Day itself, unlike the post Second World War practice of selling up to two weeks beforehand, so it seems unlikely that people would be buying more than one poppy to replace those they had lost. It therefore seems likely that the vast majority of the adult population supported the appeal.

Reasons for buying poppies would have been diverse. These included the wish to conform, to show respect, or to avoid embarrassment when passing the poppy sellers, who were on practically every street corner.[56] But it seems that the strongest motivation of all was the desire to do something practical to assist those who had been maimed in the war. This desire was firmly rooted in the rhetoric of the early 1920s which the British Legion had so successfully utilised, which held that only by helping the living could the nation avoid the charge of hypocrisy whilst honouring the dead. Indeed the British Legion had coined a slogan to this effect, 'Honour the dead, serve the living' which it adopted as its own. The power of this argument was that it drew on what Eric Leed has described as the 'economy of sacrifice'. The sacrifice of the servicemen was presented as a gift freely given. For example, an appeal on behalf of Welsh officers and men made by Earl Haig in the *Manchester Guardian* in 1921, stated that the public should give money because they would have no wealth to give were it not for the sacrifices of the men, 'who went out and faced the horrors of hell, and through their scourged bodies freed us from destruction'.[57] Much the same point was made in the broadcast speech of the Prince of Wales in 1930, which urged that: 'To wear a Poppy is to show that the wearer is not one to forget a common obligation. To pay for it generously – generously according to one's means is a proof of the sincerity of one's remembrance.'[58]

The stress on the voluntary nature of the sacrifice of the servicemen put them in a privileged position in terms of prestige to the rest of the population. This could only be rectified by a reciprocity of giving.[59] George Crosfield, writing in the *Contemporary Review* in 1937, emphasised the importance of public acknowledgement as the crucial component in the voluntary scheme: 'The fact remains that governments cannot do everything. They cannot introduce the sympathetic touch of a voluntary organisation. I believe the public in its continued and generous support of the poppy collection on Remembrance Day, does realise all the Legion is doing and has done to remove bitterness.' He went on to place a high value on this reciprocal action. 'This great work carried out unobtrusively by thousands of voluntary workers, men and women, has meant much for the unity and harmony of the nation, and in that way has made a contribution to its influence in the cause of peace.'[60] The description of the voluntary workers of the poppy appeal mirrors that of the soldiers. They carry out their work voluntarily and unobtrusively, but for great ends, for the unity and harmony of the nation and for peace. In doing so they remove the potential bitterness of the veteran. This is the reciprocity of sacrifice established.

The rectification of the 'economy of sacrifice' could become very involved in metaphors of exchange. A report on one of Haig's speeches the *Westminster Gazette* was entitled, 'Pay, Pay, Pay' and indeed used the metaphor of payment in a triple sense:

The *sale* of Flanders Poppies will in part *afford* the opportunity to-day of *paying* homage to the million men of this Empire who assured our freedom at the *cost* of their lives.

I ask one and all to *pay* as liberally for their emblems of remembrance as circumstances allow. (My italics.)[61]

Poppy Day involved a manufacturing business. It was well known that the poppies were manufactured by ex-servicemen and that the proceeds supported them. Herbert Read made this fact the central image in his poem 'Armistice Day' which is the most powerful meditation on the war to be written in the 1930s:

Gather or take fierce degree
trim the lamp set out for sea
here we are at the workmen's entrance
clock in and shed your eminence

Notwithstanding, work it diverse ways
work it diverse days, multiplying four digestions
here we make artificial flowers
of paper tin and metal thread

One eye one leg one arm one lung
a syncopated sick heart beat
the record is not nearly worn
that weaves the background to our work

I have no power therefore have patience
These flowers have no sweet scent
no lustre in the petal no increase
from fertilising flies and bees

No seed they have no seed
their tendrils are of wire and grip
the buttonhole the lip
and never fade

And will not fade though life
and lustre go in genuine flowers
and men like flowers are cut
and withered on a stem

And will not fade a year or more
I stuck one in a candlestick
and there it clings about the socket
I have no power therefore have patience[62]

One woman interviewed by Mass Observer 'J.W.' in Fulham gave her reason for supporting Armistice Day as, 'it makes work for them as makes poppies', whilst voicing doubts about everything else involved with Armistice commemoration.[63] This pragmatic attitude, of support for the living, is best illustrated with the effect on poppy sales at the start of the Second World War (a point that will be returned to in Chapter 5).

Poppy selling was the major function of the Women's Section of the British Legion which numbered 100,000 for most of the 1930s.[64] For the poppy appeal they were supplemented by up to 250,000 further female volunteers. The selling of poppies was still a female prerogative up until the Second World War.[65]

By the 1930s, the poppy appeal was a well established part of British life. It had become in effect a social cliché. It had become so normalised that apparently there was no feeling of outrage that this symbol of mass death could be used for product placement. Players cigarettes and Shell petrol used Poppy Day to run special advertisements.[66] The British Legion cultivated this practice. In 1934 the Annual Report of the Legion thanked, 'the 1,500 National Advertisers who in 1934 devoted advertising space in the press to appeal for generosity on Poppy Day'.[67] Likewise the report of the annual conference of the Women's section stated that: 'National Advertisers give great assistance. An outstanding example of this was the gift of the front page of the "Daily Mail" at a cost of £1,400 by Lord Wakefield who had booked the page for an advertisement of Castrol Oil'.[68] Prominent figures such as this could have the double satisfaction of philanthropy and a valuable public relations benefit for their businesses, a combination which further underlines the modernity of the Haig Fund as a charity.

Perhaps the most interesting piece of product placement is an advertisement for 'Ovaltine' in 1938, which is semiotically fascinating. The original is a rare exmple of colour printing in a national newspaper for the period and the vivid red poppies are very conspicuous (See Fig. 3.1.). At first sight, it is a woefully mistimed piece of unconscious irony. Ovaltine is the 'National Beverage for Health', yet it is attaching its name to a symbol which is meant to signify both death and the continuing suffering of the living. The basket of health-giving foods, fronted with a large bunch of poppies underlines this, particularly as the prime purpose of 'Ovaltine' is as an aid to healthy sleep as opposed to the drugged oblivion that the poppy signifies. The terrible, insensitive pun, 'Ovaltine appeals to everyone' and the use of an 'Ovaltine' can to collect money seems to speak of sheer cynicism.

Figure 3.1 Poppy advertising

But beneath this, there is another revealing layer of meanings, based on structural oppositions. The emphasis on health throws the concept of suffering into sharp relief, inspiring feelings of guilt and social responsibility in those who are healthy, towards those who are not. The use of a young woman (and bear in mind poppy sellers in reality *were* women) further underlines the fact that the implicit subjects are male and ageing. A smiling young woman represents the group most personally detached from the suffering of the previous war (no hint of widow or orphan here and no fear of conscription), yet clearly this group is shown as having a duty towards the still suffering veterans at the poppy factory. The whole advertisement oscillates between bad taste and profound social revelation.[69]

A similar observation could be made about the 'Poppy Day Rags' held by Cambridge University students during this period.[70] Cambridge was the exception to the rule that women sold poppies, in the town the poppy appeal was the responsibility of students. The boisterousness of the rags was notorious, but on the whole the town was willing to tolerate the irreverent undergraduates:

> At the end of a long and tiring day, six hundred undergraduates had the satisfaction that £2000 they had set out to collect for the "Poppy Day" fund of the British Legion had been obtained... In the good cause the undergraduates worked up considerable zeal... They operated for the most part in groups. Some of them were out at six o'clock in the morning collecting in dressing gowns over pyjamas...Feminine masquerade being discouraged, there were hordes in kilts. Jazz bands, brass bands, bagpipes and tinwhistles made discordant noises...There were chassis stripped and motor cars covered with property effects. The most elaborate of the carnival pieces was the arrival of Miss Jamie Tomson in her aeroplane from the Antarctic. At the conduit on the Market Hill, a mock Mayor and Corporation received her.[71]

The use of the word 'Carnival' to describe the rag raises obvious questions. Did rag week invert the usual hierarchies and challenge the social order in a ritualised way, leading to its reinforcement in the long run? The answer to this question is a circumscribed yes. Rag week should not be compared with the licensed anarchy associated with carnivals in pre-industrial societies. Nevertheless, it clearly provided an opportunity for undergraduates to dramatise frustrations by mocking figures of authority and subverting sex roles. By 1931, the University authorities were beginning to worry about the loss of respect that rag week might encourage, and enforced regulations upon it.[72] The student response combined respect for the broader sensibilities of Armistice Day with contempt for their University seniors:

> And now we have Regulations for Poppy Day.
>
> Into the vexed question whether the Cambridge method of raising money on such a day is justifiable, we do not propose to enter. Let us assume that there was good reason for some restriction this year. Why then these particular restrictions?
>
> No ragging until the Silence is over – Well, there is some reason in that... No dons, women or clergymen to be impersonated – here is a half hearted and slightly ridiculous nibble at the problem. No dons? When policemen, Rulers of the world, Ministers of the Crown can presumably be mocked? Such an elevated sense of one's importance.[73]

The solemnity of the Silence was restored and the social order maintained. In 1931, the local news paper described the rag as follows:

> A most wonderful show...There was a galaxy of brilliant stunts, rarely have the streets resounded with so much merriment; it was a day of glorious fun... broken by the most poignant of incidents – The Two Minutes Silence... Better still was the spirit behind it all. The youth of England is determined that we shall never forget what this country owes to the youth of another generation and this is well. The further we get from the war, the greater seems to be the need for the benevolent work of the British Legion.[74]

Being too young to serve imposed the same reciprocal obligation as being the wrong sex to have served. Such feelings were bound to decline as the self-perception of students changed from being the beneficiaries of those who had bled in Flanders to the frightening realisation that they might become the cannon fodder of a new cataclysm. Such thoughts occurred to many during the late 1930s until they became a horrible reality. Yet Poppy Day survived, transformed into an urgent response to a new crisis. Subsequently, in the latter part of the 1930s, a new note entered into Armistice Day activities in Cambridge, neither licensed merriment nor decorous respect, but angry dissent. In 1933 undergraduates led by Communist party activists staged a 'peace' protest meeting on Armistice Day. [75] It was a sign of the times.[76]

Notes to Chapter 3

1. P. Reese, *Homecoming Heroes: An Account of the Re-Assimilation of British Military Personnel into Civilian Life,* London, 1992, pp. 19–43. See also H. Mayhew, *London's Underworld,* (ed.) P. Quennel, London, 1950, p. 382, for a description of the 'military beggar'.

2. See, J. Hirchberger, 'Old Soldiers', in R. Samuel (ed.) *Patriotism Volume 3: National Fictions* London, 1989, pp. 50–63.

3. Reese, *Heroes,* pp. 45–61. See also, C. Kimball, 'Ex-Service Movement in England and Wales 1916–1930', unpublished PhD., Stanford, 1991, pp. 21–24.

4. Reese, *Heroes,* pp. 47–51.

5. Ibid., pp. 56–58.

6. Ibid., pp. 61–63.

7. Ibid., pp. 64–65.

8. Ibid., pp. 65–67.

9. Ibid., p. 73. Also W.G. Clifford, *The Ex-Soldier by Himself,* London, 1916, pp. 5–6.

10. D. Owen, *A History of English Philanthropy,* Oxford, 1965, pp. 485–486.

11. G. Stedman Jones, 'The Cockney and the Nation', in D. Feldman and G. Stedman Jones, *Metropolis London,* London, 1989, pp. 272–324.

12. Owen, *Philanthropy,* p. 178.

13. T. Wilson, *The Myriad Faces of War,* Cambridge, 1986, pp. 820–827. In contrast the Weimar Republic had initially intended to provide a generous level of provision for the victims of war. During the period of the inflation the burden of pensions proved to be unsustainable, representing the largest single item of expenditure. Public opinion (i.e. taxpayers), incredible as it may seem, turned on the recipients of pensions as 'scroungers'. The state was forced to scale down transfer payments. The ill-feeling generated amongst recipients was a contributory factor in political polarisation during the Republic. See, R. Whalen, *Bitter Wounds: German Victims of the Great War,* Ithaca and London, 1984. Pensions were not put under equivalent pressure in Britain during the retrenchment of the early 1920s. One reason for this was that the claim for reparations from Germany included the provision of pensions for widows and the disabled; the ability of the British and French Governments to claim reparations might have been severely handicapped by a domestic decision to reduce pension rates as pensions represented half the reparations claimed. See, D. Stevenson, *The First World War and International Politics,* Oxford, 1988, p. 260. In theory the pensions burden of the United Kingom would fall on Germany, but in practice there was not sufficient surplus to extract and by the time that there was a surplus, reparations had been re-negotiated. The British Government was placed in a position where it had accepted the commitment to state support on the principle that Germany would pay, yet was forced to find the money by more conventional means.

14. Wootton, *Official History,* pp.1–29. Also Kimball, 'Ex-Service Movement'.

15. From the poem 'The Victory Emblem', by Miss Moina Michael, cited Wootton, *Official History,* p. 39.

16. R. Moley, *The Story of the American Legion,* New York, 1966, p. 169.

17. Wootton, *Official History,* pp. 38–40.

18. *Yorkshire Post,* 5 Nov. 1921, p. 11.

19. Letter, *Yorkshire Post,* 10 Nov. 1921, p. 3.

20. *Eastern Daily Press,* 11 Nov. 1921, p. 4.

21. *Daily Mail,* 12 Nov. 1921, p. 8.

22. See for example, *Daily Express,* 12 Nov. 1927, p. 9. The King, the Queen and the Prince of Wales each paid £100 for their poppies.

23. *Western Morning News,* 12 Nov. 1921, p. 4. Similarly, 'Contrary to the usual practice of flag days, the sellers of Edinburgh were comparatively few, and those who were selling the flowers were besieged by buyers'; *Scotsman,* 12 Nov. 1921, p. 10.

This was apparently still the case in Nottingham in 1933, where, 'Poppy Day is unique among the collections in the streets by virtue of the number of people who make a bee-line for a poppy seller and ask to be relieved of money in exchange for an emblem.' *Nottingham Guardian,* 13 Nov. 1933, p. 6.

24. *Eastern Daily Press,* 14 Nov. 1921, p. 8. It is not clear why Norwich held the poppy appeal on 12 November. See also the report that, 'It was a thousand pities that the number of poppies allocated to Birmingham was not much larger, as it is quite possible that a sum of £4,000 could have been reached', in *The Veteran,* December 1921, p. 11. In Kinross, 'owing to a shortage of poppies, flags were sold.' *Scotsman,* 12 Nov. 1921, p. 11.

25. *Yorkshire Post,* 11 Nov. 1921, p. 6.

26. *Royal Cornwall Gazette,* 15 Nov. 1922, p. 5.

27. Wootton, *Official History,* p. 40.

28. Ibid, pp. 40–41. See also, A.Brown, *Red for Remembrance,* London, 1971, pp. 77–80.

29. *Eastern Daily Press,* 9 Nov. 1924, p. 9.

30. *Eastern Daily Press,*10 Nov. 1923, p. 11.

31. *Eastern Daily Press,* 12 Nov. 1923, p. 3.

32. D.L. Sayers, *The Unpleasantness at the Bellona Club,* London, 1928, pp. 117–118.

33. *Western Morning News,* 12 Nov. 1927, p. 6.

34. *Yorkshire Post,* 11 Nov. 1922, p. 5.

35. H.A.C. Godwin, letter, *The Times,* 5 Nov. 1925, p. 10.

36. Poppy Factory Wreath Catalogue, 1924. In Royal British Legion Archive: General Secretary's Circulars, (BL: GSC file 1924).

37. *Royal Cornwall Gazette,* 15 Nov. 1922, p. 5.

38. *Eastern Daily Press,* 11 Nov 1922, p. 10.

39. *Western Morning News,* 12 Nov. 1921, p. 4. See also, *Eastern Daily Press,* 10 Nov. 1923, p. 11 and *Birmingham Evening Mail,* 11 Nov. 1921, p. 6.

40. *Royal Cornwall Gazette,* 15 Nov. 1921, p. 5.

41. The British Legion was publicly visible much more on Remembrance Sunday than on Armistice Day, largely because Sunday was not a working day.

42. Pamphlet, 'The appeal work of the Legion', a lecture by Capt. W.G. Willcox, British Legion Summer School, Llandudno 1926'. pp.4–7. In BL: GSC file 1926.

43. Ibid., p. 7.

44. See Kimball, *Ex-servicemen,* and also forthcoming work by Niall Barr.

45. The Scottish Legion was an entirely independent organisation (affiliated through the Empire Service League). Wales and both parts of Ireland were included in the British Legion.

46. BL: GSC file 1924, General Secretary's Circular for December 1924 (29 Nov. 1924).

47. *Report of the Committee of Investigation of the British Legion, 2nd May 1930,* London, 1930, Statement D. In BL: GSC file 1930.

48. Ibid., Statement F.

49. Prochaska has argued that the Victorian working class were heavily supportive of charities, stating that half of a survey of working class and artisan homes in the 1890s were budgeting for charity subscription. The obvious question that arises was whether these were charities in the strict sense or mutual aid societies like burial clubs, etc. While taking the points about both kin charity and bible societies, I believe that Prochaska's picture of continuity misses a crucial change which the Haig Fund heralds. See F. Prochaska, 'Philanthropy' in F.M.L. Thompson (ed.), *The Cambridge Social History of Britain.* 3 vols, Cambridge, 1990, vol. 3, pp. 357–397, particularly pp. 358, 364–365 and 367.

50. *Glasgow Herald,* 10 Nov. 1930, p. 13.

51. *Newcastle Daily Journal,* 14 Nov. 1936, p. 16.

52. See BL: GSC file 1925: Agenda for Annual Conference 1925, Motions 52–54, p. 16. and BL: GSC file 1927: Provisional Agenda for Annual Conference 1927, Motion 10, p. 12.

53. BL, National Executive Minutes, 7 Nov. 1923, p. 17.

54. Wootton, *Official History*, appendix 13. See also p. 142, for Wootton's estimate of number of poppies sold (similar to mine). In T. Harrisson and C. Madge, *Britain: by Mass Observation,* London, 1938, 1986 reprint, p. 209, the estimate for 1938 is 40 million poppies.

55. *Daily Mail,* 12 Nov. 1937, p. 10.

56. Selling poppies in person gave me an insight into that particular motive.

57. *Manchester Guardian,* 12 Nov. 1921, p. 11. The biblical analogy with Christ's torment is obvious and revealing.

58. *News Chronicle,* 11 Nov. 1930, p. 9.

59. This idea is drawn from the work of Marcel Mauss. See, M. Mauss, *The Gift,* London, 1990, pp. 13–18, 39–40, 65–70, 81–83. It is worth mentioning that an explosion in charitable giving occurred during the war which went far beyond the usual confines of philanthropy in incorporating all classes. This underlines the connection between the sacrifices of those who volunteered and the sacrifices of those who for reasons of age, sex or occupation could or would not. See Wilson, *Myriad Faces,* pp. 158–59.

60. G. Crosfield, 'The Ex-servicemen and Peace', *Contemporary Review* CL II, November 1937, pp. 554–559, p. 556.

61. *Westminster Gazette,* 11 Nov. 1926, p. 7.

62. Herbert Read, 'A Short Poem for Armistice Day' in H. Read, *Poems 1914–1934,* London, 1935. I have quoted it in its entirety as an indulgence and because it is too good not to. The development of Read's poetry from the savage irony of the 'Happy Warrior' to his incredible message 'To a Conscript of 1940', is remarkable. This enthusiastic modernist created a personal stoicism in his reflection upon the war that makes him a far more representative figure than might be expected.

63. Tom Harrisson Mass Observation Archive, University of Sussex (hereafter referred to as MO), "J.W", Fulham Survey, 27 Oct. 1938, Woman of 50.

64. Wootton, *Official History,* p. 249.

65. Harrisson and Madge, *Britain,* p. 209. Also, Wootton, *Official History,* p. 142.

66. See *Daily Mail,* 11 Nov. 1930, p. 10.

67. *Annual Report and Accounts of the British Legion 1934,* London, 1935, p. 87.

68. *British Legions Women's Section, Annual Conference Report, 1934,* p. 13. In BL: GSC file 1934.

69. The advertisement comes from the *Daily Mail,* 11 Nov. 1938, p. 3.

70. See Chadwick 'Armistice Day', p. 327.

71. *Cambridge Chronicle,* 12 Nov. 1930, p. 1. The satire is aimed at the celebrity of the pioneering female pilot Amy Johnson. The rag was used to comment on popular crazes; an earlier example had 'excavated' the public lavatory in the Market Square as the tomb of 'Toot and Come In'.

72. See Chadwick 'Armistice Day', p. 327.

73. *The Granta,* xlii, 944, 11 Nov. 1932, p. 1.

74. *Cambridge Chronicle,* 18 Nov. 1931, p. 9.

75. *Manchester Guardian,* 13 Nov. 1933, p. 12. See also leaflet advertising the meeting in Peace Pledge Union, 'Alternative Remembrance File'.

76. It was not without precedent. On Armistice Day 1932, the debating society of University College London had passed a motion resolving 'In the event of a war this house would not support the Government' (this attracted less notice than the Oxford Union debate three months later). On the same day the Bristol University Socialist society left a wreath at the University war memorial with the inscription, 'To the dead of all nations, victims of a war they did not make – from those who are pledged to fight all such crimes of Imperialism.' See S. Hynes, *The Auden Generation,* London, 1976, p. 101.

4

The Undertones of War: Armistice Day in the Thirties

Revision (For November 11th)

In those two silent moments, when we stand
To let the surging tide of memory fill
The mind's deep caverns with its mingled flood
Of joys and griefs, I shall not think again
As I was wont of the untimely slain
Of poppies dipped and dyed in human blood,
Of the rude cross upon the ravaged hill,
And all the strife which scarred that lovely land

My thoughts shall seek, instead a hallowed place
That little leafy wood where you and I
Spent our last hour together...

Then, in those poignant moments, I shall know
That pain and parting matter not at all...[1]

Reconstructing the Memory of War

Any discussion of the memory of the First World War must take into account the chronological framework of that memory. The shifts in the way the war was perceived depended on a whole series of influences.[2] This chapter examines the development of the language of commemoration from the year 1929. To describe what occurs in that year as a paradigm shift would be to overstate the case; nonetheless it is a year of profound significance. A set of influences come into conjunction, some political, some economic and some cultural, which strengthen one language of commemoration at the expense of another. It was the year when the world economy collapsed, a disaster which finally destroyed the belief that the war

Notes for Chapter 4 can be found on page 142.

118

had created a better, saner world. In Britain it saw the enfranchisement of women on equal terms with men and the election of a second Labour government, events that seemed to threaten the 'conservative' post war order more than we might appreciate now.

Above all, for those studying the memory of war, 1929 was the peak of the 'War Books' publishing phenomenon: *Journey's End, All Quiet on the Western Front, Goodbye to All That, Death of a Hero, A Farewell to Arms* and *Storm of Steel* were all published in this year.[3] The following two years saw Williamson's *Patriot's Progress* and Sassoon's *Memoirs of an Infantry Officer,* as well as reprinting of works by A.H. Herbert, Blunden and Read and a new collection of Owen's poetry.

These influences were not simply coincidental; they represent a matrix. The onset of economic crisis was partly responsible for the popular reception received by the literature of wartime disenchantment.[4] The election of a Labour government, headed by prominent wartime pacifists, was a sharp reaction to the leadership of the other parties that had governed Britain both through war and reconstruction. There were other, somewhat more complex interconnections. Is it entirely coincidental that the year of the 'flapper' vote saw the publication of *Death of a Hero*, a fiercely misogynistic work in which liberated women betray their soldier menfolk?

Whose war? Whose memory? These are the crucial questions, for in Britain there were no undisputed guardians of the memory, in the way that the Grand Army of the Republic were acknowledged as the guardians of the memory of the American Civil War.[5] Conservatives and radicals, military and civilians, the veterans and the bereaved all had different, sometimes competing, claims.

An example of the problems emerging can be seen in one response to *Goodbye to All That*. Robert Graves received a letter condemning him as 'a member of that miserable breed which tries to gain notoriety by attacking others' and which goes on to state: 'The only good page is that quoting the beautiful letter of The Little Mother, but even there you betray a degenerate mind by interleaving it between obscenities.'[6] Of course the letter which the critic was referring to had been used by Graves as a satirical example of wartime propaganda and was quoted in an ironic mode. Yet it is possible to understand the point of view of the critic. Stripped of its literary purpose, what Graves is doing is holding up to ridicule a woman who has lost her son. To take another example, consider Sassoon's poem 'The Hero':

119

"Jack fell as he'd have wished," the Mother said,
And folded up the letter she'd read.
"The Colonel writes so nicely." Something broke
In the tired voice that quavered to a choke.
She half looked up. "We mothers are so proud
Of our dead soldiers." Then her face was bowed.

Quietly the Brother Officer went out.
He'd told the poor old dear some gallant lies.
That she would nourish all her days, no doubt.
For while he coughed and mumbled, her weak eyes
Had shone with gentle triumph, brimmed with joy,
Because he'd been so brave her glorious boy.

He thought how "Jack," cold-footed, useless swine
Had panicked down the trench that night the mine
Went up at wicked corner, how he'd tried
To get sent home, and how at last he died,
Blown to small bits. And no one seemed to care
Except that lonely woman with white hair.[7]

Despite the display of concern and compassion for the plight of the mother in the poem, the very act of writing it was an act of priveleging a view point. Speaking the truth of war, as seen from the soldier's position, becomes a moral act superior to sustaining comfortable lies for the civilian bereaved. Too often this position has been accepted at face value, a simple agreement with the moral superiority of the war writers.[8] Yet it should not take much imagination to wonder what the impact of this poem on a bereaved mother was likely to be, the questions it was likely to raise about what had really happened to her child beyond the comforting language of heroic death in battle.

The ironic tone of many war books raised this problem on a huge scale. Their destruction of the old illusions of courage, honour and patriotism was not complete, because not everyone read them and not everyone agreed with them; but they set a new standard for discussion of the war. What was not clear immediately, was how to reconcile the attack on mismanagement and propaganda with the emotional needs of those who suffered the loss of loved ones. The authors were not concerned with this problem, they were involved in creating what George Mosse has described as the 'myth of war experience', in which the position of the frontline soldier is the only valid vantage point for understanding the war.[9] Such a privileging of the soldier's experience engendered a terrible callousness towards the feelings of the bereaved. It was no comfort for a mother or widow to be told that her son or husband had died for nothing in a futile war. The old lie of 'Dulce et decorum est pro patria mori' might deserve exploding, but its devaluing had left a vacuum.

The change that these developments implied was first made explicit in a re-examination of Armistice Day policy by members of the Labour cabinet in 1929. Elements of the liberal and left-wing press had criticised the 'militarisation' of the Cenotaph ceremony the previous year claiming 'that the spirit informing it was a proud and defiant patriotism... absolutely counter to the constructive peace movement on whose imperilled success the hopes of everyone who is not drunk with nationalist emotionalism, rest'.[10] The subsequent debate in parliament reveals the trends that were to come to the forefront in the 1930s:

> Sir G. BOWYER: Asked the Home Secretary whether the usual arrangements will be made for 11th November and the Armistice service at the Cenotaph, and, if not, what are the reasons for any alterations.
>
> Mr CLYNES: The arrangements generally will follow very closely the lines adopted in previous years, but as already announced there will be a substantial reduction in the number of troops on duty at the Cenotaph.
>
> Sir G. BOWYER: Why is there going to be a substantial reduction?
>
> Mr CLYNES: Because there is an increased public feeling that, while we should continue to pay our tribute to the dead, as far as possible these ceremonies should partake of a civilian aspect more and more.[11]

Having established the fundamental point, the primacy of civilians over the services, the debate begins to reveal a more detailed picture of the desired procedure for commemoration:

> Sir H. O'NEIL: Have the War Office issued any instructions with regard to Armistice Day in provincial centres?
>
> The Secretary of State for War (Mr T. SHAW): The three services met and came to an arrangement that the relatives of deceased soldiers should play a larger part in Armistice Day celebration, but that, as far as the forces were concerned, in taking into consideration the wishes that we knew existed among the relatives of the deceased, and secondly among the comrades of deceased soldiers, the method of attendance of the military should not be changed, that there should be an alteration in numbers only, but that the arming should not be changed.[12]

The central thrust of future commemoration was to be consideration of the bereaved. In fact the formal structures of the ceremony were to change remarkably little, but the language surrounding the ceremony was to increasingly privilege the point of view of the bereaved. By 1937–8, when Mass Observation implemented street surveys, it is clear that the issue of the bereaved is foremost in the minds of those interviewed (see Chapter 5).

The bereaved were to be given the central emphasis in Armistice Day, yet at the same time denied the traditional comfort of being told that their loved ones had died for King, Country and Empire. Such rhetoric was clearly going to sound hollow in the wake of the new writing on the war. Yet the bereaved would still need consolation; meaning had to be given to the sacrifice. The war required a new purpose, one that could withstand attacks on the horror and incompetence that it had entailed. There was only one solution; the meaning of the First World War became an object lesson in peace.

H.G. Wells coined the phrase 'The War that will end War' in 1914.[13] Wells had meant the phrase as a battle cry for English liberalism against Prussian militarism, but in the aftermath of the war books boom it came to mean something else entirely. It really caught the popular imagination in the early 1930s. A purpose had been found for four years of slaughter. The deaths were an indictment of the pre-war order, they condemned the militarism of all societies, not merely the Prussian. In 1928, the editorial columnist for *The Nation* had noted, 'with all the natural sympathy of an average decent human being, the multitude of men and women who were recalling their bereavement'. He observed that 'sorrow is a sacred thing' but 'bayonets are incongrous with a scene of sorrow and repentant resolve'.[14] The sacrifice would be in vain unless the world took heed and changed its ways. For example, in the *British Legion Journal* in November 1935, Frances Lascelles linked the sense of 'national bereavement' with the loss of the men 'who fought and died believing their sacrifice would bring peace'.[15]

J.B Priestley expressed the mood, with his usual populist touch, in the *Evening Standard* :

> The real cause of the war could be set down on a postcard. It was the inevitable result of people standing around with their fingers on the triggers expecting a war...The most dangerous lunatics we have had to do with this century are the "Be Prepared" agitators. To be prepared you have to amass big guns and little guns and heaps of explosive. Once you have done that, the rest follows. Some fool gets a fright and pulls a trigger and you are off.[16]

In short, the war was presented as folly. The ultimate significance of such a view was to elevate the concept of sacrifice to new heights. No longer were the dead merely good servants to their King and Country. They had become more; men who had died for the *sins* of the world.[17] H.R.L. Sheppard had anticipated this view in a broadcast sermon in 1927; the war dead were 'martyrs' who had 'opened the spiritual eyes of the world'. It was 'a blasphemy to suggest that one single life that was laid down was given in vain'.[18] Sir Fabian Ware, the chief of the Imperial War Graves Commission, broadcast the message that, 'the millions of dead speak with one voice and they say to the statesmen of the world: "You have failed to achieve your ends by other means than war, and we have expiated your failure – fail not again, accept our atonement and give faith and life to the world." '[19] The dead were elevated to become almost Christ-like and those who survived, in particular the bereaved, became disciples.[20] Such an interpretation could take cynicism about war experience in its stride and at the same time console the bereaved with a powerful meaning attributed to the deaths of their loved ones. It was dependent for its effectiveness entirely on one thing, the maintenance of the peace. Ralph Hale Mottram made exactly this point in his 1932 collection of essays *Through the Menin Gate*: 'Those moments – and the two minutes' silence is simply a standing reverently at the grave of about a million of English-speaking people – are a mockery unless they lead to some purification, some definite resolution that such wholesale mechanical slaughter will never happen again.'[21]

Obviously the argument arose that if peace was retained the whole purpose of Armistice Day would eventually cease; this point appears in the 1929 debate in Parliament:

> Major COHEN: Does the Rt Hon Gentleman imply that when there are no relatives of Ex-Servicemen [?] left the Armistice service will cease.
>
> Mr SHAW: I cannot answer hypothetical questions, but I hope that when there are no relatives left, we shall have forgotten what war is.[22]

Indeed some believed that the time had already arrived:

> I wonder how long we shall continue our annual celebrations of Armistice Day?... Already a generation of young men are entering the life of the country who never knew the war except as a depressing topic of conversation...fewer and fewer are those to whom this annual commemoration at the cenotaph has a personal meaning.[23]

Other observers felt that the pedagogic value of Armistice Day would justify its retention:

123

More than once it has been suggested that the time will come, even that it has come already, when Armistice Day must be celebrated no longer...

It is a good argument that the celebration ought never be allowed to become a formality meaning nothing to those who take part in it. It would be impossible to imagine anything more horrible than that the last few men and women in their seventies should see the rite perfunctorily performed by another generation which does not understand what they did or what they suffered...

But is it certain that that time will come? It is said that the memory of all wars fade at last. But it must be remembered that this was a war without precedent... That impression is being transmitted to the young men and women who come after and it is hard to believe that it will be effaced from their minds even when they grow old, save by another and greater war. For those who come after, and already to-day they are standing with bared heads in the streets, the war means two things. It means a disaster that must not be repeated if by any human power that can be avoided. It means also a memory of what our race can give and achieve when the utmost is demanded of it.[24]

In 1930 the *British Legion Journal* printed the views of various senior Anglicans, all of whom except the Bishop of Durham were in favour of continuing Armistice Day. The Bishop of Ripon stated that Armistice was the 'Good Friday of the post war world' and a 'living spring of hope'.[25] In the same year the *Catholic Times* described Armistice Day as 'really a peace celebration'.[26] The secretary of the League of Nations Union in Manchester wrote that, 'the Union believes that proper observance of Armistice Day greatly helps the cause of peace'. [27]

While such views represented the main stream, there was dissent from both the left and the right. An article by Douglas Jerrold voiced the traditionalist objection:

There is nothing so displeasing to the successful as to be reminded of the greater virtue of the unsuccessful, and so we need not be surprised that this, the twelfth anniversary of Armistice Day has been precede by many suggestions from those in high places that the accustomed ceremonial is outworn and outdated.

The soldier and the sailor, we are told, if they come at all, should come unarmed. From now on the civilian should take first place.

Behind these proposals lies more than mere impertinence; people are trying to establish in the popular mind a connection between the armed forces of the Crown and the causes of war, and between the stately figures of our politicians and the peace which we all desire to ensure. It is a dastardly invention; for wherever the responsibility lay precisely for the Great War, it lay with the politicians and not with the soldiers. To try to suggest the contrary is to try to bolster up a lie about the past by an insult to the dead...

The younger generation cry aloud for the truth about the war. Let them learn it on this day. It is this. War is the inevitable price which is extracted from those who tolerate evil in the hope that good will come.[28]

The objection from the left was the charge that the form of the ceremony was inappropriate to the sentiments it was trying to convey. These sentiments differed very little from what the developing mainstream of opinion was saying; the problem was apparent hypocrisy:

There are young men who omit, after passing Horse Guards, to salute the Cenotaph. They respect the dead, but not the obelisk, for they have no illusions about war. They say the Cenotaph celebrates victory and is an excuse for proud emotion, and is not a symbol of old, unhappy, far off things.

Are they wrong? I wish I could be sure they are altogether wrong...

Yet I don't want to be near it today, when bearskins and bayonets and rich slow music surround it. They are not appropriate.They disturb and disfigure one's memory...

We ought to hate the ceremonial and assuaging solemnity of Armistice Day. The ritual is an outrage to common sense when we know that, so far from having got our lesson from our million dead, we welcome opportunities to attend Hendon where our children can gaze heavenward at bombing planes.[29]

This was to become the key argument in the development of 'alternative Armistice Day' and the author of this piece, H.M.Tomlinson, would be an important figure in that movement.[30] The reference to Hendon is more than a simple rhetorical device. During 1930, the League of Nations Union and the Fellowship for Reconciliation and Peace were engaged in a campaign to abolish the Hendon Air Display, because it stirred 'martial impulses', in children.[31] This is a little-known landmark in the development of the culture of British pacifism.

It should be stressed that the disagreement over Armistice Day was more one of form than content, Hamilton Fyfe in *Reynold's Illustrated News* expressed similar doubts to Tomlinson, while voicing his approval of the general concept:

What is it we celebrate on Armistice Day. Not "victory". God knows not that...

But there lingers on in the mind of humanity still, the old idea that war may bring gain or security or prestige to a nation.

What the celebration of Armistice Day means to me is the trampling down of such a foolish notion.

The sentiment is approved, but there is no question that the form ought to be changed, as far as this commentator is concerned: 'If the Labour cabinet had followed up their action in stopping the purely formal tributes to the unknown soldier, by keeping the military element out of next Tuesday's ceremonial, they would have won widespread approval.'[32]

The views of the left might be dismissed as marginal, even when expressed by a populist Sunday paper like *Reynold's,* but for comparison, the following piece from the *Daily Mail* in the same year indicates the broad acceptance of this new interpretation of Armistice Day (co-incidentally from the same edition which printed Jerrold's piece above):

> Twelve Years have not dulled the significance of the recurring solemnity of Armistice Day...The men whose death we mourn to-day went to war with the love of peace in their hearts. They believed that by taking upon themselves the doom, they might save their children from the curse of war... "If you want peace" we used to say "prepare for war"; we have bitterly learnt that that maxim is too narrow; we would rather say now "If you wish for peace remember war."[33]

In November 1933 the *British Legion Journal* had as a cover photograph, a statue of a mourning mother holding her dead son with the word 'disarm' inscribed on the base.[34] Across the ideological divide a common language was emerging, one in which there were differences in nuance but which controlled what could reasonably be said on Armistice Day and which shared many elements of a common vocabulary. The form of commemoration changed little between 1928 and 1931, but the meaning was being transformed all the same.

The Organisation and Performance of the Cenotaph Ritual

To understand the nature of Armistice Day in the 1930s it is necessary to examine in more detail the bureaucratic routinisation of the Cenotaph ceremony during the 1920s. Until 1924 the events at the Cenotaph were the responsibility of an annual Cabinet committee dominated by Lord Curzon. When Labour formed a minority government in 1924, this experienced and forceful personality was lost to the organisation of the ritual. It became important to place the annual commemoration on a permanently organised basis. The responsibility fell upon Arthur Henderson at the Home Office.[35]

It was decided that the most efficient form of organisation would be an annual Home Office Committee co-ordinating the various interested bodies and departments.[36] The Government departments involved included the Service Departments, the Colonial Office, the Board of Works, the Metropolitan Police and the Lord Chancellor's Office. The involvement of so many different bodies tended towards a natural conservatism when regarding the ritual, a conservatism reinforced by fear of public controversy in the press. It was also felt that once the ritual at the Cenotaph had been perfected it was most unwise to attempt to innovate.

By the late 1920s most of those involved with the ceremony, including the leaders of the political parties had attended the ceremony on several occasions and knew exactly what they were supposed to do and when. The early 1920s had been a learning process. For example, on the second occasion on which he attended the Armistice ceremony at the Cenotaph as Prime Minister, Stanley Baldwin had, 'in spite of careful explanation as to exactly what he had to do, laid his wreath not only at the wrong time i.e. before some of the royal personages, but in the wrong place.' To add to the farce, 'Sir Hugh Trenchard too went wrong and laid his wreath entirely out of turn before the High Commisioner for India and also before Lord Beatty and Lord Cavan. Probably he was not thinking of what he was doing, but he realised he was at fault and apologised afterwards to Sir Atul Chatterji.' The civil servant writing the description then adds with impressive understatement, 'apart from this the wreath laying was very good.'[37]

Subsequently, the Home Office minimised alteration in the service to help avoid confusion. This bureaucratic conservatism meant that the ceremony at the Cenotaph was highly resistant to any form of innovation, so that even though there were many calls to change the nature of the ceremony to bring the symbolism into a closer relationship with changed thinking about the meaning of the war, the ceremony was to remain surprisingly unchanged in form throughout the 1930s. This was rendered even more significant because through the increasing importance of a new medium, radio, the Cenotaph ceremony was to obtain a more central position as the universally significant ritual.

Old Forms and New Meanings; Armistice Day in Transition

Antoine Prost describes Armistice Day in France in the following terms:

Pour les combattants, aucun doute en effet: ce sont bien les poilus qu'on les fête le onze novembre. C'est à eux que l'on rend hommage, à eux que s'adresse la reconnaissance public. Leur attachement à cet anniversaire tient à ce qu'il constitue le principal geste de gratitude de la patrie envers eux, qui l'ont sauvée.[38]

It seems unlikely that even the majority of members of the British Legion in the 1930s would have considered Armistice Day in Britain to be essentially a festival of veterans.[39] The formal ceremony at the Cenotaph in Whitehall was a grand state function, just as it had been from the outset. The monarch was intended to be present, although on two occasions after 1930 George V was too ill to attend (or possibly lacked enthusiasm) and one of his sons substituted on each occasion.[40] In 1936 the still uncrowned Edward VIII presided and in 1937 his brother took over. The leaders of the major political parties and the heads of the armed services were present as well as representatives from Dominions and Colonies. Dignitaries from the former allies also laid wreaths on several occasions. Prior to the Silence,[41] the massed bands of the Brigade of Guards played folksongs and laments. Representatives from the army, navy, marines, airforce and the merchant navy marched to the Cenotaph along with a representative contingent of veterans in civilian uniform. These groups formed a hollow square around the Cenotaph. Shortly before 11.00 a.m., the monarch would lay his wreath, followed by other members of the Royal Family,[42] then the Prime Minister and the leaders of the opposition parties, then the dominion and colonial representatives, and finally the armed forces representatives. After the Silence, signalled by maroons and sirens, there would be the two haunting trumpet calls 'Last Post' and 'Reveille'. A Church of England dignitary, usually the bishop of London, would deliver a short homily and a prayer after which the representative detachments would march off. Simultaneous with the Cenotaph service was a religious service in Westminster Abbey, climaxing in the observance of the Silence there.[43]

The ritual was not always impeccably performed. In 1931, 'by some mistake the Airforce, who led the way from Wellington Barracks, instead of turning off at the end of Birdcage Walk and approaching Whitehall by the Horse Guards Parade marched straight along Great George Street and entered Whitehall via Parliament Square.' This spectacular wrong entrance was 'due to a mounted constable who took it upon himself to lead the Airforce wrong.'[44] Such errors had become less frequent since the 1920s, organisation had been largely perfected and the annual meetings at the Home Office analysed past errors in order to anticipate problems. It was natural that tried and tested procedure would be preferred and fearing the furore which the press was believed capable of generating on the subject of ill-considered innovation, there developed a strongly conservative bias amongst those in charge of the ritual forms. This led to a head on clash with the Prince of Wales in 1932 which was repeated when he ascended to the throne as Edward VIII in 1936.

The Prince of Wales believed that the public as a whole would prefer to see the Cenotaph ceremony demilitarised. The second Labour government had made steps in that direction in its short term of office, arousing strong opposition from the British Legion and other interest groups who accused them of wishing to de-emphasise the day. The Government had compromised and confined itself to reducing troop numbers at the Cenotaph. The Prince of Wales suggested a different approach. He sounded out General Maurice of the British Legion with the suggestion of removing the service contingent entirely and replacing them with members of the British Legion. Space was to be found on one side of the Cenotaph for widows and orphans. Maurice passed on the suggestion to H. R. Boyd at the Home Office. Boyd raised the objection that the press would attack any such innovation and that the armed forces were eternal organisations in which each generation was entitled to publicly honour their forbearers.[45] Boyd anticipated that the Prince of Wales would not let the matter drop and in his report on Armistice Day in 1933 he described the efforts made to pre-empt a repetition. 'It is very doubtful that the King would listen to such a proposal and General Sir Frederick Maurice has been told that if the Prince wishes it discussed, HRH must go to The King about it. Except on HM's instruction the HO is not prepared to consider the question.'[46] The Home Office knew from experience that George V had a very conservative attitude towards the ceremony, disliking any innovation.

When the Prince of Wales came to the throne as Edward VIII in 1936, it was inevitable that the subject would re-emerge. Early in the reign the new King put forward his views once more. Towards the end of June the Home Secretary discussed the matter with the Prime Minister and agreed to recommend that the ceremony should proceed 'on the same lines as in King George's time'. The still uncrowned monarch proved hard to convince and it was only when

Sir John Simon arranged a personal audience that the King 'eventually agreed that it would be unwise to attempt any alteration for the present'.[47] The conclusive argument that Simon presented was that 'the last thing which the British Legion and ex-servicemen generally would want would be a change which would be resented by the fighting forces'.[48] Colonel Heath, both the organiser of the British Legion contingent at the Cenotaph and General Secretary, and Sir Frederick Maurice the Legion President had agreed on this point.

At the Home Office, H.R. Boyd had prepared a memorandum for the Secretary of State on the feasibility of the plan. In it he intimated that the British Legion leadership had become more hostile to the plan since first suggested, quoting Heath describing it as 'the end of Armistice Day'. He also stressed that the Beaverbrook and Rothermere press would be hostile as would the *Morning Post* and the *Daily Telegraph*, although the King would probably have the *Daily Herald* and *News Chronicle* on his side, a point that seems to be an implied further criticism.[49]

The significance of this flurry of activity is that it shows the difficulty of adapting the ceremonial form of Armistice Day to bring it into line wth new meanings assigned to it. In retrospect it seems that the King was more attuned to popular feeling on the subject than the bureaucrats. Mass Observation reports from the late 1930s show that there was substantial feeling against an armed military presence at the Cenotaph. Furthermore the assumption that the Beaverbrook and Rothermere press would have automatically opposed the move is dubious; it seems more likely that if the initiative had been known to be a royal one, they would have supported it on loyalist grounds. The same is certainly true of Reith at the BBC. The churches would probably have proved favourable and the ordinary membership of the British Legion had an enormous affection for their honorary leader, a King who was also a veteran of the Western Front.[50]

At the same time the Home Office was in one essential respect correct. The King's proposal would have inevitably led to the transformation of Armistice day into a veteran's celebration. The Legion itself admitted that it would be quite difficult to assemble more than the existing contingent of 2,000 members on a working day. In equity, so as not to disadvantage provincial and working class Legion members in attending the ceremony, the King's proposal had it been followed would have meant moving the

Cenotaph ceremony to a Sunday or declaring it a public holiday. By the 1930s even the British Legion had effectively given up the latter demand, perhaps realising that the true impact of the Silence was felt most on a working day. Even at the Cenotaph there was no question that it was the Silence which was the heart of the ritual.

The Silence made the Armistice commemoration distinctly different from other occasions of what might be described as British civil religion. At a royal funeral or coronation it would be possible to distinguish clearly between participants and spectators, but the shared silence for two minutes on Armistice Day destroyed this distinction. The crowd participated in the central ceremony at least as much as those who held centre stage. It was the crowd who gave the Silence force.

The crowds were huge, filling Whitehall and overspilling as far as Trafalgar Square, the Mall and the Strand. Figures in excess of 20,000 seem likely and 30,000 is plausible.[51]

There is some evidence that public interest revived in 1930 after showing signs of declining: 'The police authorities estimate that the crowds around the Cenotaph to-day were larger than in any year since the first anniversary of Armistice Day', ran one report in 1930.[52] Clearly the revival in interest in the war indicated by the sales of war books and the long theatre run of *Journey's End* had extended itself to the Armistice Day ceremony.

What motivated this crowd to attend the ceremony? Some may have had the simple motive of attending a good show, a chance to see the military bands perform and to look at the monarch[53] and the leaders of the political parties. But the continuing criticism of the 'pomp and circumstance' aspect suggests that a good number may have attended despite these things, rather than because of them. Both the *Daily Herald* and the *Evening Standard* noted in 1930 that the crowd seemed younger than in previous years, but differed in their description of the mood and motivation of those present. According to the *Herald* :

> Pilgrims honouring the war dead queued at the Cenotaph last night many hours before the official act of remembrance was due to take place...Young men and women, whose sorrow for fathers or elder brothers killed in a war of which the mourners themselves had no first hand knowledge formed a large proportion of the procession...Typical of the wreaths was one inscribed "To Daddy from Doris, Aged 16"... But for them this act was primarily the observance of Peace Day – the recording of a vow that others should not be bereaved as they had been.[54]

This a description which fits perfectly with the developing bereavement – peace paradigm. But the *Standard* puts a completely different interpretation on the same observation:

> This Cenotaph crowd differs from its predecessors, in part because time heals the wound of war and partly, it may be, because of the sunshine... No the crowd is not an unhappy one and the mourning note is not present, many men wear black ties, but few women are in black, and blue hats and red predominate. But all remember.[55]

(It should be noted that this is not simply a case of the journalistic predilections of the commentators. The first account describes the evening before Armistice Day in the gloom outside the Abbey, whilst the second account is of the 11.00 a.m. ceremonial in bright sunshine.)[56]

The prominence of young people in 1930 appears to have surprised observers, the continuing prominence of women in the crowds did not. In fact it is hard to gauge with any precision the male–female ratio in the crowd. Women were often mentioned as the typical crowd members in press reports, yet the photographs of the crowd nearest to the Cenotaph show this group to be at least two-thirds male (this issue will be discussed further in Chapter 5).

Armistice Day was, of course, not simply a ceremony in London. It was also a national charity drive (as Poppy Day) and a whole series of local ceremonies. Crowds gathered by the War Memorials in the major provincial cities, in small market towns and in villages. It was also an imperial event, participated in by city dwellers in Vancouver, in Durban, and in Brisbane and by families in front of their radios from the Manitoba prairies to the New Zealand sheep stations.[57] Local variants could have powerful meanings of their own; for example in the Irish Free State, clashes between ex-servicemen and Nationalists became a regular feature of Armistice Day, with the IRA accusing the British Legion branch in Dublin of holding an 'Imperialistic demonstration' and threatening retaliation: 'To imperialist leaders, we give a last solemn warning. Too tolerantly have the people suffered insults on Armistice and other days. There is a limit to our patience. Those who fly the Union Jack or sing the British Anthem on Irish soil tonight do so at their own risk.'[58]

Within Great Britain it seems plausible that generalisations about the mood of the participants at the London service would hold good for most other areas, although local pride doubtless had a role to play. Certainly outside London the views of the local British Legion branches could be expected to carry more weight, but nonetheless the local churches and civic authorities by and large seem to have controlled proceedings. Besides this, it is clear that during the 1930s the balance of significance was shifting very sharply away from the local ceremonies to the Cenotaph commemoration.[59] The reason for this is clear and can be expressed in one word: radio.

Broadcasting the Silence

In 1927 there were 2,178,259 radio licenses issued in the United Kingdom, by 1939 there were 9,082,666. By the latter date there were 73 licenses for every 100 households in the UK. It would be no exaggeration to describe this development as a social and cultural revolution. Even during the worst years of the depression the number of license holders increased, doubling between March 1929 and March 1933. The social composition of the audience was transformed in these years, from the original, largely middle-class wireless enthusiasts to a broad cross section of the population. Cheap commercial wireless sets and an increase in the availability of hire purchase, meant that well over half of the licenses issued in 1939 were bought by those with an income of under £4 per week and 2,000,000 by those with an income of under £2 per week.[60]

Officially, broadcasting during this period was the monopoly of the BBC (since 1927 a public corporation rather than a company). Unofficially, European stations were beginning to make an impact, particularly Radio Luxembourg with its commercial English language service and its more unabashedly populist style. But when discussing the broadcasting of Armistice Day in this era, broadcasting and the BBC are synonymous.

Almost from the start of broadcasting in the United Kingdom, Armistice Day was felt to be an event worth marking with special programming. In 1923 there was a special broadcast which marked the beginning of the silence with 'The Last Post' and its end with 'Reveille'. At 3.00 p.m. there was a 'national call to righteousness' sermon, preached by Rev H.R.L. Sheppard of St Martins-in-the-Field, this was followed by the mass bands of the Coldstream Guards and the City of London Regiment.[61] The following year the broadcast was planned to include speeches by the Prime Minister (although in the event Baldwin did not attend) and Viscount Grey.[62]

Even so, the cherished ambition of the BBC was to obtain permission to broadcast the Cenotaph service. In particular the

Chairman, Lord Reith at the height of his near dictatorial powers, wanted the service covered. Many facets of Reith's complicated personality[63] could have contributed to this wish. He was fascinated by and deeply drawn to the monarchy, he clamoured to cover any royal occasion and took inordinate pride in being a servant of the crown. He had been intrigued by the military since boyhood and would have been drawn to the pageantry, an enthusiasm which he would share with few in the 1930s. He was himself a veteran who had been wounded near to death. It is even possible that the event appealed to his deep seated streak of morbidness. All these factors may have played a part, but primarily, Armistice Day was exactly the kind of national event that Reith saw as being the responsibility of the BBC to cover.[64] Reith stated as much in his column in the Radio Times in 1923, 'If broadcasting is a national service our function is revealed on occasions such as these.'[65]

In 1927 negotiations with the Home Office looked close to success.[66] In August a memo, apparently from the Director-General, was sent to the Head of Engineering and to the Programme Executive (Peter Eckersley and Cecil Graves):[67]

> I understand the O.B. Department has been making enquiries as to the possibility of broadcasting the Cenotaph Service proper on November 11th. This seems more likely to become an established fact this year owing to the success in connection with the broadcasting of the British Legion Service, and some of the Office of Work's prejudices may be broken down.[68]

By early September the corporation was clearly feeling confident in its ability to get permission to broadcast and was sending out memoranda to that effect to the regional stations.[69] But by 7 October, a note of doubt began to creep in. Gerard Cock reported to Eckersley:

> I went to see Mr Boyd of the Home Office this morning, as it was obvious that the question of permission for the broadcast was proceeding very slowly.
>
> I spent about an hour and a half with Mr Boyd, and in the course of the interview got the impression that opinion in official circles as to the advisability of granting us permission was very much divided.
>
> I was particularly warned by Boyd that we were not to consider the matter by any means decided on yet. My interview gave me the impression that we would eventually get permission though, but that it would be a long and wearisome business, and despite the necessity from our point of view of having an early decision, that we should not be

given the word go (if at all) until the end of next week...A great many difficulties were made tending to show that the broadcast should not be undertaken, but I think I have succeeded in getting Boyd to look at the thing from the public rather than the Home Office point of view.[70]

This is never a safe assumption when dealing with Whitehall and in fact the next item in the BBC archive is a press release stating that permission to broadcast from the Cenotaph had not been granted.[71] The Cenotaph service was broadcast for the first time in 1928.[72]

Why so much effort to broadcast two minutes of silence?[73] One might wonder whether simply turning off transmission for two minutes would not amount to the same thing. Contemporaries were also aware of the peculiarity: 'Here is one of the great paradoxes of radio, that no broadcast is more impressive than the silence following the last dashing strokes of Big Ben.'[74]

In fact, the crucial element in broadcasting the Silence was that it was not silence that was being broadcast, but rather the absence of deliberate noise:

The climax of the ceremony is, of course, the Silence. Its impressiveness is intensified by the fact that the silence is not a dead silence, for Big Ben strikes the hour, and then the bickering of sparrows, the crisp rustle of falling leaves, the creasing of pigeons wings as they take flight, uneasy at the strange hush, contrast with the traffic din of London some minutes before. Naturally vigilant control of the microphone is essential. The muffled sobs of distressed onlookers, for instance. Audible distress too near a microphone would create a picture out of perspective as regards the crowds solemn impassivity and feelings.

Our job is to reduce all local noises to the right proportions, so that the Silence may be heard for what it really is, a solvent which destroys personality and gives us leave to be great and universal.[75]

Not everyone agreed that broadcasting was capable of dealing with the problems of broadcasting a solemn silence. Filson Young suggested an inevitable technical paradox:

The effect of the Silence of Armistice Day is possibly least effective through the medium of a microphone. What it gives you is a picture in sound of the movements of the crowd and all the military and devotional accompaniments. It is a wonderful sound picture, which piles up in effect until the actual moment when the last note of the hour on Big Ben hums away to silence.

But to get a real impression of the Silence, you must I think be among the throng itself, which for two long minutes so strangely and so impossibly seems to emit no sound whatsoever. It is one of the most impressive experiences in life; and I hope that no misguided impulse of future generations to whom the dead we commemorate will not even be a memory, will be allowed to deprive the world of a kind of salutation that is unique in its history.[76]

Despite such doubts it is certain that a great many people listened to the Silence on their wireless sets and found it intensely powerful. The crucial feature of the radio Silence was less the actual broadcast than the knowledge that the listener was one of millions doing exactly the same thing. Benedict Anderson has written on the importance of print media in allowing individuals to imagine a community with their countrymen. On the act of reading the morning newspaper he writes :

> It is performed in silent privacy, in the lair of the skull. Yet each communicant is well aware that the ceremony which he performs is being replicated by thousands (or millions) of others whose existence he is confident, yet of whose identity he has not the slightest notion...What more vivid figure for the secular, historically-clocked imagined community can be imagined.[77]

A still more vivid figure is a wireless listener who knows, with absolute confidence, what all of her compatriots should be doing at that exact moment. It is an incredibly powerful idea that a whole nation should stop, in silence, at the same moment; and radio, by capturing that immediacy, was the most effective way of transmitting that idea.[78] David Kertzer states that, 'one of the most potent and widely found, mechanisms for tying local groups to a national entity is the simultaneity of symbolic action'. He goes on to cite the enormous efforts made by French revolutionary leaders to make sure that the entire population pledged allegiance at the same moment.[79] Twentieth century technology has greatly eased the process of organising ritual.

It is important to remember that prior to radio broadcasting, the perfect co-ordination of time throughout the country would have been impossible. Clocks vary and getting the Silence to start and finish everywhere at precisely the same moment, so important in producing the psychological impact of total communion, would be impossible.[80] Radio time-checking changed that. The Silence in Leeds would precisely match the Silence in Exeter and in Edinburgh. All three Silences would gain in impact in that knowledge.[81] The impact of this was to strengthen the role of the London Cenotaph service which would define the correct moment for the Silence.[82]

This process initially met some regional opposition, some areas wished to continue broadcasting local Armistice Day services which they had started to cover before permission was gained to broadcast from the Cenotaph. From Hull Relay Station a letter was sent to BBC Head office stating:

> We cannot help thinking that there will be a very strong local feeling in favour of the usual service from the local Cenotaph here. Many people look upon their own ceremony in the light of a family sacrament, and it is very much doubted if the National ceremony would be a fitting substitute for it.
>
> The National conception will doubtless come later but we do not think the time is yet ripe.[83]

Likewise, Manchester also had its doubts on the subject of a compulsory broadcast from London:

> We have broadcast the local Armistice Ceremony and service for the last two years and these have certainly been very successful. All the chief religious, civic and military dignitaries of the City play a part in these services. I realise of course the value of a national rather than a local relay, but there really is a sort of feeling that the local gathering, is so to speak, a gathering in the Manchester churchyard for the fallen. I think we may come up against a great deal of local feeling if we take the national service.[84]

Initially London Head Office was prepared to take a tolerant line:

> I quite understand the situation and it seems quite possible that the majority of your listeners would prefer to hear a broadcast from their local Cenotaph, which after all is a very intimate business and may mean more than hearing a relay from London...
>
> Sitting here in London the way I look upon it is that the local cenotaph service will be attended by a great many of regular Hull listeners and that broadcasting from your aerial of the London ceremony is at the same time affording your people an opportunity of taking part in the national ceremony from which they are prevented from attending in person owing to inability to leave the district...
>
> Please don't be influenced by anything I say. I leave the choice entirely to you and if you are certain that the right thing is to broadcast the local ceremony, then by all means do so.[85]

However, once the national broadcast was established any attempt to return to regional variation[86] was frowned upon:

> Armistice Day is Universal in its significance and I can't help feeling that the B.B.C. should underline that universality by confining itself to

commemorations of the day, both religious and secular, in London, the centre of the Empire. If Scotland, Wales and Northern Ireland are to do their own programmes the force of the celebration tends to dissipate itself, which seems to me to be a great mistake.[87]

This hardening of attitudes is an indication of the extent to which the London Cenotaph service had gained central place in Armistice Day by the middle 1930s, involving a substantial part of the country in a single event, so that even the larger provincial services were becoming signs pointing to the national service which co-ordinated them. In Taunton in 1930, the local service was simply a public broadcast of the Cenotaph service from London, with the crowd joining in the singing of the hymns.[88]

BBC Armistice Day programming involved more than the Cenotaph service, which was not in any case part of the annual broadcast for the first few years. In 1927, it was decided to broadcast a memorial concert on the evening of 11 November, with verses from Ecclesiastes read by Sir Ian Hamilton and Pericles' Funeral Oration read by Lord Balfour. The discussion surrounding the appropriate music for the evening indicate that wartime prejudices about German culture had by no means run their course:

All the composers represented in the programme are British, except Chopin and Handel, and Handel was as good as British and Chopin as good as French, although actually a Pole. In any case I don't think that any petty considerations of a composer's nationality should be allowed to govern us.[89]

The concert appears to have been a substantial success. It was followed in 1928 by a full orchestral rendering of Elgar's *Spirit of England*. In 1929 the Productions Department got involved by broadcasting *Journey's End*. Looking back on this two years later, *Radio Times* stated that:

The innovation was a significant (some said a dangerous) one. It seemed magnificently appropriate that a war play, with a peace lesson, the world famous work of an English soldier, should be heard on Armistice Day, and yet it was feared that the effect upon many listeners of recalling actual scenes of war might be unduly painful and create protest. Permission for the experiment was won with difficulty, it was entirely justified by results. *Journey's End* drew more letters than any single broadcast of the last two years; only one of these hundreds of letters protested against the play being included in the programmes for Armistice Day.[90]

The production department had scored a triumph at their first attempt. It followed up with two efforts in 1930; with a play on 10 November (interestingly based on the the German novel *Brigade Exchange,* an indication, perhaps, of how far *All Quiet on the Western Front* changed attitudes in the space of a year). On Armistice Day evening, there was a production called *In Memoriam – 1914–1918: a chronicle,* using the music of Elgar and the poetry of Rupert Brooke, Herbert Asquith, Laurence Binyon, Julian Grenfell, Siegfried Sassoon, Robert Graves, Wilfred Owen and Richard Aldington amongst others.[91] Many letters of appreciation were apparently received for this programme as well. One to the *Radio Times* is worth quoting:

> Please let me thank you for the beautiful "In Memoriam" selection you have given us on the evening of Armistice Day. After all the horrid, sordid, so called "war books", of which one hears so much even if one does not read them, it is heartening to be lifted back to the heights and glories of vision which these poems recalled and deepened.[92]

A letter like this serves to remind us that, to a large extent, the function of radio was seen as solace[93] (although the content of the programme, with poems by Sassoon and Aldington seems less than reassuring). In 1931, in response to the crisis resulting from the collapse of the Labour administration and the abandonment of the gold standard, the programme became much more specifically directed at the present. Val Gielgud, Head of Drama, put forward a proposal that:

> In view of the generally critical situation, I think if possible ,it would do the Corporation credit to present on this occasion, a programme of more than usual significance, and probably this can best be done in terms of poetry and music. I suggest therefore that we present a programme of this sort as a sequel to 'IN MEMORIAM' broadcast last year on the same occasion. Whereas, however 'IN MEMORIAM' looked backward, 'RESURGAM' or ' I WILL ARISE' – the suggested title – would look forward, in so far as it would be, first of all, a statement of the parlous condition in which we find ourselves, and then an invocation of an ideal commonwealth, the attainment of which given enthusiasm on the part of the people is not so remote as the prevailing apathy would lead one to think.[94]

This programme, based on the works of Milton, was indeed produced and broadcast on 11 November 1931.[95] It may not have been a great success because programming seems to have been less innovative through the rest of the thirties. *In Memoriam* was repeated in 1932 and 1937, and a very similar poetry and prose compilation 'We shall Remember Them' was broadcast in 1933 and 1938.[96] In 1935 the evening production was 'Scott of the Antarctic'.[97] This, however, is not the whole story. Various productions were mooted, but fell through, for one reason or another. For example, the original idea for the production that became 'We shall Remember Them' was for a programme of a much more radical sort, one that would use extracts from English and also French, German and Austrian war literature, 'at last giving Armistice Day the international flavour which we have all hankered for', as was said in the proposal.[98]

In 1934, the difficulties involved in dealing with the current situation on Armistice Day produced a flurry of memos that became increasingly entertaining. Someone (unnamed) had suggested 'Miracle at Verdun' as the Armistice Day production. The C(P) (Colonel Alan Dawnay,the Controller of Programmes) objected, 'I do not think that "Miracle at Verdun" with its bitterly destructive satire, would do at all for production as a special Armistice Day programme.'[99] Instead the C(P) suggested that:

> The time has come, I feel sure to introduce into our observance of this anniversary a straightforward element of constructive idealism; and falling this year on a Sunday, it seems a particularly good opportunity to start the new orientation.
>
> I would like to see a programme based upon the idea of the spirit of intense mutual cooperation and personal self denial, which inspired the war effort of those who took part in the "War to end War" – bringing out in dramatic form the fusion of purpose, the elimination of class and personal prejudice and subordination of individual interests born of the belief that people *were* fighting for an ideal...
>
> Meanwhile, if we could only apply to the present problems of peace anything approaching the spirit of common endeavour which carried the nations, particularly this nation, through the ordeal of war, most if not all these problems would now be more than halfway to a solution...
>
> I feel it should not be beyond the creative genius of somebody to work this idea up into a programme, the message of which – and on this point I lay special stress – should be in the form of an appeal to the individual, not a diatribe against the incompetence or illwill of governments.[100]

This memorandum was passed on to Lionel Fielden, Head of Talks, who felt that the proposal was misconceived:

I do not see how it is within the bounds of anyone's creative ability to construct an intelligent programme on the lines of constructive idealism unless the forces in the modern world which effectively obstruct constructive idealism are, directly or implicitly, attacked. It seems to me rather like asking someone to write a play on the eternal triangle without mentioning anything so unpleasant as a third party. C(P) speaks of old hatreds and conflicts reasserting themselves, but I cannot understand whether by this he suggests that there was a time when they did not assert themselves, and if that is so, I should like to know when that time was. We can hardly take the common endeavour to murder people of other nations as an example for an Armistice Day programme. Common endeavour, however, is a straw at which I feel I can clutch. If a programme on the lines of common endeavour and constructive idealism is to be made without offending anyone, I can only suggest that we might try to dramatise peace by pointing out that "Peace hath her victories" and showing what they are.[101]

The C(P) disagreed strongly with Fielden's analysis; whilst at the same time admitting that the project had to be abandoned for that year:

> Notwithstanding all Fielden's shafts of ridicule, I am not in the least convinced that a programme of "constructive idealism" on the broad lines I suggested, is incapable of production. On the contrary, in the hands of, say J.B. Priestley, Phillip Gibbs, or (from a different angle) Noel Coward, I believe that it could be well done and done effectively.
>
> However let that pass. Since we have now decided to build our evening programme on Armistice Day this year upon the special service and the Albert Hall relay... the question does not arise...
>
> Again, whatever Fielden may say (and possibly feel) about the "common endeavour to murder people of other nations", the fact remains that the impulse of war <u>did</u> bring out among millions of people, of all nations and all classes, human qualities of self sacrifice (in the material no less than in the physical sense), of co-operation and of real brotherhood on equal terms in a common cause, which the no less urgent problems of peace have unhappily so far totally failed to inspire...What a pity it is that Fielden cannot be inoculated against the bug of somewhat petty sarcasm which infects so many of his memoranda![102]

This could stand as a perfect example of the clash of discourses for framing the memory of the war. The traditionalist framework put forward by Dawnay is shot down by Fielden's irony and the result is impasse. The only way around it is to emphasise the achievements of peace. This BBC internal debate is a microcosm of the broader debate in society.

In fact the subsequent course of BBC programming attempts to move in exactly that direction. In December 1934 it was noted that, 'in view of the present militaristic tone of the public ceremonies broadcast on Armistice Day...something might be done in the Corporation's own programmes to restore the balance', and it was resolved to emphasise 'the idea of peace and comradeship'.[103] In practice in 1935, the problem of dramatising peace was approached obliquely by broadcasting a drama on 'Scott of the Antarctic'. This was a cunning compromise, emphasising peaceful pursuits and comradeship, but also being part of the national patriotic myth. [104]

The embryonic television service also gave consideration to Armistice Day, by broadcasting live from the Cenotaph for the first time in 1937. The year before a special television broadcast, using poems by Archibald Macleish and Siegfried Sassoon with music by Elgar and a commentary by Cecil Lewis, had been broadcast. The visual images were drawn from the film 'Westfront 1918' and from a 'Peace sequence' specially commissioned from the Strand film company.[105] The broadcasting of a German war film on television can stand as an image of how far the priorities of Armistice Day broadcasting had changed since the suspicion that broadcasting music by German composers might be deemed offensive in 1927.

An interesting programme which was seriously considered for Armistice Day in 1939 was a special 'Children's Hour' broadcast with participation by children in London, Paris and Berlin. It was vetoed, in July 1939, purely on grounds of cost.[106]

Notes to Chapter 4

1. Eileen Newton, in C. Reilly, *Scars upon my Heart*, London, 1981, pp. 81–82.

2. As Dominic Hibberd has remarked, 'Aldington, C.E. Montague, Siegfried Sassoon, Robert Graves and many other volunteers who have had such a lasting effect on posterity's view of the First World War, wrote their memoirs in the twenties when the dismal realities of peace...had supplanted the desperate hopes of war.' *The First World War*, London, 1990, pp. 2–3.

3. Hynes, *A War Imagined: The First World War and English Culture*, London, 1990, p. 424. See also Eksteins, *The Rites of Spring*, pp. 368–398. Eksteins' argument is deeply flawed. For example, 'of the unemployed between the ages of 30 and 34 in Britain at the end of the Twenties, 80 % were ex-servicemen.' *Rites of Spring*, p. 390. This apparent over representation is used to indicate the failure of ex-servicemen in

Britain to adjust to civilian life. However, it was this age cohort that was most heavily represented amongst *servicemen*, corresponding to those who were 20–24 during the war. Perhaps *60 per cent* of this age group *were* ex-servicemen; it is hard to say because of the imprecision of 'late Twenties'. Of those who were not, it might be assumed that many were exempted from the draft because they possesed skills vital to the war effort, these skills would make them less vulnerable to unemployment later. Therefore what Eksteins presents as a significant piece of supporting data for his argument about alienation is nothing of the sort. The whole chapter is riddled with unsupported statements and misuse of evidence.

4. The Wall Street crash occurred in October; the worst economic effects were not felt in Britain until well into 1930. It could be argued that the larger crisis in Britain was coming off the gold standard two years later. Nonetheless, the crash contributed to a sense of unease in the condition of capitalism. Unemployment reached 2 million by July 1930. For a discussion of this see C. Cook and J. Stevenson, *The Slump*, London 1977, pp. 1–3. Hynes makes a persuasive case for placing the change a little earlier, with the General Strike in 1926, citing T.S. Eliot: 'The period immediately following the war is often spoken of as a time of disillusionment: in some ways and for some people it was rather a period of illusions. Only from about the year 1926 did the features of the post-war world begin clearly to emerge – and not only in the sphere of politics.' *War Imagined*, p. 419. I would argue that the impact of the General Strike was ambiguous, unsettling, but also reassuring in its relative lack of violence. It was a disillusioning experience for the working classes, but its failure was a comfort to the middle classes. By contrast the 1929–1931 crisis had no reassuring aspects. The precise chronology may matter less than an acknowledgement that the years around the turn of the decade had a crisis feel about them.

5. See for example, M. Dearing, *Veterans in Politics: The Story of the GAR*, Baton Rouge 1952.

6. Quoted in Fussell, *The Great War and Modern Memory*, p. 217.

7. Siegfried Sassoon 'The Hero', *The War Poems*, London, 1983, p. 49.

8. The growth of feminist criticism has begun to make commentators on this subject more sensitive to the inherent gender bias of the 'myth of war experience' which is exhibited even by the authors who have been sometimes interpreted as anti-war. It is certainly arguable that the central theme of much of the writing is less anti-war than anti-civilian; see, M. Adams, *The Great Adventure: Male Desire and the Coming of World War 1*, Bloomington and Indianapolis, 1990, pp. 113–133.

9. G.L. Mosse,'Two World Wars and the Myth of War Experience', *Journal of Contemporary History*, 21 (1986), pp. 491–513. See also Leed, *No Mans Land*.

10. 'KAPPA', *The Nation*, 17 Nov. 1928, p. 249.

11. *Hansard*, 231 (31 October 1929), p. 318.

12. *Hansard*, 231 (31 October 1929), p. 319. There had been a call for the soldiers to assemble unarmed, ' at the solemn gathering held to remember the sacrifice of the dead that brought us peace' this 'would indeed be eloquent symbolism'. *The Nation*, 3 Nov. 1928, p. 170.

13. Hynes, *A War Imagined*, p. 20.

14. 'KAPPA', *The Nation*, 17 Nov. 1928, p. 250.

15. Hon. Frances Lascelles, *British Legion Journal*, November 1935, p. 174.

16. J. B. Priestley, 'The Lost Generation', *Evening Standard*, 11 Nov. 1931, p. 7.

17. The poem 'I vow to thee my country', is significant in this context. Written by Sir Cecil Spring-Rice in 1918, shortly before he died, it was attached to a section of Holst's 'Jupiter' from the 'Planets Suite' (the tune was also referred to as 'Thaxted'), and used as a hymn. Its two verses may be said to sum up the development of the memory of the war; the first is an expression of traditional patriotism, the second a vision of a transcendent duty to God's Kingdom where 'her ways are ways of gentleness and all her paths are peace'. The hymn first appears in a hymnal in 1925 and grows in popularity in the 1930s. See, L. Adey, *Class and Idol in the English*

Hymn, Vancouver, 1988, pp. 218–219. Also, E. James, 'I vow to thee my country' in *Bulletin of the Hymn Society of Great Britain and Ireland,* no. 135, 10:1, January 1982, p.4.

18. *St Martins Review,* December 1927, p. 615. See also *Nottingham Guardian,* 11 Nov. 1933, p. 6.

19. Maj. Gen. Sir Fabian Ware, 'The Empire's Homage: Memorials of a million Dead', *Listener,* 9 Nov. 1932, p. 651. George Mosse has argued that the British war graves after the Second World War were regarded as a sermon to peace, but: 'Needless to say, this was not how they had been officially regarded before the Second World War.' This broadcast by the official voice of the War Graves Commission demonstrates that Mosse's argument is completely unsupported by the evidence. See, Mosse, *Fallen Soldiers,* p. 222.

20. This statement should not be taken to mean agreement with George Mosse's view that there existed a 'cult of the dead'. Mosse argues that a cult of the dead reaffirmed traditional values of masculine honour and patriotism. What is meant here is something quite different, a commemoration of the soldier as the innocent *victim* of these same values. The characteristic discussion of the Unknown Soldier stressed ordinariness, rather than heroism, and placed him in a specific individual context, as husband, father, son or comrade. In other words the significance was retained by the living, who were provisionally redeemed by the sacrifice if they kept faith. The imagery suggests that of the Christian church, where the significance of the crucifixion is in the hope of resurrection for the followers of the true way, rather than, for example, the more directly mourning orientated practises of Shia Islam. See Mosse, 'Myth of War Experience' and additionally *Fallen Soldiers.*

21. R.H. Mottram, *Through the Menin Gate,* London 1932, pp. 203–204.

22. *Hansard,* Vol 231, 31 October,1929, p. 320.

23. *Radio Times* (Southern Edition), 7 Nov. 1930, p. 372.

24. *Evening Standard,* 11 Nov. 1930 , p. 6. See also *Birmingham Evening Mail,* 11 Nov 1930, p. 6; *Newcastle Daily Journal,* 11 Nov. 1936, p. 5.

25. *British Legion Journal,* December 1930, p. 174.

26. *Catholic Times,* 14 Nov. 1930, p. 12.

27. Letter from C.E. Clift to *Manchester Guardian,* 8 Nov. 1930, p. 7.

28. Douglas Jerrold, *Daily Mail,* 11 Nov. 1930, p. 10. Jerrold was the author of a pamphlet attacking the 'War Books'. See Hynes, *A War Imagined,* pp. 451–2. The bastion of Ultra Toryism, *The National Review,* could still claim in 1928 that: 'Those who have seen the price paid for the highest citizenship...will be most anxious for their children to be brought up under the influence of Armistice Day and the Khaki vision.' Yet it is evident that such traditional 'patriotism' was a relic of a past epoch by the beginning of the 1930s. See Viscount Sandon, '11 November', *National Review,* November 1928, pp. 371–376.

29. H. M. Tomlinson, 'The Two Minutes Silence and What Then?' *Daily Herald,* 11 Nov. 1930, p. 8. Tomlinson was a war correspondent and the author of the anti-war novel, *All Our Yesterdays.*

30. His name is mentioned as an organiser of the 1937 Armistice Peace Rally in *The Times,* 12 Nov. 1937.

31. Graves and Hodge, *The Long Weekend,* p. 269.

32. Hamilton Fyfe 'What Armistice Day Means to Me', *Reynold's Illustrated News,* 9 Nov. 1930, p. 3. This view had been foreshadowed in the *Methodist Recorder,* 10 Nov. 1927, p. 12.

33. *Daily Mail,* Editorial, 11 Nov. 1930, p. 10.

34. *British Legion Journal,* November 1933.

35. One of Henderson's first moves was to request a file to be put together on the Cenotaph ceremony as it had been performed to that date. This file is a valuable source in itself. Henderson's son David had been killed at High Wood on 15 September 1916, exactly the same day as the death of the son of Asquith, the Prime

Minister at the time. Bonar Law, the leader of the Conservative Party, was to lose two sons later in the war. What impact these personal losses had on these crucial figures in wartime politics is a matter for interesting speculation. It is clear that Henderson took a strong personal interest in organising Armistice Day for 1924 and was disappointed that he was not present in an official capacity on the day. For the death of David Henderson, see C. Wrigley, *Arthur Henderson,* Cardiff, 1990, p. 84.

36. This Home Office dominance represents an almost classic case of the need for bureaucracy as described by Weber: 'Precision, despatch, clarity, familiarity with the documents, continuity, discretion, uniformity, rigid subordination, savings in friction, material and personal costs... The possibility of an honorific administration of notables only exists for any length of time when business can be adequately attended to as a sideline. Once there is a qualitative increase in the range of tasks confronting the administration – as is happening even now in England – it reaches its limit.' M. Weber, 'The Development of Bureaucracy' in *Weber: Selections in Translation,* trans. E. Matthews, ed. W.G. Runciman, Cambridge, 1977, pp. 341–354, 350.

37. PRO: HO45/12329/481781/48.

38. A. Prost, *Les anciens combattants et la société Française 1914–1939,* Paris, 1977, vol. 3, p. 62.

39. For example, an incident in Bootle in 1937 did lead to veterans boycotting the civic ceremony. Close examination of the event leads to the conclusion that the reason for this was a classic sectarian feud between the British Legion head, the Protestant ex-mayor and the new Roman Catholic mayor. This was Lancashire politics, not veterans' politics. See account in the *The Times,* 12 Nov. 1937. p. 10.

40. In 1934, the King went to Sandringham where he was well enough to go shooting on the 13th. J. Gore, *King George V: A Personal Memoir,* London, 1941, p. 435.

41. 'The Silence', when used as a proper noun, will be capitalised according to contemporary practice.

42. The role of the Royal family on Armistice Day was changing, as perceptions of that family changed. Prior to 1914, the Royal family was part of a Pan-European elite, having extensive connections with the major dynasties of Europe. War and revolution broke these ties and redefined the Royal family as the House of Windsor. In 1932, George V made his first Christmas broadcast, a direct message from the head of the nuclear Royal family to the families of Britain and the Empire. Likewise Armistice Day, being about families because of the stress on bereavement, was an appropriate moment for a display of the family virtues of the House of Windsor. In one sense, it was a message of sympathy from a family that had not suffered bereavement, to families that had. See D. Cannadine, 'The British Monarchy c.1820–1977', in Hobsbawm and Ranger, *The Invention of Tradition,* pp. 101–162. For discussion of family image see pp.142–3.

43. See extract taken from Home Office statement, 16 Sept 1936 : BBC, Written Archives Centre, Caversham, (Hereafter WAC) File R30/275/1. See also Home Office communication to BBC, 19 Oct. 1933, File R 30/275/1. Also much material in PRO: Files HO 45/14357/584723 and 14866/599975 for the years 1931 and 1932.

44. PRO: HO45/14357/584723/58; Report on Armistice Day 1931, Minute 12 and handwritten addendum.

45. See minute by H.R. Boyd, 20 June 1932, PRO: HO 45/14866/599975/3.

46. Report on Armistice Day 1933, Minute 6, PRO: HO 45/15305/657655/55.

47. Report on Armistice Day 1936, Minute 1 (26.11.1936), PRO: HO 45/16743/687673. The report concluded that the issue was likely to arise again next year and the King would be likely to prove more determined. Ironically the memo is dated the day on which Baldwin received the Morganatic marriage proposal from the King, the beginning of the so-called 'Abdication Crisis.'

48. Submission from Sir John Simon to HM Edward VIII, 14 July 1936, PRO: HO 45/16743/687673.

49. Memo, H.R. Boyd to 'S of S', 2 July 1936, PRO: HO 45/16743/68763.

50. There is little doubt that the Legion was shocked by the abdication. The relationship between Edward VIII and the Legion was intimate. The former Prince of Wales had been active on the Legion's behalf and had regularly attended the Festival of Remembrance. Apparently, when he attended the Festival in 1936, a number of knowing looks were made in his direction when the band played 'Hello, Hello, Who's your Lady Friend.' This was an intimacy which George VI did not share, much as he came to be respected. The Legion was dominated by Army veterans and although the former Duke of York had more claim to combatant status than his brother, having actually been under fire at Jutland, there was a strong Western Front prejudice against Navy personnel as being little better than fancily dressed civilians. See, M. Bloch, *The Reign and Abdication of Edward VIII* , London, 1990, p. 88.

51. Estimate based on photographic records of Armistice Day through the Thirties in *Daily Mail, Evening Standard* and other newspapers.

52. *Evening Standard,* 11 Nov. 1930, p. 13. See also, *British Legion Journal,* December 1930, p. 176.

53. David Cannadine cites Armistice Day as one of the three major occasions in redefining the monarchy, the others being the Christmas broadcast and Royal weddings. See Cannadine, 'British Monarchy', p. 140. Phillip Ziegler has noted that crowds at Royal weddings and at Royal funerals appear to have behaved in surprisingly similar fashion, suggesting that to some extent curiosity and a day out to look at the monarch may have been more important than the nominal reason for the parade. This may have been held for the Cenotaph ceremony as well amongst some of the crowd. P. Ziegler, *Crown and People* , London, 1978, p. 92.

54. *Daily Herald,* 11 Nov. 1930, p. 1.

55. *Evening Standard,* 11 Nov. 1930, p. 1.

56. Photographs of Armistice Day from the early thirties onwards tend to indicate good weather, this is not necessarily the case, as the development of infra-red photography was already well advanced. James Jarché describes in his memoirs the first use of an infra-red plate on a gloomy afternoon at the Cenotaph, which made the pictures appear 'as clear as though they had been taken on a sunny morning.' See, J. Jarché, *People I Have Shot* , London, 1934, p. 142.

57. See for example the reports on Armistice Day in Canada in PRO: HO 45/14357/584723, Sub-files 3–4.

58. Extract from *The Republic,* quoted in *Evening Standard,* 11 Nov. 1932, p. 2.

59. It is very difficult to demonstrate this from evidence in local newspapers. Reporting on Armistice Day had become conventional and cliché ridden. A refreshing exception is the following account from Burry Port in Wales: 'It was rather a surprise to find so few ex-service men in the procession in a district where so many claim to have served...The general public gave but little support to this annual celebration. The younger section of the community were conspicuous by their absence...Despite the apathy and indifference of this locality, "The names of those who made the supreme sacrifice liveth forever." '*Llanelly and County Guardian,* 15 Nov. 1928, p. 2.

60. A. Briggs, *The Golden Age of Wireless,* Oxford, 1965, pp. 253–254.

61. BBC programme records, WAC.

62. BBC programme records, WAC; see also *Radio Times,* 7 Nov. 1924, p. 296.

63. Some would argue a warped personality; very few public figures believe with absolute certainty in their own damnation. Reith is a peculiar example of a Calvinist who spent his entire life convinced that he was not amongst the Elect.

64. See, A. Boyle, *Only the Wind Will Listen: Reith of the BBC,* London, 1972.

65. Quoted in P. Scannel and D. Cardiff *Serving the Nation: A Social History of British Broadcasting Volume One 1922–39,* Oxford, 1991, p. 29.

66. Negotiations had begun in 1923. Initially the Home Office objected in the belief that outside broadcast equipment would be too intrusive. The objection then became that the Broadcast would discourage people from attending local services. See

PRO:HO 45/11557/392664/41 generally and letter from Joynson Hicks to Reith, 27 Aug. 1925 in PRO: HO 45/12329/481781.

67. This is assuming these to be the correct identities, Eckersley had a brother working for the BBC at this time. Cecil Graves may be Robert Graves's first cousin of that name. See Briggs, *Golden Age,* p. 20 and R.P. Graves, *Robert Graves: The Assault Heroic 1895–1926,* London, 1986, Family Tree, p. xv.

68. Memo, 11 August 1927: WAC File R34/227/1.

69. Memo from Hull Relay Station, 9 Sept.1927, and reply , 12 Sept. 1927: WAC File R34/227/1.

70. Internal Memo, 7 Oct. 1927: WAC File R34/227/1.

71. Press release, 20 October 1927: WAC File R34/227/1. The Home Office end of this correspondence is in PRO: HO 45/12840/511682/4.

72. See PRO: HO 45/13091/517330/ sub-files 2, 6, 10 and 11 the latter including the permission sent to Reith on the 27 April 1928.

73. It is worth noting that from 1928 onwards every issue of the *Radio Times* for the week covering Armistice Day had a picture of the Cenotaph service on the cover – until 1939.

74. *Radio Times,* 8 Nov. 1935, p. 7.

75. H.H. Thompson, *Radio Times,* 8 Nov. 1935, p. 7. See also *Radio Times,* 3 Nov. 1933, p. 319. This expresses an idea very close to what Turner describes as *Communitas* .

76. Filson Young, *Radio Times ,* 22 Nov. 1935, p. 14.

77. B. Anderson, *Imagined Communities,* London, 1983, p. 39. See also p. 31.

78. Scannel and Cardiff argue that broadcasting was the decisive influence in creating a unified 'national' culture by fusing the late nineteenth-century developments (national education, a refurbished monarchy, sport, national music) and bringing into being the concept of a general public interested in such things. See Scannel and Cardiff, *Serving the Nation,* p. 277.

79. D. Kertzer, *Ritual, Politics and Power,* New Haven, 1988, p. 23.

80. See *Evening Standard,* 12 Nov. 1928, p. 6. The commentator welcomed the technical possibilities inherent in wireless for this purpose.

81. See Memo from Leeds relay station, 15 Oct. 1928: WAC R34/227/1. This memorandum requests the time signal at 10.55 a.m. as opposed to 10.30 a.m. in order to provide a still greater level of precision and to make sure that all the town clocks could be stopped so that none would chime during the silence. The idea was rejected as impractical as the 10.30 a.m. time signal was considered adequate for this purpose.

82. There were fears in 1928 that the broadcasting of the Cenotaph service would discourage people from attending local services and an official appeal was made to those who would normally attend a local commemoration to continue to do so. *Manchester Guardian,* 10 Nov. 1928, p.13.

83. Hull Station Memo, 9 Sept. 1927: WAC R34/227/1.

84. Manchester Memo, 12 Oct. 1927: WAC R34/227/1.

85. C. Graves, Memo to Hull, 12 Sept 1927: WAC R34/227/1.

86. This is also part of the ongoing process of centralisation at the BBC during the years 1929–34, a process well described in Scannell and Cardiff, *Serving the Nation,* pp. 323–329.

87. R.E.L. Wellington, hand written addendum to internal Memo, regarding Scottish Armistice Day Broadcast, 20 Oct 1934: WAC R34/227/2.

88. *Western Morning News,* 12 Nov. 1930, p. 7.

89. Nicolls to Director-General, WAC: R34/ 227/1.

90. 'A History of Broadcasting on Armistice Day', *Radio Times,* 6 Nov. 1931, p. 453. At Caversham I could find no *evidence* of any internal controversy over the play, perhaps a little institutional myth making is going on. Also, unfortunately, none of the listener responses were saved, this being before the time that the BBC was particularly concerned with audience research.

91. *Radio Times,* 7 Nov. 1930, p. 395.

92. 'M.P.B., Petersfield', in *Radio Times,* 28 Nov. 1930, p. 587. See also, *Radio Times,* 6 Nov. 1931, p. 453.

93. Briggs, *Golden Age,* p. 255.

94. Memo, Harding and Gielgud to Wellington, 4 Sept. 1931: WAC R34/227/1.

95. *Radio Times,* 6 Nov. 1931, p.456.

96. Illustrating that BBC repeats are not a recent development.

97. *Radio Times,* 4 Nov. 1932, 3 Nov. 1933, 9 Nov. 1934 , 8 Nov. 1935, 5 Nov. 1937, 4 Nov. 1938.

98. Memo, Wellington to ?, 29 July 1933: WAC R34/227/1.

99. Private memo, 25 June 1934: WAC R34/227/1.

100. Memo, C(P) to D.T., 25 June 1934: WAC R34 / 227/2.

101. Memo, Fielden to D.T., 28 June, 1934. See also Memo, Salt to Fielden 27 June 1934: WAC R34/227/2.

102. Memo, C(P) to D.T., 2 July 1934: WAC R34/227/2. The full correspondence is much funnier.

103. BBC Internal circulating Memo, 20 Dec. 1934, See also Northern Regional Office Memo to Head of Drama, 8 April 1935: WAC R34/227/2.

104. The particular symbolic relationship between the Scott expedition and the war was presented in Chapter 1 above. It should be clear from this that my interpretation both supports and departs significantly from that put forward by J.M. Mackenzie in an article on the BBC and Empire. He tends to see Armistice Day broadcasting as part of a broad policy of imperial propaganda programming. I would agree with Mackenzie on two points; first the theme of the "Empire of peace" was of paramount importance and second that there was clearly a clash between imperialist minded conservatives in the hierarchy and more radical personnel at production level. However, as I hope is evident, the resulting deadlocks and compromises in the case of Armistice Day were more complex than Mackenzie's picture admits. See J.M. Mackenzie, 'In touch with the infinite, the BBC and Empire, 1923–53' in J.M. Mackenzie (ed.), *Imperialism and Popular Culture,* Manchester, 1986, pp. 165–192.

105. See script for this: WAC T16/191/1. See also letter to Strand Film Company, 27 Oct. 1936, in the same file.

106. Memo, D.P.P. to C.H.D., 28 July 1939 and reply C.H.D. to D.P.P., 31 July 1939: WAC R34/227/3.

5

The Irony of History: Armistice Day from Peace to War

We have never had Peace. We have not even got Armistice. What we have now is War without the engagement of great armies and fleets... Night and day the forges roar, the hammers descend, the hellish implements of slaughter pour out to the multitudes of training troops. Statecraft is bankrupt, the unity of Christendom is a mockery... Dictators ride to and fro on tigers and the tigers are getting hungry...Yet what is it that three hundred million Europeans want. They want Peace and comfort. They want a larger share of life. They want to cast to the ground some of the needless burdens which they bear... Is it not worth their while to make the great effort, the supreme effort on the grandest scale to prevent Armistice lapsing into actual War, and to make Armistice ripen into real Peace?

These are my thoughts for Armistice Day.

– Winston Churchill, 1937[1]

'When There is No Peace...'

The development of a broad based 'Peace Movement' is a notable feature of British society in the 1930s. 'Militant anti-war protest has (with the possible exception of the early 1980s) never been so widespread in Britain as in the years immediately before the Second World War.'[2] It fused together a group of competing, sometimes mutually hostile, traditions in a common fear at the prospect of repeating a European war. Communist groups following Soviet propaganda, which presented capitalism as predatory and aggressive, could find themselves in alliance with those who followed the view of the heirs of Cobden and Bright, who saw war as economically irrational. Fascist sympathisers who wished to defend the actions of Italy (and later Germany), could find common ground with Christian idealists. Socialist internationalists might act the same as Tory isolationists, but for very different reasons.

Notes for Chapter 5 can be found on page 178.

These different agendas could produce an extraordinarily confusing impression. For example, in 1935 the Labour party conference held a debate over whether support should be given to League of Nations sanctions against Italy after the invasion of Abyssinia. The left of the party, led by Stafford Cripps and supported by the leader George Lansbury, condemned sanctions. Cripps argued that the League was, 'an International Burglar's Union' and that, 'every war entered upon by a capitalist government, is and must be a capitalist and imperialist war'. In return, Bevin argued that the best way of preserving peace was to remain loyal to the League and was so harsh in his attack that he destroyed the Christian pacifist Lansbury as leader of the party.[3]

This has been recorded as an important clash between two wings of the Labour Party further examination reveals a much more complex picture. The League of Nations Union called for national protests on Armistice Day 1935. These protests were vehemently attacked by the *Daily Mail,* a newspaper not noted at any time for its enthusiasm for Cripps. 'Electors should ascertain which candidates attend these meetings and should refuse to support those who thus desecrate this day of national sorrow' (a strange unintentional endorsement for the most left wing element of the Labour party!) This might appear to be straightforward pacifist bashing, after all the League of Nations Union was a body committed to peace through collective security. The reason for condemnation therefore comes as something of a surprise, 'The League of Nations Union, it is scarcely necessary to add, is a war mongering institution, dominated by war-mongering politicians and prelates.' The editorial goes on to state how the protests are an insult to the British war dead and their Italian allies. It also argues that Italy had a perfect right to invade Abyssinia as compensation for the Italian effort in the First World War, because Britain and France had gained ex-German colonies![4] In the run up to a General Election, the honesty of this editorial could be challenged, but the fact remains that the appeal was made, however disingenously, to anti-war sentiment.

Martin Ceadel, the historian of the peace movements in early twentieth century Britain has attempted to clarify the elements in the debate about war and peace by creating a typology of 'ideal types' of thinking on the subject. His typology runs from militarists who welcome war as a positive good, through 'crusaders' who dislike war but will accept it for idealistic aims, 'defencists' who dislike war, but are sceptical about the possibility of its elimination; 'pacificists' who seek the elimination of war, but are not unconditionally opposed to participation *in extremis* and finally pacifists who will not participate in war under any circumstances.[5] In Ceadel's opinion, British debates have principally been between 'defencists' and 'pacificists', the former being more pessimistic about the way international politics operates than the latter. It could be argued that the line between these two and between them and the other strands as well, became blurred during the 1930s.

Conservative thinking was certainly 'defencist'. The National government pushed through rearmament and maintained a scepticism about the efficacy of 'collective security'. However, it was forced to be remarkably circumspect on both these issues in dealing with public opinion. Most Conservatives also seemed to believe that it was possible to permanently avoid entanglement in warfare through bilateral agreements and accomodations with aggrieved powers. Appeasement was not purely a matter of buying time to strengthen the national defence, although this has been a retrospective defence of the policy.

'Pacificist' attitudes could also be complex. A disdain for the traditional elements of patriotism did not prevent the possibility of approval for certain varieties of military action. As the example cited above makes clear, support for the League of Nations could appear bellicose under certain circumstances. Pacificism could slip quite easily into what Ceadel describes as 'crusading'. Malcom Muggeridge maliciously quoted a report that 'the pacifists from the English universities' made 'excellent machine gunners' for the Spanish Republic.[6]

In order to clarify the popular cultural consensus during the 1930s it is perhaps more helpful to look at what was being rejected, rather than the mixed aims and motives of the 'peace movement' and the many who sympathised with it. The principal difference between the 1920s and 1930s, is that up until the late 1920s the notion of 'patriotism' still had a powerful, if residual, appeal. This appeal fell apart during the late 1920s. In rejecting war the peace movement of the 1930s was principally rejecting the popular picture of the patriotic urges of 1914. The Oxford Union resolution not to fight 'For King and Country' should be understood in the most literal sense. Few were willing to fight for an Edwardian notion of patriotism.[7]

In 1935 the results of the League of Nations Union 'peace ballot' were announced. 11.5 million people replied, more than 10 million agreed with the pacifist tone of the first four questions. At the same time 6 million answered the fifth question by stating that the League of Nations should meet aggression with force, as opposed to 2 million who disagreed. It delineated the main split in the peace movement between absolute pacifists and the proponents of collective security.[8]

These policy divisions in the peace movement have been stressed by some to suggest that the British public was not as pacifist as a superficial reading might suggest. Against this it could be pointed out that these nuances, significant as they might be, hide a wider area of agreement in the desire to create a culture of anti-militarism. That 'war mongering' institution, the League of Nations Union, had been trying to ban warplane displays at Hendon (See chapter 4). This common ground both within the peace movement and with the general public outside it as evidenced by the tone of the *Daily Mail* editorial, was emphasised by the common language that could be used on Armistice Day. The use of this language could go a long way towards healing the policy divisions by reminding pacifists of their common aims. In fact it went further, setting up a completely phoney target, a 'militaristic', 'establishment' Armistice Day; which allowed the peace movement to rally around their more genuine, pacifist alternative. This ignored the fact that a few soldiers marching down Whitehall, did not make the commemoration militaristic, not when almost every voice in print and on the radio was beginning to read the significance of the day as a pledge against war. In 1934, when the Catholic Herald gave a profile of St Martin, the Saint commemorated on 11 November, the piece was headed 'St Martin of Tours – Patron Saint of Conscientious Objectors' and went on to state that 'the unwilling recruit and conscientious objector has no title to that place among the soldier Saints which the irony of later devotion has conferred upon him'.[9] There was a widespread belief that war would be prevented when people refused to be belicose.

1933 marks an important year in Armistice commemoration, as it was the year when the Women's Co-operative Guild produced and sold the first white poppies. The Guild had been involved peace propaganda on 11 November since the mid-1920s. At the 1926 conference a resolution was passed that, 'Armistice Day should be observed as a National and International Peace Day', which urged 'all Guild branches to arrange... public Peace meetings and other forms of propaganda...'[10] In 1928 the guild established a 'Peace Agenda' for use in Armistice week.[11]

The idea of the White Poppy originated with Edith Pavitt of the Guild. Visiting France in 1928 she was told by French guildswomen that they would like a peace symbol for use on public occasions. She discussed the idea some years later with Mrs Lloyd of the Guild, who had the first poppies made by a Mrs Miller who was 'crippled with arthritis'. Eleanor Barton, president of the Guild approved the idea and subsequently commissioned the CWS to manufacture them.[12] In 1936 the white poppy was taken up by the newly founded Peace Pledge Union as 'a definite pledge to peace that war must not happen again'.[13] Then as now, the white poppy signified all the dead of the war, military, civilian, allied and enemy .

What was the significance of white? Detractors have linked the white poppy to defeatism and the white flag of surrender, but this is clearly not the reasoning of its originators. Bill Heatherington, a present day P.P.U. activist and a historian of the movement, argues that it was the one colour without a political connotation, unlike blue, orange, green or yellow.[14] Ingenious as this explanation seems, it seems that the connotation of moral purity would be a simpler explanation.

The wearing of white poppies became an integral part of what may be described as 'alternative Armistice Day'. The alternative war commemorations, and indeed in some important respects the whole pacifist movement in Britain during the 1930s, grew out of earlier official Armistice Day commemoration.[15] For example, Vera Brittain addressed meetings on behalf of the League of Nations Union several times on 11 November during the early 1930s. Although commited to the doctrine of collective security, the League of Nations was still congenial at this time to many who would later come to see themselves as unconditional pacifists, as Brittain was to do. At the Armistice Day evening meeting in 1932, she states in her diary that she had 'one hell of a scrap' with Brendan Bracken, who was presumably advocating the conventional strident patriotism which made him something of an eccentric in 1930s political life.[16] Such incidents may have pushed Brittain towards the absolute position she later espoused.

It was not only prominent people who were drawn into commitment. One local example of this comes from Lewes in Sussex where in 1934 there was a 'sensational climax to an otherwise unexceptional Town Hall Armistice Day service'. A sermon preached 'with eloquence and passion' by Father Kenneth Rawlings denounced war as 'barbaric, immoral and unchristian' and called on the congregation to rise to their feet if they would refuse to participate in any war and would actively oppose it. Almost the entire congregation of eight hundred did so. The hard core of the Federation of War Resisters branch in Lewes was formed from those who pledged themselves on Armistice Day.[17]

Nationally, Armistice Day played an even greater role because of its influence on the key individual for the British Peace movement. The key figure in British pacifism in the 1930s was Canon H.R.L. Sheppard, sometime army chaplain and vicar of St Martin in the Fields. Sheppard was the man who preached the first radio sermon on Armistice Day (see Chapter 4). In 1925, Sheppard had been outraged at the plan for a 'victory ball' to be held by on 11 November, an activity which he felt was totally out of keeping with the solemn nature of the day (see Chapter 2). He had mounted a campaign to prevent the ball taking place and had been successful.[18] Furthermore as editor of *St Martin's Review*, the nation's most influential parish church magazine, he had promoted an Armistice Day supplement in 1927 and 1928.[19] This involvement in defending the correct tone of Armistice day was probably what started Sheppard thinking about the contemporary meaning of the war experience.

In 1927, Sheppard announced his conversion to pacifism.[20] His first major act of pacifist publicity was the 'peace rally' which he organised in Trafalgar Square on the afternoon of 11 November 1928. It was apparently an Armistice Day sermon preached by the American Dr Henry Fosdick, which provided Sheppard with the Peace Pledge of 1935, 'I renounce war and will never support or sanction another'.[21]

It was in the wake of the Peace Pledge that the first major 'alternative' Armistice events were held in 1935. With the foundation of the Peace Pledge Union in 1936 there came into being an organisational and publicity structure for making such events more effective.[22] In 1937 there was a large alternative ceremony in Regent's Park.[23] This was organised by Sheppard, although he died shortly before the event, and was sponsored by Isaac Foot MP, Ellis Roberts, Storm Jameson and H.M. Tomlinson among others.[24] According to the *Times* :

> Few of the crowd were of more than middle age. Women slightly outnumbered men and nearly all wore white "peace" poppies as well as the scarlet poppies of Earl Haig's Fund. Nowhere was a medal to be seen. There was no address and instead of the customary bugle calls

after the silence, an anthem "o lovely peace", was sung by a choir of men and boys.[25]

The official programme described the event as a ceremony of remembrance,'for people of all schools of thought who wish to keep faith with those who died in the World War and to to honour the principles for which they suffered.' The slogan for the day was 'not peace at any price but love at all costs'.[26]

The wearing of Red *and* White poppies was significant; obviously the organisers were not going to be laid open to the charge of denying money to crippled ex-servicemen. In Sunderland in 1936, the pacifist mayor Alderman Summerbell wore a white poppy, a Haig Fund poppy and for good measure, his war medals.[27] Elsewhere though, some people did substitute white poppies for red:

> The wearing of white poppies instead of Flanders poppies at the Leeds war memorial by the Lord Mayor (Alderman J. Badly) and the Lady Mayoress (his daughter Mrs Hammond) caused comment. Afterwards Alderman Badly and Mrs Hammond, both of whom are members of the local Labour party, emphasised that the white poppy stood for peace.[28]

Although arguments about white poppies in the 1930s lacked the vehemence of the controversy that has attended them in more recent times, there was still substanial opposition to the idea in some sections. One veteran woman co-operator recalled years later that, 'between the wars it was absolutely unthinkable not to wear a red poppy on 11 November. Public opinion was such that you were likely to be tarred and feathered,' while another stated that, 'in various areas white poppy wreaths were laid on cenotaphs in 1937, '38 and '39. They were immediately taken off and jumped on by irate people.[29] In 1937, the exasperated General Secretary of the Women's Co-operative Guild had a pamphlet published chronicling the persecution of the white poppy movement. In Old Bexley a white poppy wreath was removed by a special constable from the local memorial, in Royston a wreath was removed by persons unknown and at Strood in Kent it was the chairwoman of the local Haig appeal who removed the white poppy wreath and proceeded to trample it.[30] The pamphlet also cites the example of two underwriters at Lloyds who were fired for wearing white poppies on 11 November.[31]

There is no doubt that the British Legion as an institution was hostile to white poppies. At the National conference in 1934 a motion was passed stating that, 'this conference views with alarm the proposed selling of emblems on 11 November by other organisations and instructs the council to take all steps to have these sales stopped'.[32] In 1935 a further motion was carried that an instruction should be issued forthwith that members of the Legion should be 'discouraged by all possible means' from wearing white poppies.[33] The British Legion's principal argument against white poppies was that they were a competitor to the red poppy and therefore threatened to deprive the Haig Fund. This was a point on which the Legion was historically sensitive; there had been a series of conference motions in the 1920s condemning non-Legion manufacturers of poppies who were selling them for private profit and a deep concern that the public should recognise the authorised Haig poppy. The Legion had also condemned other charities including the British Red Cross for collecting on 11 November. By the mid 1930s the white poppy, which was manufactured by the CWS and the proceeds of which were used to aid war resisters and conscientious objectors in Europe, was seen as an unwelcome competitor.

The WCG contended that the Legion only had itself to blame. Repeatedly, WCG sources claim that the Guild had approached the Legion in 1933 and had asked that the poppy factory manufacture white poppies with the Legion taking the proceeds for the Haig Fund.[34] The difficulty of establishing the truth of this claim is considerable because the Co-operative Women's Guild, the Peace Pledge Union and the Royal British Legion are still functioning organisations with limited office space for archival purposes. In all three cases the archives are patchy. The British Legion has no evidence of this approach by the Guild in 1933. The Peace Pledge Union, which collects most information on white poppies, did not exist at that time. But on balance the claim is probably true. The Co-operative Guild witness is remarkably consistent and plausible. It would have been natural to approach the Legion, because of the sensitivity of public opinion on the matter and because of the experience of the Legion in artificial flower manufacture (most artificial flower manufacturers were notorious for the use of sweated labour and would have been anathema to a co-operative movement). Furthermore the improvised nature of the Guild effort in 1933 suggests the Guild had counted on Legion assistance. The speed with which the Legion condemned the white poppy suggests that the Legion had been forewarned of the Guild's intent and the most likely source of the information would have been an approach from the Guild. Evidence from the PPU minutes shows that an attempt to approach the Legion about the manufacture of White Poppies was made in April 1939 proving that even at that stage the peace movement was not ideologically averse to trying to do business with the Legion.[35] Finally there is Motion 53 at the British Legion conference in 1934, which demands that Haig poppies should only ever be red, a motion which makes no sense unless someone had suggested an alternative.[36]

The peace movement felt that the Legion had been unreasonable on this issue. Yet the Legion had its reasons. As far as the British Legion was concerned the Flanders poppy *was* a peace symbol, there was no need for any other and it was a slur on the Haig Fund symbol to suggest that it needed to be replaced or supplemented. They believed that the general public felt the same way; the symbolism of the poppy was popular and was already hallowed by tradition, helped by the popularity of John McCrae's poem. The Legion was also highly sensitive about direct involvement in party politics. The Co-operative movement and to some extent the PPU were closely connected with the Labour party while George Lansbury led the party. It is certain that Conservative Legion members would have seen manufacturing white poppies as assistance to Labour policy propaganda.

Above all, the symbolism of the white poppy jarred. Veterans' pacifism was based on personal experience and sacrifice. It could not accept the moral equivalence of conscientious objectors with servicemen, let alone any claim to the superiority of the former. The peace movement revered the memory of the war resisters of 1914–18; for the ex-servicemen they would always be damned as 'conchies'. The red poppy symbolised the experience of veterans' suffering. The white poppy was too close to the white feather for comfort; an analogy that some in the peace movement were prepared to promote.[37]

The climax of the alternative remembrance movement was probably the WCG rally in Hyde Park in 1938. Organised in conjunction with the Peace Pledge Union, it was originally scheduled for Regent's Park as the 1937 rally had been.[38] The procession to the park was headed by a banner inscribed with the slogan 'S.O.S WOMEN CALLING THE WORLD NO MORE WAR'. A veteran woman co-operator described the rally years later: 'We all met on the Embankment with a banner saying "Women's Peace

Movement" and we all marched to Hyde Park I suppose it was. The women in those days would embroider banners and this was a big banner which stretched across the road... I think most Guild members were pacifists... They had lost sons and brothers hadn't they.'[39] As a counterpoint to John McCrae's poem 'In Flanders Fields' which was associated with the red poppy, an anonymous 'poet' of the peace movement wrote a hymn to the white poppy, which was probably circulated on this occasion:

> White poppy, white poppy, you signify peace,
> On this day of Rememb'rance all war will cease;
> The red one beside you for memory is laid,
> To honour the millions who sacrifice made.
> "Never again!" is the cry of the day,
> Never again will we ask them to pay;
> So forward you women, let your voices be heard.
> Advance into action, but let Peace be the word
> That will lead and inspire you in the ages to come,
> When the darkness has passed and your goal has been won.
> White poppy, white poppy, you shall signify Peace
> In the new world to come when all war has ceased.[40]

Despite the tensions chronicled above, perhaps the most interesting thing about these 'alternative' ceremonies was the way they generally co-existed with the official commemorations without particular hostility from those involved in the latter; indeed at the end of the 1937 rally, representatives of two WCG branches laid White Poppy wreaths at the Cenotaph in Whitehall, having obtained permission from Scotland Yard to do so.[41] Alternative commemoration showed respect for the central tenets of mainstream Armistice Day, particularly when it came to honouring the dead and sensitivity to the bereaved. In an article in 1930, significantly for the *Women's Pictorial*, Dick Sheppard stated that: 'For very many this day cannot help being a day of sorrow rather than rejoicing... we must never give in to the belief that the sacrifice of countless lives given with no thought of self has been in vain... "For Christs sake don't let it happen again" '.[42] The central themes of the piece would have been acceptable to the British Legion at that date.[43]

The compliment was returned in 1937 when Dick Sheppard's memory was honoured with a cross planted in the Garden of Remembrance at Westminster Abbey, one of the central points of British Legion activity.[44] Another example of official tolerance came when the police in Royston mounted a guard on the white poppy wreath at the memorial in 1937 to prevent its removal.[45] Again according to the Women's Co-operative Guild, an Army colonel passing a young woman at the 1937 rally in Regent's Park pointed to her red poppy and said 'you should not wear that. That is a debt the War Office should pay'. He then asked for her white poppy and pinned it on his coat. The story is apocryphal but plausible.[46] This official tolerance was quite natural given that official Armistice Day, as described earlier, was being hedged around with a rhetoric of peace. In 1933, the mainstream position was expressed by John Drinkwater in the *Daily Mail* :

> I have said that this should be a day of no contention. But if it is not to put to fine a point on it, may we hope that in this hour of memory, that contention will cease among the contending....The militarist who accuses the pacifist of weakness and pusillanimity is talking nonsense; but the pacifist who declares that the apologist for security by arming is eager for a conflict that must end in another inconclusive peace does his own cause no good.[47]

Likewise, Reverend R.L. Hussey, speaking in Salford on Armistice Day 1937 dissasociated himself from unconditional pacifism, yet expressd his sympathy with its expression on Armistice Day, 'Our War Cenotaphs are not altars to Mars...They are rather memorials to the victims of the Juggernaut of war. If there is one day more than any other on which the complete pacifist will find the justification he seeks, I imagine that day will be Armistice Day.'[48] But for some on the left, the matter was simply too serious, to be settled by a gentlemanly system of live and let live with the status quo:

> There grew in our minds from the first anniversary the resolve that this should be the last massacre of youth....
> We were less happy in the ceremonies that were added to give dignity to our resolve in silence. They became a military pageant. That was mistaken and out of tune with the day. This is not the day of the young soldier trained for the next war that we have renounced in pact after pact. It is the day of the demobilised who never want to form fours again. It is the day of the mothers and widows who hear in the marching feet no assurance that the sacrifice of their men has borne fruit... If I dared to suggest what we shall do in to-morrow's silence, it would be this: Let us retire into ourselves; hear nothing; see nothing; feel nothing, unless it be the inarticulate sorrow of the millions around us, make an inner silence, and from it draw assurance that this massacre will never come again.[49]

This was comparatively mild compared with Hannen Swaffer's comment in 1933 'I am beginning to think it is time we stopped. It does not seem true you see. It is beginning to look like humbug. If we really meant it, it would have become a different world.'[50] Raymond Postgate pitched his criticism in a different way, one that acknowledged the appeal but argued for a total change in practice on Armistice Day:

> Steel yourself all you can against the hypocrisy of some who celebrate Armistice Day, remember how the chief actors behaved during the war, tell yourself just this same sentimental wave of feeling can be turned the other way towards war when the time comes – all the same the pipes, the songs will get you whether you like it or not.
>
> Anyway is this the right way to celebrate Armistice Day? This church service atmosphere, and decorous, respectable regret. Certainly on August 4th there is no lamentation that would be too extreme, but November 11th is a day of rejoicing, a day at last when a great crime and folly was ended.[51]

But had the folly ended? For some of the left it was obvious that false prophets were crying out peace when there was no peace. Against this, the weapon of irony came into increasing use. Spike Hughes described the Cenotaph service in 1936 in these terms: 'I felt that in that atmosphere, it would only have needed a couple of bugles and a recruiting sergeant to have turned Whitehall on Armistice morning 1936, into the Whitehall of August 1914; the crowd would have turned its back on the Cenotaph, not only metaphorically but literally. It would have had to, because the war office is at the other end of Whitehall.'[52] A favourite example of irony in the left wing press, was the image of the Silence being observed in armament factories.[53] It gave rise to a poem in the *New Statesman* in 1932:

> The buzzer sounds, and, at our benches, we
> Stopping the lathes, two minutes silently
> Mourn for the lads who fell; then turn again
> To making arms for killing other men.[54]

The silence also inevitably became the subject of a cartoon (see Fig 5.1).[55] It should be remembered, in the light of subsequent events, that a major reason for this fear of rearmament in the early 1930s, was the belief on the left that the National government was more likely to ally with the Fascist states against the Soviet Union, than oppose Fascism.[56]

"KNOCK OFF FOR A COUPLE OF MINUTES, BOYS"

Figure 5.1 An Ironic View of The Two Minutes' Silence

More subtle is the irony contained in two short stories, published for Armistice Day in the *Daily Herald*. The first in 1935, by Aird Galloway, concerns a man waiting for the birth of his child on 11 November. He worries about his wife and thinks back to his wartime experience, the death of his brothers and his mother who, 'wilted like a fine plant with the roots cut.' The war had not ended for him, because it 'would go on like waves of dying echoes; for suffering did not stop when peace came'. These macabre thoughts continue until he is informed by the midwife that his wife has given birth to a son, and that mother and child are well. Then, 'The eleventh hour rang out. And the peace of the world outside was no more. Through the open doorway came again the cry of his man-child. From the street came the sound of music, of a quick stepping, intoxicating, military march.' [57]

The second story was by H.A. Manhood, in 1938. A shepherd and a gamekeeper wait for the Silence on a remote hillside. As they wait the shepherd reminisces about his war experiences, some humorous, some horrifying, 'but the gamekeeper wasn't particularly interested. Sourly he brooded over a lost pension and irritated by the low whining of the shepherd's dog, he swore fiercely at it.' The dog continues to growl and the gamekeeper attempts to silence it. He struggles with the dog until the clock begins to strike eleven, when: 'Angered in turn that the moment be spoilt the shepherd moved swiftly, hitting the gamekeeper once with his great fist'. The gamekeeper is knocked unconscious and the shepherd observes the Silence, 'with half shut eyes, remembering his dead son, gone too young to fight so stupidly, remembering grief, how life had been dulled for his wife and himself'. After the Silence ends, the gamekeeper comes round and, 'lifted his stunned bruised head, slowly, spitting viciously, fighting angry but respectful of the shepherd's strength'. The last line is the gamekeeper swearing revenge on the shepherd and his dog.

This story, in the context of 1938, feels like allegory, of force begetting force and insult leading to dreams of revenge. It is not difficult to picture the gamekeeper as a metaphor for Germany brooding on its defeat and waiting for its moment. There is nothing hopeful at all in this story, bleak from start to finish, with an ending almost as menacing as that of the earlier story.[58] It is also worth noticing that although the main protagonists of each story are veterans, the central meaning of the Silence for each of them is their bereavement through the war.

By this time irony had even begun to permeate the news coverage of Armistice day in the *Herald*. For example, in 1937 a series of stories were printed together which illustrate the folly and malice of humanity at this solemn moment: 'Rowing on a lake in Regent's Park N.W, a middle age man tried to stand in his skiff for the Silence. He overbalanced, and observed the two minutes standing with water to his waist.'[59] This illustrates the folly, whilst the malice is shown by a young man who stole a tray of poppies and a collecting box from a depot. But the biggest story of the year was Stanley Storey, the man who broke the Silence.

Silence Broken and Silence Observed

The action of Stanley Storey on 11 November 1937 shocked the nation. The *Manchester Guardian* described the incident:

> And then suddenly there was a commotion on the pavement outside the Home Office and behind the line of Cabinet Ministers. The rigid line of sailors at the edge of the crowd was abruptly broken, and a thick set fair haired man, bare headed, and wearing a mackintosh, rushed out into the roadway, shouting in a high tormented voice, "All this Hypocrisy!" and after it another phrase that sounded like "preparing for war".
>
> He ran forward in the direction which would have taken him past the Prime Minister, but half a dozen policemen burst through the gap after him and brought him down in a struggling heap two yards away from Mr Chamberlain...
>
> The Silence still held everyone else rigid and dumb. Mr Chamberlain never moved though all this was happening. The King turned his head slightly towards the disturbance for an instant, then looked to his front again and stood motionless... Not another sound or movement came from all those thousands of people; the Silence still held for them...A few excitable people are said to have said "Kill Him" but as far as one could judge there were not many people who made any noisy protest.[60]

The man who had broken, perhaps for ever, the illusion of unanimity was an escaped lunatic. Stanley Storey, a forty-three year old ex-serviceman, had been commited the previous January after causing a disturbance in the House of Commons. When this was discovered it would have come as a considerable relief to the authorities, who must have feared that a trial on a public order offence would have opened up a substantial debate on the subject of Armistice Day and government sincerity. Even so, the screams of the madman articulated what a number of unquestionably sane people thought. Hannen Swaffer, who had been arguing for some years in the *Daily Herald* that Armistice Day had become worse than meaningless, wrote: 'Armistice Day's formal Empire service at the Cenotaph, with its Two Minutes' Silence should never be held again! Yesterday's events made this even more obvious.'[61] He evoked the memory of the recently deceased leader of the peace movement: 'I thought during yesterday's ceremony of dear 'Dick' Sheppard. He at least had the courage of his convictions, "If I can avoid it I do not pass the Cenotaph, I am ashamed." '[62]

It is possible to gauge public response to the Storey incident and to many other aspects of Armistice Day in the late 1930s due to the implementation of that pioneering experiment in social surveying, Mass Observation. Initiated by the left-liberal Tom Harrisson and the communist Charles Madge, Mass Observation was part of the 1930s left-wing attempt to come to an understanding of the ordinary people of Britain, an enterprise that ranged from Wigan Pier to the history of Cole and Postgate.[63] Given that left-wing intellectuals were demonstrating a considerable hostility to Armistice Day, it might be argued that Mass Observation constitutes a biased source. In answer to this, a comment by Angus Calder is worth repeating: 'Mass Observation's role is to describe rather than to prescribe, to mediate rather than to agitate.'[64] In fact the advantage of using Mass Observation compared to some more 'scientific' survey techniques is its relative lack of structure. Observers tended to ask a simple trigger question and then take down the sometimes almost incoherent comments made by their subjects, more or less verbatim. As a result the terms of reference of those interviewed, their instant presuppositions and prejudices, shine through in a way that is rare in surveys that structure thought around detailed questionnaires. The 'language' is that of the interviewed rather than the interviewer.

That Mass Observation chose to conduct large-scale interviewing about popular attitudes to Armistice Day, and furthermore to include the results in the first major publication of its data, is an indication of Armistice Day becoming a question worthy of attention. The years that the survey ran, 1937, 1938 and 1939, were a time when the possibility and finally the fact of war were in everyone's mind. The Storey incident was followed the next year by both the relief and the misgivings raised by the Munich agreement. Even for the least articulate, Armistice Day had become a powerful cultural text to meditate upon.[65]

The Storey incident cast shadows over Armistice Day 1938. Some drew the moral explicitly, like one young middle-class man who stated that: 'It should be stopped. The lunatic last year was very near the mark when he shouted against the hypocrisy of it all.' The cry of hypocrisy had struck home. A middle-class woman in her thirties stated that: 'It's shocking that all the politicians and clergy should be pretending to pray for peace while all the time they are preparing for war', while a working-class man of similar age said: 'It makes my blood boil, there ought to be capital punishment for organised hypocrisy'.[66] The shadow of Munich still hung heavy, and a middle-class woman of twenty-seven referred to it: 'It's disgusting, the crisis showed they might very well have had us fighting again by November the 11th', while a working-class man of forty was unconvinced that there would be peace in his time: 'It don't mean anything now that we are so near another war.'[67] The horrors of war had been a recent, continuing nightmare; one young man remarked: 'It's the idea that I am only capable of imagining the horrors of war for two minutes in the year that I resent, I don't like being publicly sensitive to order.'[68] The surveys in 1937 and in 1938 revealed a strong body of opinion in favour of ending Armistice Day altogether.[69] But the reasoning behind much of that opinion was not to do with hypocrisy. Once again the bereaved return to centre stage.

The number of those interviewed who were themselves actually bereaved by the war was small. Only four out of the total of seventy-one interviewed in London in 1938 stated that they had lost a close relative in the war (one brother, three brothers, a husband and a father respectively). This was equalled by the four interviewed who explicitly stated that they had lost no one (in itself an interesting reaction). Of the four who had lost a close relative, two were in favour of continuing the Silence and two against. A man of twenty-three who had lost his father was ambiguously favourable: 'I'm working most of the time....I think of my father in the war...they might make it less military now...I just think of my father and how he died there.'[70] The woman who had lost her husband clearly found the day stressful, and she described her reactions as follows: 'It brings back memories, my husband was killed in it. It makes me miserable all day, I stop at home for the day, listen in...My second husband goes all of a tremble when it comes, he was shell shocked then...My poor pop jumps out of his boots at it.'[71] A younger woman, in what is perhaps the most moving testimony of all, expressed the opposite opinion:.

Keep on with it... we don't ever want it [the war] again. My God, I lost my father, my mother and three brothers... the shock killed them, of the lads being killed...how can I ever forget it all (cries). I pray every night about it... On Armistice Day I take the children and we kneel down and pray....I tell them about what it means then, they know now.... I tell them what an Air Raid was like. It makes me think of all the family.... we can't live with the dead but we can think of them that day... nobody knows the struggles I've had through the war...I had to bring up three brothers and go and scrub steps. Had to be a mother to them.... I nearly went mad when they told me there was no mask for the baby.... see them two medals, well I always tell the children what they represent in death in our family.[72]

Some of the strongest opinions were expressed by those who were not themselves directly bereaved, but were related to those who were. These opinions were generally hostile to Armistice Day. For example a woman of forty-five stated: 'I don't think we ought to have it... My sister's husband was killed, she goes all to pieces that day...My chap was there... they ought to stop it.' A woman of sixty expressed similar sentiments: 'I don't care so much for it now. Makes everybody sad, all the poor people who have lost theirs. I have an Aunt who lost her lad, it's terrible for her on that day.'[73]

The idea that Armistice Day was too painful for those who had 'lost theirs' is a common theme. A man of twenty-eight expressed it succinctly: 'I think it should be stopped, it brings unpleasant memories for the people who lost their people', whilst a woman of forty-five put it more strongly: 'I think them as lost anybody go through hell that day, it's all brought back, there are other ways of showing it, they could have some form of charity.' Yet another forty year old woman in Fulham felt that 'people should stay at home and listen to the service, it is too sad for those who lost their husbands and sons', implicitly identifying the bereaved with women.

Those who supported the idea of continuing Armistice Day also tended to phrase their support in terms of the bereaved: 'It's for the people who lost theirs, it should be kept for them to think of the ones they lost', according to a woman of sixty. Likewise a sixty year old man felt that, 'if it gives some people comfort it should be continued'.[74] A woman of twenty-five phrased her answer interestingly: 'Oh it's a good thing, I didn't lose anyone myself, but it's right that we should shed a tear for those who did'. Noticeably the tear is shed for the bereaved rather than for the fallen.[75] In a work on 'Old English Customs and Ceremonies', published in 1938, the reference to Armistice Day argues that the 'deriders of tradition' would surely not wish to see 'the memory of their fathers, brothers and cousins pass away'.[76] But the popular attitude appears subtly different in that it was the living bereaved who were being shown consideration, rather than the memory of the dead.

Many of those in favour of Armistice Day felt that it was justified for bringing back the memory of the war if it provided a lesson for peace. A woman of thirty stated that: 'It's a good thing. Makes people think about the horrors of it all', whilst a middle-class woman of sixty said that, 'it's good surely for people to continue to thank God for the Armistice and to pray for peace.'[77] A middle-class woman of fifty-seven had a direct interest: 'I have two boys who would have to go and I think it is a good thing to think of peace'.[78] By this stage peace was quite simply defined compared with the ambiguity of the early 1930s. Collective security was no longer an issue following the failures with Abyssinia and Spain. Peace was both an overwhelming emotional need and, in the autumn of 1938, a policy position, in favour of Munich. It was the former that received most stress in conversation about Armistice Day.

The pedagogic value was stressed by some: 'The woman said that we should keep it up, to teach the children about the war',[79] and a man of sixty agreed that, 'it makes the younger generation think about war'.[80] Doubts about the presence of the military at the Cenotaph ceremony were expressed by a number of people, a woman of thirty-five stated: 'I stay at home... I don't like the soldier part', and a man of forty-five (quite probably an ex-serviceman) made his opinion clear' 'Yes, it should be carried on for the lads who died... But keep the army out now from the services, makes me think of the war.'[81] A few people showed indifference or contempt, a middle-class man of forty-seven said that: 'I don't bother with it, I expect sentimental and stupid behaviour from other people', and a man of fifty said: 'Let the dead rest with the dead.' A man of forty said: 'I done my bit then, I've got no opinion about it now, it's the living I worry about now, how to make it.'[82]

It is curious that these comments all came from men of the war generation. Does it represent a strong undercurrent of indifference to Armistice Day on the part of veterans? Certainly a discussion reported in 1937 by an 'observer' suggests that this may have been the case:

> I am alone in the staff room quietly processing books. The janitor comes in. I ask him: 'You're an ex-serviceman, aren't you?' He says Yes. 'What do you think about this Armistice business? Don't you think it ought to

be stopped? It means nothing to people like me. Does it mean anything to you who were in the war?' ' It ought to be stopped' he says.

'It's only the people who weren't in the war who want to keep it going. The average fellow who was in the thick of it wants to forget all about it.' [83]

The relative absence of veterans from the discussion is an interesting feature. Few talk about war veterans as part of Armistice Day. In one case, a war veteran makes the only belligerent remark recorded by Mass Observation on Armistice Day (at least the only one to have survived in the record): 'Sam has just told me that we should have gone right into Germany and wiped them all out.'[84] Even more interesting is that the rhetoric of King, Country and Empire at this level is totally extinct. None of these words come up in discussion during the 1938 interviews.

Given the high level of indifference and hostility reported in these interviews, it seems a little surprising that 80 per cent of Mass Observers reported that they had kept the Silence in 1937. This may approximate to the tendency observed by Phillip Ziegler when reading Mass Observation material relating to Royal occasions, where 'indifference tinged with disapproval' gave way to enthusiasm on the actual day.[85] Significantly those who were on their own were twice as likely to not observe the Silence as those in company.[86] Social sanctions played a part in enforcing the Silence, and blatant infringement incurred widespread censure. A woman who kept her car engine running during the Silence in London in 1937 had her life threatened.[87] In Manchester the same year, 'The droning of an aeroplane displaying an advertisement streamer while circling over Albert Square during the civic commemoration of Armistice Day, and particularly during the Two Minutes Silence was a cause of annoyance and indignation to thousands assembled in the square and a group of ex-servicemen present signed their names later to a written protest.'[88]

Even so, the majority of those observing the Silence were doing so uncoerced. The popularity of the radio broadcast is attested to by the number of those interviewed by Mass Observation who said that they intended to 'listen in' and by the report from one Mass Observer who stated, 'All the way down the street I could hear the wireless in various houses tuned in for the service'.[89]

Because 11 November usually fell on a working day, the radio may have been more significant to women than men (although radios were beginning to appear in workplaces). Women were in fact quite prominent in a number of ways on Armistice Day. Although the crowd at the Cenotaph may have been predominantly male, the congregation at Westminster Abbey was clearly female. At the early service in 1938, eighty-seven out of one hundred and thirty-five were women; of those entering for the Armistice service proper, an observer sampled five minutes in which fifty-seven out of eighty-eight were women.[90] This may reflect the greater religosity of women at this time, as another observer reported three times as many women as men at the parish church Armistice service[91]. On the other hand, it may well be that women had definite reasons for preferring the Abbey. The Tomb of the Unknown Soldier may have been a more accessible and meaningful symbol than the Cenotaph; furthermore, the service at the Abbey would avoid all the military display at the Cenotaph, which many women appear to have objected to. It was also noted that women were predominant among those who made the full 'pilgrimage'. This proceeded from the Cenotaph to the Garden Of Remembrance and on to the Tomb, a route which moves from the most abstract symbol to the symbolic individual crosses and finishes in front of a real body.[92]

For the vast majority of men, and a substantial minority of women, the Silence was something that occurred at their place of work. The most dramatic example of this might be the case of the party of Tyne Improvement Commission workers who observed the Silence in a diving bell underwater. According to one of them, 'the electric lights faded out; that was the stopping of the dynamo, and the three of us stayed down below with heads bowed. Never was there such a silence, I think and it was the longest two minutes I have experienced.'[93] This is an extreme case, but indicative of the universal nature of the observance. The following description comes from an office: 'Only one other man in the room. We have our backs to each other. Dead silence, heard clock ticking. First time I have ever heard it. My colleague and I did not speak. 11.10. Third man came into the room. First remark was "Cold two minutes." They started discussing business.'[94]

This description is from a factory:

> I have during previous years made a rule of going down into the workshop and observing the silence with the men and to this end I had endeavoured to arrange my morning's work. A certain amount of tension was evident towards 11.00 and I felt we had the correct atmosphere [But]... I'll be hanged if the phone didn't blare out it's nerve-wracking call for attention. No time to go down the shop now, I had just time to place

myself by a lorry underneath which one of my men was working.... The man under the lorry was evidently more concentrated on his job than on silence for he went on hammering until I requested him to observe the silence.[95]

It is interesting to speculate how the mechanic under the lorry would have described that interaction! Something of the other side of the picture might be gained from this description by an apprentice 'trimmer', a car upholsterer from Staines:

> When the hooter blows at 11, I am on my feet outside the car, so I "down tools" and assume a more or less upright position, and watch the others. There is a painter who has been on his back blocking a chassis. He is an old man, and he wriggles his way out and lays there, propped on one elbow, with his brush in hand. In crawling out, his cap was pushed over one side. He goes to put it straight – seems to wonder whether to leave it on or not – leaves it on and lies there – in an uncomfortable position, and therefore what I suppose he thinks – a good enough one. He is less comfortable than if he were at attention, so I suppose he thought that much about it.
>
> A few seconds after our hooter go the whistles and sirens of nearby factories and then the gun. Our works is quiet by this time, and there is only the noise of the self stoking heating plant. I looked around me. There were only about 5 men in sight, and two of these had taken off their caps and were standing stiffly to attention. One of these is a proper 'old soldier' and is looking forward to a trench supper to which he has been invited. The other was a very old man – 70 or more, and for the first time I saw him bareheaded. His hair was white and he stood there thinking perhaps of a son or relation who was killed. These two were the only two who seemed to treat the silence for what it was – remembrance. The others seemed bored...
>
> The general impression of the chaps was I think that it was a bit of a nuisance and to some an embarrassment to stand still for two minutes, but the only comment came from the men who had memories of the war – "If you'd seen so and so and been through what we did some of you young chaps would feel different about it."[96]

This perhaps is the real influence of war veterans on Armistice Day; not as organised members of the British Legion, but in ten thousand work places compelling others to show respect for the Silence simply by their presence. This may explain the observance of the Silence in deep mine workings which was regularly reported in the press.[97]

Not only those at work, but those in transit were drawn into the silence: 'The people on top of the bus are sitting, but the driver is standing hatless beside the bus. So are most car drivers.'[98] Trains and underground railway services were not affected.

One place of work where the observance had an additional significance was in schools. The pedagogic purposes of the commemoration were being brought into line with the broader social interpretation of the day:

> The London County Council is issuing to its teachers a notice that Thursday may be celebrated in the schools as Armistice and Peace Day. At the discretion of head teachers, children may be withdrawn from school to attend a service at a place of worship during the morning...much excellent teaching dealing with the spirit and achievements of those who have set up and are operating the machinery for the prevention of war is already given in schools (says the notice) and it is hoped that Armistice and Peace Day will come to be seen as the culmination of efforts in this direction.[99]

How far such a message was actually transmitted in the school environment, is more open to question:

> Assembled in hall. Head gives a talk on "The war to end war". Children quiet, eyes straight ahead, evidently held... No emotion, I should say, in children, but interest in something that is spoken of so much in their hearing.....No joking, whispering, this is very noticeable. Dismissal to class rooms. I felt disposed overwhelmingly to talk on the war and events in Spain and Japan.[100]

This appears to be a more liberal school than the one described by another teacher:

> The Head, "I want you to keep your thoughts on the service at the national war memorial in London. What is it's name?" Children, "Cenotaph". "The King and his ministers are there and not England only but the whole British Empire is keeping the two minutes silence. Afterwards we will have God save the King".[101]

At the level of Higher Education it seems that Armistice Day was more of a curiosity than a solemn event:

> As the Lecturer went on with no signs of stopping, people began to get a little more restive, and to begin shutting up their books. At last, about 10.56, he finished, and I made a rush for the door. Armistice Day does not thrill me, but I had always heard what large crowds gathered in the market place and I thought I might go and see how big they really are.[102]

Such dilettantism was frowned on in certain circles: 'Graduates like me never bother about it and just stay in their respective places going on with their work.'[103]

It is unsurprising that students should (except perhaps in Cambridge, due to the rag) seem unimpressed by Armistice Day. Young men from the middle classes seem in all accounts to be the least impressed by Armistice Day. Of those in the crowds passing Westminster Abbey in 1938 who were observed not to be wearing poppies, all eleven were young men.[104] Perhaps they had other things to think about. Ominous signs were everywhere; the Dean of Westminster said prayers for the victims of 'Kristallnacht' at the Tomb of the Unknown Soldier.[105] At Victory House on Kingsway 100 recruits queued to join the RAF, a record number.[106]

Most of the young men would be wearing poppies on the next Armistice Day, whatever their views. Their commanding officers would insist.[107]

Silence Suspended

The outbreak of war was the ultimate ironic comment on Armistice Day as it had developed during the 1930s.[108] The editorial of *The Times* in 1937 can be taken as representative of the official interpretation of the meaning of Armistice Day:

> The heart of today's commemoration lies not in the prayers publicly recited or the hymns sung, but in the two minutes silence. This in each year anyone is free to employ as they will...Thoughts will turn this morning to the future rather than to the past; they will concern themselves less with bygone victory than with the hopes of peace to come. Yet to devote the two minutes to silent prayer for peace is certainly not to show forgetfulness for the fallen or ingratitude for their sacrifices. It is, on the contrary, to commemorate them in just the way they would wish.[109]

Paul Fussell has argued that the Great War ushers in a modern consciousness, in which our perception becomes ironic. Yet there is no irony in the language of this editorial. The irony is in the events that followed, which make us read it now with a feeling of loss. The outbreak of the Second World War destroyed the meaning of the First for a generation. If Armistice Day had been a celebration of patriotism and national strength, it is inconceivable that it would have been cancelled in November 1939, just when it was necessary to evoke those emotions. But it *was* cancelled:

> The Home Secretary raised the question of the observance this year of Armistice Day. He had been in touch with the Archbishop of Canterbury and all interested Departments. As a result it had been agreed that no

general celebrations could take place in present circumstances. No obstacle would however be placed in the way of local observance of the day if desired by small communities. It was agreed that the usual Poppy Day collection under the auspices of the British Legion should take place on the 11th of November, and that Sunday, 12th of November should be observed as a day of dedication.

If the War Cabinet approved this suggestion, the Archbishop of Canterbury would get in touch with the Heads of other churches, and concert the necessary plans. And simultaneous announcements would then be made by the Government and the Archbishop. The Home Secretary added that the King had already been pleased to signify his agreement.[110]

Armistice Day was in fact partially observed through the broadcast of a service from Westminster Abbey and through a broadcast by Queen Elizabeth to the women of the Empire.[111] Poppy Day would continue, its signification detached for the time being from the general context of Armistice Day. Poppies were now primarily support for the living rather than commemoration of the dead, with the need for the services of the British Legion being greater than ever (see Fig.5.2).[112] The gross yield of Poppy Day in 1939 was a record £595,887.[113] More people than ever before were wearing poppies; out of one hundred observed, eighty-two were wearing them. The Mass Observer who recorded this concluded, 'a very high proportion of people had bought poppies' but, 'few if any regarded Armistice Day as anything other than a way of raising money for a good cause'. There was a feeling that the symbolism of the poppy was incongruous; a forty year old working-class man was overheard saying, 'Buy two poppies this year, eh? Why not three, one for 1914, one for this war and one for the next.' Such cynicism was unusual, and gentle resignation may have been more typical: 'They still need money for the last war relief and a new one started. What a life! But it's right, it would be a farce to celebrate the "war to end war" with a new one started.'[114]

It is curious that despite this tone, twenty-five people interviewed out of twenty-seven stated that they intended to keep the silence when interviewed on 10 November. A private ceremony replacing a public one?[115] People lost in their own thoughts and worries, unsure if anyone else was performing the same act?[116] Or simple inertia? It is impossible to know.

In the relief following the Munich crisis, British Movietone news produced a newsreel of Armistice Day. The commentary accompanying it was a poem by Gerald Sanger. It hammers home

Figure 5.2 Memory and Charity in 1939

the theme of peace defended from the threat of war with a
minimum of subtlety:

> Peace that is in England – blessing these favoured isles;
> Steeping the placid acres of content;
> Peace – bounds the sky and sweeps the fallow miles
> where Autumn's beauty fades divinely spent...
>
> Peace at the Cenotaph. The tranquil scene
> Of hallowed memory, and pledge renewed.
> No blare of triumph breaks the quietude
> Of spirits knit in fellowship serene.
>
> This is our anniversary of – Peace.
> How should we celebrate this sacred day
> Other than in the mood of men who pray
> Thanksgiving for miraculous release.
>
> We've seen it grow inevitable – War,
> Then like a miracle it passed away
> Not yet are free men fated to betray
> The martyrdom of twenty years before...
>
> This year of fate, this nineteen thirty eight,
> That pushed the world to Armageddon's brink,
> That's made of Might a noble thing again
> What would the Unknown Warrior think –
> Would not his sacrifice seem all in vain
>
> Pity his grief, who brought the world relief.
> How shall we seek and earn our comrades pardon?
> Only by vowing – till Remembrance cease,
> And there will be no more crosses in the Garden –
> That we will keep the thing he gave us – Peace.[117]

This poem would be of no particular interest if it were not for the
fact that the author wrote a similar poem in 1939, which illustrates
both the continuities and the change of mood brought by the
outbreak of war:

> This fateful year the crowds will not assemble
> To pay their loving tribute to the shrine,
> Of that last war we thought to be the last.
> Multitudes will not gather mute and vast;
> But in the sanctuary of your heart and mine
> The chords of faithful memory will tremble...

The lucky warrior forsook his burrows,
Returned to ease and joy of civil life
Leaving behind his unlucky fellow –
To whom a grateful nation built memorials
Framed in the mood of merciful release;
Greatest of them all the Cenotaph.

At which each year, we vowed to keep the faith
And thought to keep it best by keeping peace
Inspired by speeches, pictures, editorials.
Eleven o'clock, The hour spelt Armistice...

Eleven again! The peace we loved is broken
The tyrants heel stalks mightily abroad...[118]

The Cenotaph service was not performed again until 1945.

Implications

Studying Armistice Day during this period provides insights into wider questions of British history. In assessing the 'era of appeasement', two schools of thought tend to emerge.

The first is the traditional approach, political, institutional and intellectual history.[119] It stresses the role of a Germanophile and anti-communist political elite or the pragmatism of government, depending on ideological taste. It examines the internationalist idealism of the Labour party under Lansbury and the institutions of the peace movement, finding them admirable or foolish depending on the authors' standpoint. It examines the Oxford Union debate or the Hoare-Laval agreement depending on whether domestic or international politics are the authors' speciality.

The other approach stresses public reaction to the events of the 1930s[120] and the themes that arise. It analyses the reaction to the rise of Hitler, the Spanish Civil War and the Munich agreement. It looks at the developing fear of bombing[121] and the speculative accounts of 'the next war'.[122]

Both approaches have long traditions. Michael Foot published his polemic *The Guilty Men,* in 1940, setting the standard for attacks on the National Government's policies. Mass Observation and Gallup were providing almost instant analysis of the public reaction to Munich. Both traditions can be synthesized to produce general accounts in which government responds to public opinion or public opinion responds to government action, or even in which the two are locked in a feedback system.[123]

What both approaches have in common is the belief that the memory of the First World War was a crucial element in determining attitudes to the possibility of a Second World War. What neither has done is examine how that memory was constructed. It is simply assumed that the 'war books' of 1929–33 created a revulsion towards the prospect of another conflict.[124] This is a vast oversimplification.

The memory of war was not simply constructed in this period, it was reconstructed. The stimulus provided by the war books interacted with the needs of the bereaved and, to a lesser extent, those of veterans to formulate a new meaning for the war. This new meaning was the idealistic position that the suffering and sacrifices were not in vain because they were made to end war all together. The British people tried to cling to this interpretation through the 1930s, in the face of increasingly overwhelming evidence to the contrary, because they had been left with no other meaning for the war which could provide comfort.

The French ultimately knew that between 1914 and 1918 they had driven an invader from their soil, and their pacifism was 'patriotic' (to use Antoine Prost's assessment). In Britain, where so little apparently changed between 1910 and 1920 (much *had* changed, but the continuity was more apparent), there would always be the fear that the war had been for nothing.

It was around Armistice Day that meaning coalesced. It answered the question 'What was it for?' by saying 'Peace'. The opponents of Armistice Day attacked it in the same terms as those who supported it; they simply argued that with the military present it was not peaceful enough, that the spirit of the day was violated by the Silence being kept in armaments factory. The rhetoric of peace, poured out once a year for ten years, reshaped the popular memory of the war and provided the deep strata of assumptions which determined public opinion in the 1930s.

Then the war came. The assumptions were shattered and in their place came gloomy resignation. There was a sense of hatred for 'the tyrant' who shattered those assumptions and brought all the good-will to naught. When the hand of friendship is refused, when trust is betrayed, the bitterness that emerges can create a powerful anger out of all proportion to common sense. Armistice Day may provide insights not only into appeasement, but also into the Second World War.

It would be ludicrous to argue that the British people were willing to continue an apparently hopeless fight in the autumn of

1940 simply because Hitler had shattered their comforting illusions about Armistice Day. Nonetheless, it would be wrong to discount the power of hurt sensibilities.[125]

Notes to Chapter 5

1. W.S. Churchill, 'Armistice or Peace?', in Churchill, *Step by Step 1936–1939*, London, 1939, pp. 176-179.

2. J. Hinton, *Protests and Visions: Peace Politics in 20th Century Britain*, London, 1989, p. 89.

3. A.J.P. Taylor, *English History 1914–45*, Oxford, 1965, p. 470.

4. Editorial, *Daily Mail*, 11 Nov. 1935, p. 12. For an analysis of the complexities of the Rothermere approach to foreign policy see P. Addison, 'Patriotism under pressure: Lord Rothermere and British Foreign Policy', in C. Cook and G. Peale (eds), *The Politics of Reappraisal 1918–1939*, London, 1975, pp. 189–208. Particular reference to Abyssinia and the League is found on p. 203.

5. M. Ceadel, *Thinking About Peace and War*, Oxford, 1987, pp. 4–5.

6. M. Muggeridge, *The Thirties*, London, 1940, p. 175.

7. See, J.H. Grainger, *Patriotisms: Britain 1900–1939*, London, 1986, pp. 329–360.

8. Taylor, *Engish History*, pp. 467–468.

9. *Catholic Herald*, 10 Nov. 1934, p. 6. See also *The Fiery Cross* (Official organ of the Anglo-Catholic conference), November 1935, p. 173.

10. *43rd Annual report of the Womens Co-operative Guild*, London, 1926, p. 17.

11. *45th Annual Report of the Womens Co-Operative Guild*, London, 1928, p. 6.

12. Photocopy of undated testimony by G.E. Lloyd in PPU archive file on 'Alternative Remembrance'. There is a slightly different account in J. Gaffin and D. Thoms, *Caring and Sharing; The Centenary History of the Co-Operative Women's Guild*, Manchester, 1983.

13. A statement made by the Women's Cooperative Guild in 1933, quoted in a P.P.U. pamphlet 'About White Poppies', 1988.

14. *Peace News*, January 1983, p. 5.

15. The 'No More War' movement in the twenties was already aware of the potential of Armistice Day for pacifist propaganda and had held meetings on that date. See their monthly newspaper, *No More War*, November 1924, p. 6. 'This is a splendid opportunity for our propaganda among the crowds at war memorials everywhere AFTER the Great Silence'. See also *No More War*, November 1925, November 1926. In 1927, 17,000 copies of the journal were claimed to have been sold on 11 November. See *No More War*, December 1927.

16. V. Brittain, *Chronicle of Friendship; Diary of the Thirties 1932–39*, (ed.) A. Bishop, London, 1986, pp. 107–108.

17. E.J. Bowen, 'Sussex Peace Groups 1914–45', *Journal Of Southern History*, 9, 1987, pp. 141–157.

18. R.E. Roberts, *H.R.L. Sheppard, Life and Letters*, London, 1942, p. 80. Bill Hetherington of the PPU infers from various evidence that Sheppard was actually an unconditional pacifist from 1919, but refrained fom publicly saying so. I am not convinced of this, but this is partially a semantic argument on the exact meaning of pacifism in the 1920s.

19. 11 November was the 'Saint Day' of St Martins-in-the-Fields Church.

20. M. Ceadel, *Pacifism in Britain: 1914–1945*, Oxford, 1980, p. 67.

21. PPU pamphlet, 1988.

22. The League of Nations Union appears to have sponsored peace meetings on Armistice Day prior to 1935. As early as 1926 the point was discussed by the publicity committee of the LNU who decided that a national effort would be too difficult to organise and instead left the initiative to local branches. See BLPES, LNU IV 50 c.13., minutes of meeting of the League publicity committee, 9 March 1926, p. 2.

The tenth anniversary of the League in 1929 was heavily publicised in Armistice week see LNU IV 21 c.58, publicity committee, 27 March 1929 and 21 Oct. 1929.

23. There was also a major peace rally in Manchester, see *Manchester Guardian*, 12 Nov. 1937, p. 13.

24. It was not purely a Peace Pledge Union demonstration but was designed to appeal to a wide range of pro-peace sentiment.

25. *The Times,* 12 Nov. 1937, p. 10.

26. Official Programme for Regents Park, 11 November 1937, in PPU: 'Alternative Remembrance File'.

27. *Newcastle Daily Journal,* 12 Nov. 1936, p. 9.

28. Ibid., p. 10.

29. Salt (ed.) *Of Whole Heart Cometh Hope: The Centenary History of the Co-Operative Womens Guild*, London, 1983, p. 38.

30. R. Simpson, '81, 000 women want to know the reason why' (undated but clearly 1937), p. 2. In PPU: 'Alternative Remembrance File'.

31. Ibid., p. 1.

32. BL: GSC, 1934: 'Agenda for British Legion Conference 1934', motion 51 Proposed Farsley and Yorkshire Area, p. 16. Marked as carried. There is also motion 53 that, 'In the opinion of the conference red poppies are symbolical of the blood of the nation and this colour only shall be used in British Legion Poppies.' This motion may be significant for reasons discussed below.

33. BL: GSC, 1935: 'Agenda for British Legion Conference 1935', Motion 9 proposed Wales area, p. 8. See also: 'Annual Conference Resolutions 1935'.

34. See, Simpson, '81, 000 Women', p. 3. Also testimonies in, Salt, *Of Whole Heart Cometh Hope,* p. 38. and *51st Annual Report of the Women's Co-operative Guild,* London, 1934, p. 12.

35. PPU Archive, Sponsors Meeting 4 April 1939. Item 170, report by Stuart Morris. There is no record of this approach in the Royal British Legion Archive.

36. See note 30.

37. See correspondence in *Peace News*, 12 Dec. 1936, p. 6, particularly letter from K.H. Bond. The debate continued in *Peace News,* 26 Dec. 1936, p. 7. Here the analogy was decisively rejected, even so Miss E. Newman, whilst rejecting the white feather, stated that 'a man who refuses to fight for conscience sake may be braver than one who enlists', which illustrates the gulf between the positions, as the British Legion could not have accepted this.

38. See circular letter 4 Oct. 1937 from Rose Simpson (General Secretary WCG) to interested organisations, copy in PPU: 'Alternative Remembrance File'.

39. Salt, *Of Whole Heart Cometh Hope*, p. 37. The fundamental connection between bereavement and peace, central to Armistice Day in the thirties, is stressed by another Guild member in this book: 'Peace was predominant in the WCG because at the end of the war – the 1914–18 war – the bereavement of the millions of soldiers that had died, the mum's sons who had not come back. And so the tremendous surge of these women "never again, never again." The men had a certain amount of patriotism – there was a certain amount of military bands and this kind of thing. Tottenham beat West Ham and we beat the Germans. But for the women – sadness only sadness. And determination that – "OK no grandson of mine has got to go through this" ', Ibid., p. 39. See discussion of Mass Observation material below.

40. Undated, but almost certainly 1938, printed on card, kept in PPU: 'Alternative Remembrance File'.

41. *55th Annual Report of the Women's Co-operative Guild,* London, 1938, p. 2.

42. *Womens Pictorial,* 15 Nov. 1930, p. 15.

43. I believe that Sheppard's attitude to the war was largely consistent with the idea of redemptive sacrifice from 1919 to his death, although Bill Hetherington disagrees with me. Sheppard was not at all afraid of controversy and I suspect that when he said, as he did repeatedly through the 1920s that the soldiers had not died in vain, he meant it. Exactly what he meant by that may have changed around the late 1920s, but I have argued in a previous chapter that this was probably true for many people.

44. *The Times,* 11 Nov. 1937, p. 11.

45. Simpson, '81, 000 women', p. 2.

46. Ibid., p. 3.

47. J. Drinkwater, 'What I Think About in the Great Silence', *Daily Mail,* 11 Nov. 1933, p. 10.

48. *Manchester Guardian,* 12 Nov. 1937, p. 3.

49. H.N. Brailsford, 'A Vow for the Great Silence', *Daily Herald,* 10 Nov. 1934, p. 10.

50. *Daily Herald,* 11 Nov. 1933, p. 10.

51. *Reynold's Illustrated News,* 15 Nov. 1931, p. 19.

52. *Daily Herald,* 12 Nov. 1936, p. 12. See also *Daily Herald,* 12 Nov. 1935, p. 9; *Daily Herald,* 12 Nov. 1938, p. 8; *Reynold's Illustrated News,* 12 Nov. 1933, p. 1. It might be tempting to dismiss such ideas as marginal, it should therefore be pointed out that the *Daily Herald* had the largest circulation of any national daily in 1935. The radicalisation of the *Daily Mirror* began in the same period and began to draw readers away by 1939. See C. Seymour-Ure, 'The Press and the Party System', in Cook and Peele, *Politics of Reappraisal,* pp. 232–258.

53. Naturally this did happen; 4,000 workers employed at Euxton munitions work near Chorley took part in an Armistice Day ceremony in 1937. *Manchester Guardian,* 12 Nov. 1937, p. 12.

54. Wilfred Gibson, 'Armistice Day 1932', *New Statesman and Nation,* 12 Nov. 1932.

55. *Reynold's Illustrated News,* 11 Nov. 1934, p. 13.

56. R. Shepherd, *A Class Divided,* London 1988, pp. 40–41. See also A.J.P.Taylor, *A Personal History,* London, 1983, p. 162.

57. *Daily Herald,* 11 Nov. 1935, p. 14.

58. *Daily Herald,* 11 Nov. 1938, p. 22.

59. *Daily Herald,* 12 Nov. 1937, p. 9.

60. *Manchester Guardian,* quoted in Harrisson and Madge, *Britain,* p. 201.

61. *Daily Herald ,* 12 Nov. 1937, p. 8.

62. Ibid., p. 9. This may appear to contradict my earlier comments about Sheppard. Yet the clear meaning is that Sheppard had become ashamed of betrayal of the ideals for which he believed the Cenotaph stood.

63. See for example, J. Clark, M. Heinemann, D.Margolies and C. Snee (eds), *Culture and Crisis in Britain in the 30's,* London, 1979.

64. A. Calder, in the Introduction to the 1986 edition of Harrisson and Madge, *Britain,* p. xv.

65. According to Harrisson and Madge, *Britain,* p. 200; 1000 Mass Observers participated in the 1937 survey. If this is so, remarkably few (fifty!) of those reports were placed in the archive now at the University of Sussex. I could only find one of the reports cited in *Britain* at Sussex. However, the initial cataloguing of these files was confused; for example, some 1938 material was filed under 1940. This was through no fault of the excellent archivists at Sussex. What may have happened is that, when the 1937 interviews were collected to write the book, they were not returned to the file they were taken from. I can think of no reason to believe that the

material cited in *Britain* is not authentic, particularly as it agrees broadly with the more plentiful material in the files for 1938.

66. MO; all three quotes are from Camden Town, 27 Oct. 1938. The 'class' description of the respondents is that given by the observer.

67. MO; first quote Camden Town, second Fulham, both 27 Oct. 1938.

68. MO; Camden Town, 27 Oct. 1938.

69. See Harrisson and Madge, *Britain,* p. 200; for 1937. Of the 69 interviews conducted in 1938, for which there are records at Sussex, which posed the question 'Do you think the Silence should be continued?' 33 expressed the view that Armistice Day should be scrapped against 29 clearly in favour (7 unclear).

70. MO; Fulham, 27 Oct. 1938.

71. MO; woman of 40, Fulham, 27 Oct. 1938.

72. MO; woman of 40. See also woman of 30 who lost a brother, both Fulham, 27 Oct. 1938.

73. MO; Both Fulham, 27 Oct. 1938.

74. MO; all interviews, Fulham, 27 Oct. 1938.

75. MO; Camden Town, 27 Oct. 1938.

76. F. Drake-Carnell, *Old English Custom and Ceremonies,* London, 1938, p.110.

77. MO; both Camden Town, 27 Oct. 1938.

78. MO; Camden Town, 27 Oct. 1938.

79. MO; woman of 55, NW1, 27 Oct. 1938.

80. MO; Camden Town, 27 Oct. 1938.

81. MO; both quotes Fulham, 27 Oct. 1938.

82. MO; first two quotes Camden Town, third quote Fulham, 27 Oct. 1938.

83. Harrisson and Madge, *Britain,* p. 208.

84. Ibid., p. 206.

85. Ziegler, *Crown and People,* p. 83.

86. Harrisson and Madge, *Britain,* p. 202.

87. *Daily Herald,* 12 Nov. 1937, p. 9.

88. *The Times,* 12 Nov. 1937, p. 10. *Manchester Guardian,* 12 Nov. 1937, p. 13. The advertising company, the sponsors and the pilot all subsequently apologised in the *Manchester Guardian* for the incident.

89. MO; S27, 11 Nov. 1937.

90. MO; Westminster Abbey, 11 Nov. 1938.

91. MO; S17, 11 Nov. 1937.

92. *The Times,* 12 Nov. 1937, p. 10.

93. *Newcastle Daily Journal,* 17 Nov. 1936, p. 8.

94. MO; S29, 11 Nov. 1937.

95. Harrisson and Madge, *Britain,* p. 203. Neither of these examples are the in the Sussex archive, but are obviously reliable first hand reports from 1937.

96. Ibid., pp. 204–5.

97. See for example the report from a Leicestershire mine, *The Times,* 12 Nov. 1937, p. 10.

98. MO; S11, 11 Nov. 1937.

99. *The Times,* 9 Nov. 1937, p. 13. See also report on the peace pageant, Armistice Day 1937, at Shirebrook Girls school, Mansfield in *Peace News,* 27 Nov. 1927.

100. MO; S43, 11 Nov. 1937.

101. MO; S44, 11 Nov. 1937.

102. MO; S46, 11 Nov. 1937.

103. MO; S33, 11 Nov. 1937.

104. MO; Hand written MSS 'LT', 11 Nov. 1938.

105. *Daily Herald,* 11 Nov. 1938, p. 1.

106. *Evening Standard,* 11 Nov. 1938, p. 15.

107. See *Daily Mail,* 11 Nov. 1939, p. 2; 'Remembrance Day poppies will be worn by most of the British troops in France.'

108. Mona Ozouf has stated in her work on French revolutionary festivals that, 'Ending was the ambition of the Revolutionary festival and its evident failure.' M. Ozouf, *Festivals and the French Revolution*, trans. A. Sheridan, London, 1988, p. 186. A similar point can be made about Armistice Day which had proclaimed the finality of the event it was commemorating. How could there be a second war to end all wars?

109. *The Times*, 11 Nov. 1937, p. 15. See also the editorial of *St Agatha's Parish Magazine*, Sparkbrook, Birmingham, November 1938, p. 1. In this the priest, G.D. Rosenthal, thanks God and the Prime Minister for having saved the nation from catastrophe and having been 'spared the ignominy of failing the men who in 1914–18 gave their lives in the war to end wars'. Birmingham Public Library DRO 43/121.

110. Record of telephone conversation, 10 Oct. 1939, WAC. R/34/227/3.

111. See, S.Hibberd, *This – Is London...* London, 1950, p. 180.

112. *Daily Mail*, 11 Nov. 1939, p. 3.

113. Wootton, *Official History*, p. 258. Naomi Mitchison noted in her diary in 1942 that most people were wearing poppies. D. Sheridan (ed.), *Among You Taking Notes: The Wartime Diary of Naomi Mitchison*, Oxford, 1986, p. 217. British Legion figures suggest that in real terms 1942–45 may have been the most successful collections ever.

114. All the above from; Mass Observer 'HJN', Streatham High Road, 11 Nov. 1939. Surprising as it may seem, white poppies were also sold in 1939; personal communication from Bill Heatherington at the PPU.

115. It may be worth noting that in her book on customs published in 1941 the doyenne of English folklorists, Christina Hole, does not mention Armistice Day at all. It is possible that it was believed at the time that the public commemoration had ended permanently. C. Hole, *English Custom and Practises*, London, 1941.

116. Some unplanned local ceremonies occurred in 1939, for example: 'On his own initiative a Nottingham Salvation Army Officer conducted a short service in the old market square where the two minutes silence was reverently kept by several hundred people.' *Nottingham Guardian,* 13 Nov. 1939, p. 3.

117. Printed in *Daily Mail*, 11 Nov. 1938, p. 11. I have spared the reader six further stanzas.

118. *Daily Mail,* 11 Nov. 1939, p. 3.

119. The literature is enormous. On diplomatic history and collective biography, see M.Gilbert and R. Gott, *The Appeasers*, London, 1963; J. Charmley, *Chamberlain and the Lost Peace,* London, 1989; L.W. Fuscher, *Neville Chamberlain and Appeasement,* New York 1984; K. Middlemass, *The Diplomacy of Illusion: The British Government and Germany 1937–9,* London, 1972. On the elite's mentality, see R. Shepherd, *A Class Divided*, London, 1988. On intellectuals for and against appeasement, see A.L. Rowse, *All Souls and Appeasement,* London, 1961. On the peace movement see Ceadel, *Pacifism.* This is a very partial list.

120. See for example, P. Kyba, *Covenants Without Swords: Public Opinion and British Defence Policy,* Ontario, 1981; R.Douglas, *1938: In the Year of Munich,* London 1977; M. Ceadel 'Interpreting East Fulham', in C.Cook and J.Ramsden (eds), *Bye Elections in British Politics,* London, 1973; K.W. Watkins, *Britain Divided: the Effect of the Spanish Civil War on British Political Opinion,* London, 1963.

121. See first chapter of J. Terraine, *The Right of the Line: The Royal Airforce in the European War,* London, 1985.

122. See I.F. Clarke, *Voices Prophesying War 1763–1984*, Oxford, 1966, pp. 163–178. Clarke points out that 1930s 'imaginary wars' were aimed to promote peace, unlike their pre-first world war equivalents which tended to be military propaganda; see p. 176. Also see M. Ceadel, 'Popular Fiction and the Next War', in F. Gloversmith (ed.), *Class, Culture and Social Change*, Brighton, 1980.

123. A pioneering work in this repect was M. Gilbert, *The Roots of Appeasement,* London, 1966. It also has the virtue of taking a long view, being primarily concerned with the 1920s.

124. For examples see Gilbert, *The Roots*, pp. 20–21 and Shepherd, *A Class Divided*, p. 17.

125. Angus Calder's brilliant cultural history of the crucial years 1940–1941 appeared shortly after I first wrote this. In it he stresses the importance of the dichotomy of peace loving Britons, as opposed to militaristic Germans, as a propaganda theme of the early war years. The English, 'conquerors of a vast empire...must now be portrayed as gentle, pacific until provoked'. It is implied that the love of peace makes the British stout fighters in defence. Such mythology was as much for home consumption as for overseas use. See A. Calder, *The Myth of the Blitz*, London, 1991, pp. 195–196.

6

God Our Help: The Churches, Armistice Day and Remembrance Sunday

The Frontiers of Heresy

Early in 1923, an ex-serviceman from Slough declared himself to be the Primate of the 'Independent Church of the Great Sacrifice'. 'Archbishop Banks, patriarch of Windsor', claimed full equality with Randall Davidson, Archbishop of Canterbury and head of the Anglican communion. In a statement to the press he informed the world that he intended to attend the Cenotaph ceremony on 11 November and be crowned as patriarch immediately afterwards. The date was chosen because, 'Our great festival day is November 11 – Armistice Day.'[1]

A typical piece of newspaper trivia, yet one that indicates the very real problems which Armistice Day could pose to established religion. Banks, a self proclaimed medium, was tying together two of the most powerful quasi-religious responses to the Great War, the ritual of 11 November and the surge of interest in spirit communication. Had he been a little less obviously deranged, or alternatively a little more charismatic (in the Weberian sense), it is possible that his independent church might have gained a measure of success. His was not the only effort to connect the two phenomena. Psychic photography was used to show the spirits of the dead in attendance at the Cenotaph.[2]

Yet even without the possible added attraction of spiritualism, the language that surrounded the Armistice commemoration quickly took on spiritual overtones, ones that were in certain respects threatening to orthodox christology. The fundamental definition of Christian Orthodoxy is the Nicaean Creed to which all important Christian communions subscribe. At the heart of the creed is the

Notes for Chapter 6 can be found on page 207.

assertion that mankind has fallen from Grace and can only be saved by faith in the incarnate, crucified and resurrected God. There is one single cosmic redemptive sacrifice. Groups that reject this dogma, whether Cathar, Quaker, Unitarian or modern sects such as spiritualists and Jehovah's Witnesses are not regarded as Christian by the orthodox majority they are clearly either heterodox or heretical, depending on the generosity of the observer. Other dogmas can be considered fundamental by churches and schism is sometimes treated as akin to heresy, but the redemptive sacrifice is a point on which all churches with a claim to orthodoxy would be in agreement.

The 'folk theology' of the redemptive sacrifice of the war dead naturally veered towards heresy, the heresy which Banks proclaimed. That this heresy drew on Christian tradition would be no comfort to the major churches, indeed the threat would seem all the greater.[3] The difficulty that the churches faced was having to acknowledge the popular need for a transcendant meaning for the 'sacrifice', whilst at the same time protecting the orthodox insistence on the singular and eternal quality of the redemptive sacrifice at the heart of Christian belief.[4] The Anglican, Methodist, Nonconformist and Roman Catholic communions faced the same problem in this respect. How they dealt with it was determined by their church organisation, their theology, their congregations and their history.

The Dilemmas of Establishment: The Church of England, Armistice Day and Remembrance Sunday

The first anniversary of Armistice Day, as has already been noted, was a somewhat improvised public commemoration. A special service was held at Westminster Abbey for 'St Martin's Day, the first anniversary of the Armistice'. A prayer said on that occasion drew attention to the Abbey containing, 'memorials to Great Britain's most illustrious dead', which offered a dedication to the great glory of God and 'the memory of our dear Brothers departed', asking God to 'Grant them eternal peace' and to give, 'all that mourn the blessing of Thy perfect comfort'.[5]

By 1920, when it was clear that the commemoration would be repeated, the Church of England began to prepare for the possibility that some people would want a local religious framework for their commemorations. The Society for the Propagation of Religious Knowledge printed a service form for commemoration on 7

November, the Sunday preceding Armistice Day. This service is the direct progenitor of Remembrance Sunday services to this day.[6] The suggested form of service began with Hymn 447 (A&M), followed by an address by the priest. This was followed by a General Confession, Absolution and the Lord's Prayer, by Psalms CXXIII, CXXIV and CXXV[7] and by a first lesson (either Daniel III 16–28 or Ecclesiastes XLIV 1–14).[8] The service continued with the Benedicite, a second lesson (Revelations XXI 1–5 or Hebrews X 32–50),[9] then the Bendictus and the Apostles' creed. The service would conclude with Hymn 222 (A&M) and four prayers.

In 1921 SPCK produced a new service sheet, which was substantively similar to the previous year except for the following: the Hymns were altered (217, 298,439 and 437 in the A&M), a choice of sentences preceded the address (Ps.CXLII 2 or Deuteronomy VII 2 or John XI 25–26), the address was changed and either a Te Deum or a Magnificat Anima Mea was replaced the Benedicite. A Nunc Dimitis could replace the Benedictus. Instructions for a procession to a war memorial were also incorporated and the place for the Last Post, the Reveille and the National Anthem in such a practice were indicated.[10]

Such services of remembrance attempted to remind the congregation of orthodox belief whilst they remembered the dead. The lessons and psalms chosen are evidence of this. Yet the prayers and addresses show the difficult balancing act the church was engaged in when it tried to reconcile orthodoxy with popular sentiment:

> During this week two years ago our prayers for peace found their fulfilment and with one accord those to whom victory had been given rendered their heartfelt thanks, and in a brief but noble silence the deep significance of Armistice Day was widely observed. For a like purpose to-day we meet once more in the sight of God on this Sunday before the Anniversary of the Armistice, that our memories might be renewed by Him and our wills again directed in all that He holds good: for if there be any virtue, if there be any praise, it is to Him that it is due and to the lives laid down.[11]

The tension is readily apparent between giving all credit to God and incorporating the sacrifice of the war dead. Equating the sacrifice of the war dead with Christ's passion would be heresy, the heresy known as patri-passionism, but it was a heresy that many, particularly the bereaved, wanted to hear. Archbishop Davidson in his sermon at the Tomb of the Unknown Warrior walked a fine line:

'we have lived through large days, large doings, at a great juncture in the history of Mankind...we are not afraid, as we ponder the sacrifice and all that it means... to link it with our prayers for the bettering of the world.' Yet he ended the Sermon with impeccable orthodoxy, 'it is within our grasp if we only trust *not in our strength*, but in His who lived for us, died for us and who rose again, who is alive & present with us here tonight.'[12]

Part of the popularity of spiritualism in the aftermath of the war was that it was a more comforting doctrine concerning the dead than that held by either of the wings of the established church. Justification by faith, the position of hardline Evangelicals, was obviously less than appropriate for the vast majority of British servicemen and families would find it difficult to believe that it was applicable to most ordinary soldiers and sailors. On the other hand, the doctrine of purgatory was still little understood and frequently disliked; what was acceptable to Roman Catholic congregations was seen as alien by many of those who were under the pastoral care of Anglo-Catholics. It seems probable that the broad centre of the Church of England evaded the issue by concentrating on the love of God as comfort to the bereaved and by stressing the secular achievements of the sacrifice. Hence the rhetoric of secularised redemption (see Chapter One) was often voiced by churchmen in terms not greatly different from those of politicians or the press. The address in the 1921 SPCK service talked of 'those who fought a manful fight in the war which we waged to save the world from cruelty and wrong'.[13]

The established nature of the church made it natural that many felt that it should give its blessing to 'secular' commemoration and also made churchmen feel obliged to get involved. Archbishop Davidson was apparently insistent that he should participate in the unveiling of the Cenotaph, despite ill health, 'On Thursday 11th, I was well enough to take part in the Cenotaph unveiling and the burial of the Unknown Warrior. It was important on all accounts that I should be there. I had some keen controversy with the Prime Minister and the Cabinet, especially Curzon about the proceedings at the Cenotaph.' Curzon and Lloyd George had argued that the Cenotaph ceremony should be 'wholly secular' because, 'Mohammedans and Hindus were among those in whose memory it stood.' Davidson in his diary stated that, 'as a matter of fact I believe it was the fear of Nonconformist criticism'. This may have been true of Lloyd George, but Curzon was probably genuinely concerned to make the event appropriate to all peoples of the Empire.[14] Nonetheless Davidson 'prevailed and we had prayer and "God our Help". Instead of anybody disapproving, there was thankfulness that we had marked thus our Christian fellowship.'[15] Davidson must also have been gratified to hear that his rendition of the Lord's Prayer at the Cenotaph was so powerful that, 'every word was distinctly heard at the top of the Clock Tower Westminster', which was no mean feat from Whitehall.[16]

In 1923, Armistice Day fell upon a Sunday for the first time. The growing religosity of the ritual was given a distinct boost. At the Cenotaph the Bishop of London, Winnington-Ingram, infamous for his wartime belicosity, gave a short prayer.[17] The Archbishop of Canterbury took the service at St Paul's. According to one church newspaper: 'The general testimony, both from London and the provinces, is that the churches were fuller than on any occasion since the war, indeed were crowded out more than once during the day.' While this might be an exaggeration, it seems clear that churchmen were impressed by the willingness of the population at large to attend a church service of remembrance. The same newspaper asked whether it was possible 'to capture and conserve what might be called the Sunday spirit of the day' and suggested that 'without interfering with the actual date... Armistice Day should be solemnly commemorated in all churches on the Sunday immediately following November 11th.'[18] Archbishop Davidson was profoundly impressed, 'I imagine that nothing for many years stirred the country so deeply as this Sunday Armistice Day. It makes one wonder whether some arrangement ought not to be made for an Armistice Sunday near Nov. 11 every year.'[19]

In fact it was not so much the general public as the ex-servicemen, particularly the British Legion, who took to commemorating the war on the Sunday before Armistice Day. Even before 1923 it seems that the Legion was taking an interest in the church service on the Sunday preceding 11 November, partly because the Poppy Appeal coveted the church collections on that day. Writing to the Bishop of Winchester in 1921, Davidson pointed out that, 'wherever possible a special service will be arranged on Armistice Day, or the Sunday preceding it, for ex-servicemen and their friends at which addresses may be given by ex-padres and others calling upon them to remember their duties to Church and State. Selborne, Horne and others have been in correspondence with me for months about this.'[20]

Remembrance Sunday was more suitable for the assembly of veterans as a collective presence than 11 November when the two did not coincide. Ex-servicemen attained greater prominence in the Sunday commemorations, whether they were held at the civic memorial or in church. Ex-servicemen's services followed a pattern similar to those which have already been described for most of the inter-war period. The programme has survived for an afternoon service at the village of Uckfield. It is from an unknown date, but as the hymn, 'The supreme sacrifice' was sung it cannot be earlier than the late 1920s. The sermon and shape of the service are clearly based on the 1921 service plan mentioned above.[21] An undated service programme from Brighton, which was collected by Bishop Bell, appears to be from the 1930s. It is more innovative, including the Russian Contakion for the departed, but it still shows a distinct lineage from the earlier services.[22]

The ex-servicemen's service would centre on the memorial whether it was in the church or not. This is an example of a service where the memorial was in the church:

> The choir moved down the nave to the Memorial Tablet with its twelve names of the men of the village who laid down their lives in the Great War. Behind the choir walked the ex-service men from their block of pews in front of the church. At the appropriate moment one of them came forward with a plain wreath of moss entirely covered with laurel leaves and decorated with a wreath of red white and blue ribbon; this he placed beneath the Memorial Tablet, stood smartly to attention and returned to his comrades. Twelve of these each held a Flanders Poppy. The time arrived for the rector to read the names on the roll. He pronounced the first and one old soldier stepped forward and put the poppy he held in the wreath; the second name was read, and another man fixed his poppy in position, and so on down through the twelve names.[23]

In larger communities the memorials, and hence the services, would be in a public space.[24] Don Haworth remembered from his childhood in Lancashire: 'On two Sundays of the year, Armistice Sunday and Mons Sunday, we lined the main thoroughfare of the park to watch the parade of men who had served in the Great War. They marched in fours behind the bugle band of the Boy's Brigade to the white marble Cenotaph which overlooked a small ornamental pond.' It is clear from his account that this was a ceremony particularly for the veterans, in which others were on the margins: 'There was a ceremony which we were too distant to hear. The Last Post sounded among the trees. They formed fours and marched back through the park. To us children they looked like old men, though most had not passed forty. They belonged to a time before we were born and shared an experience of which we knew next to nothing.'[25]

Armistice Sunday in the countryside took on a particular importance due to the nature of rural work: 'you cannot shut down a farm like you can an office, a shop or a factory. The shepherd, the carter, the woodman and most of the workers are scattered over the farms at eleven o'clock in the morning, so, when the eleventh of November falls on a weekday, they parade in remembrance on the nearest Sunday.'[26] As was generally the case, the 1938 Sunday ceremony in the Wiltshire village described by A.G. Street provided an opportunity for veterans to assemble which was not possible on a weekday. In a village the size of Ditchampton, Armistice Sunday was 'such an intimate affair. One knows everyone.' The officers and men of the British Legion, the members of the village band, the parson, the choir and the onlookers were 'more or less intimate companions the year through'. At the centre of the Sunday ceremony were men like 'Caleb Toomer, head dairyman at Elm Tree farm, now rather tubby and grey-haired, once a dashing young sergeant' and Shepherd Hardiman who usually looked 'every inch a shepherd, but not in the least like a soldier.' These veterans were reunited once a year in church 'to remember their fallen companions and to recapture the fellowship of their young manhood.'[27]

By contrast, Tom Harrisson's report of Remembrance Sunday in Bolton in 1937 appears to describe a less veteran-centred commemoration, 'most of the procession are women, but men are mixed up indiscriminately among them'.[28] Nonetheless the majority of newspaper accounts of the period bear out the impression that Sunday was the day for ex-servicemen.

When priests had doubts about military or paramilitary displays, they often attempted to justify the services on the grounds that it was theologically analogous to All Souls Day, a festival which was being avidly promoted by the Anglo-Catholic wing of the church which was increasing its influence in the 1920s. Editorials in the Parish Magazine of St Agathas, Sparkbrook (where the vicar was the extreme Anglo-Catholic G.D. Rosenthal), used the stimulus of Armistice Day to encourage the parishioners to think about Catholic doctrines of purgatory.[29] More mainstream Anglicans linked Remembrance Sunday to the tradition of All Saints which had retained a residual Anglican significance.

The compounding of images from Armistice Day and All Saints Day was not merely a clerical conceit. According to Edward Short: 'All Saints Day lost a great deal of its separate identity in the early 1920s because of the newly established Armistice Day...We always had a service of remembrance at the war memorial with the vicar officiating, wearing his overlong surplice and biretta, though the latter was regarded by the low church element as a papish affectation.' In Short's mind, 'so mixed up did All Saints and Armistice become, that to this day my image of the countless host streaming towards the gates of pearl is a column of men marching across the heavens in First World War uniforms'.[30]

The suspension of Armistice Day activity on the outbreak of war in 1939 brought a new emphasis to the church-based commemorations of Remembrance Sunday. An editorial in the *Guardian* entitled 'Martinmas' shows the way in which the suspension of the routine civic commemoration gave added power to the church festival:

> This holy day as specially observed through the British Empire on twenty anniversaries of November 11 will be differently kept this year, and offers a temporary mark of Herr Hitler's iconoclasm. Consistency with the avoidance of large public gatherings(no better or worse cause is put forward) forbids the solemn service at the Cenotaph in Whitehall. But the day will not therefore be neglected in thousands of parish churches and chapels or around the village crosses and memorials set up in 1919. If less is made of the hour of 11 o'clock on Saturday, more should be made of "Armistice Sunday" at the church services the next day.[31]

It was the outbreak of the Second World War that saw the shift of the principal war commemoration to Remembrance Sunday. It is clear that commemoration continued through the war years on the Sunday nearest to 11 November. The changed date of commemoration was already traditional by 1945. By chance, 11 November 1945 was a Sunday. This masked the fact that an alteration had already occurred in the usual practice.

At the Parochial Level: Three Birmingham Parishes

How important was Remembrance Sunday to the church at local level? Was it a major festival? The following figures drawn from parish returns for communicants, are available for three sample parishes in the Birmingham Diocese.[32]

Table 6.1 Average Number of Communicants in Three Birmingham
Parishes 1923–1938

	Easter Sunday	First Sunday of December	Remembrance Sunday
St Alban, Bordesley	323.6	64.4	63.4
St Bartholomew, Edgbaston	357.4	82.6	45.9
St Edburgha, Yardley	334.1	37.4	36.8
Three Parish Average	338.4	61.5	48.7

(Source: Parish Returns at Birmingham Diocesan Records)

The immediate conclusion which could be drawn from these figures is that Remembrance Sunday was not a particularly significant date for churchgoing. Indeed the average communicant figure is somewhat lower than for the control chosen here (the first Sunday of December was usually, although not always, Advent Sunday).[33] At first sight it would appear that the Easter congregation must have dwarfed the congregation for Remembrance Sunday.

However, the figures for communicants are a very unreliable guide to the numbers in church, as any clergyman would confirm.[34] The figures are themselves often innaccurate or even invented. Most important of all, they only refer to those who take communion. For a non-communion service there is often no accurate method of ascertaining numbers and as is clear from other sources many Remembrance Services were not communion services. Many were inter-denominational services which would include non-Anglicans. The figures can also give no guide to the number of children attending.

An alternative method for attempting to gauge numbers is to examine the size of the collection, where figures are available. For St Edburgha's a substantially different picture begins to emerge. Thus in 1926, there were 37 communicants at the Remembrance Day service as opposed to 214 for Easter. But the collections on the respective occasions were far less disproportionate £4–16s and £13–14s respectively. Likewise in 1929, there were 35 communicants on Remembrance Sunday as opposed to 38 on the first Sunday of December, but more money was collected on Remembrance Sunday, £11–16s as opposed to £10–14s. In 1932 the contrast is even more noticeable there were 34 communicants on Remembrance Day as opposed to 385 for Easter but the collections were £23–8s and

£27–14s respectively. Whenever the First Sunday of December was not being used for a Baptism or Confirmation class, the collection on Remembrance Sunday was greater, often substantially greater. The collection on Remembrance Sunday was usually at least half the collection for Easter Sunday.[35] This suggests that communicant figures were masking a real increase in churchgoers for Remembrance Sunday in this parish.

It might be argued that the larger collections on Remembrance Sunday were a result of higher *per capita* giving, rather than greater numbers attending church. After all the church collection on Remembrance Sunday was donated to ex-service charities, which were popular causes. But in 1931 there were 31 communicants at the Remembrance Sunday service and a collection of £ 20–1–4d. This represents more than 12 shillings per communicant as opposed to 1 shilling and sixpence per communicant at Easter in the same year. The discrepancy is simply too large to be explained by a variation in the amount that was given by individuals.

On the basis of these figures, the number attending the Remembrance Sunday service would have to be adjusted upwards by at least a factor of five and anything up to a factor of ten would be plausible. Taking the more conservative figure, the attendance at St Edburgha would be approximately 187 on Remembrance Sunday or somewhat more than half the Easter communicant figure. This seems to be in accordance with more impressionistic evidence that Remembrance Sunday was a reasonably large event in the church calendar prior to World War Two, but not a *very* large one. In urban centres the church commemoration on Sunday would be overshadowed by the civic commemoration on 11 November, which in turn was increasingly overshadowed by the national commemoration at the Cenotaph in broadcast form. Religion, or more accurately a form of non-denominational piety, permeated these outdoor commemorations and the state church had a role to play in them, but church-going as such was relatively marginal to war commemoration in urban centres prior to 1938.

There appears to be a change in the pattern during the Second World War. In the parishes of St Alban and St Bartholomew there was a clear decline in regular churchgoing during the war years. St Bartholemew averaged 215 Easter communicants between 1939 and 1945 compared with 357 for the interwar years.[36] St Alban averaged 152 compared with 323.[37] Various factors were probably involved; the blackout, evacuation, transport restrictions, fear of bombing and

Sunday working may all have contributed to this decline. It is noteworthy that for St Alban the decline in attendance on Remembrance Sunday was much less steep. An average of 39 communicants were registered for Remembrance Sunday during the war years as compared with 63 for the interwar years. As usual this understates the numbers attending. In 1942, St Alban held an evening Requiem for the first time on Remembrance Sunday and in 1945 an 11 a.m. Requiem service to commemorate the war dead.[38] There was no communion in 1944 at St Bartholomew on Remembrance Sunday, but the collection was double the figure for the first Sunday of December when 75 communicants were registered.[39] Once the change from 11 November had been institutionalised in 1946, the upgrading of Remembrance Sunday as a church festival became clear. The average communicant figure at St Alban for Remembrance Sunday 1946–50 was 43 compared with an average of 162 for Easter and 35 for the first Sunday of December.

If these figures are compared with Table 6.1, then the growth of the relative significance of Remembrance Sunday in the parish becomes clear even when the fall in the absolute numbers of communicants is acknowledged. Furthermore the institution of a regular sung requiem at 11 a.m. on Remembrance Sunday at St Alban, means that the post war communicant figure is even more likely to be a serious underestimate than the pre-war figure.[40] At St Bartholomew the evidence is such as to suggest a packed church on Remembrance Sunday 1946 for a non-communion service. The collection was £41-1s-6d as compared to £10-18s-4d on the first Sunday of December. As 95 communicants were registered for the latter date, it seems reasonable to assume that at least three times that figure attended on Remembrance Sunday. This would comfortably exceed the *Easter* communicant figure of 204. In 1947 the collection on Remembrance Sunday was £23-8s-9d, substantially less than in 1946, but even larger proportionately than the collection for the first Sunday of December, when £7-2s-6d was collected with 43 registered communicants.[41]

The difficulties of using parish returns and the highly speculative nature of any conclusions drawn from them should be readily apparent from the evidence above. Any conclusions would have to be extremely tentative. The following points are made with these reservations in mind. Remembrance Sunday during the inter-war years in these parishes may have been marginally better attended than an average Sunday service. There is no clear evidence from any of the churches concerned that veterans' organisations or youth organisations were involved with the Remembrance Sunday service during these years, which would probably have boosted attendance substantially, but invisibly as far as parish returns are concerned, because many would not take communion. There is no suggestion that church attendance on Remembrance Sunday prior to 1939 came close to church attendance on Easter Sunday in numbers. The highest communicant figure for a 'Remembrance Sunday' service in any of the churches during this period is for St Alban in 1920.[42] In that year 103 took communion on Remembrance Sunday compared with 338 at Easter (the latter was a low figure for the early 1920s at this church).[43] When church leaders referred to Armistice Day as the 'Easter of the post-war world', this did not imply Easter attendance figures in church.

Some churches continued to divide their effort between Armistice Day and Remembrance Sunday. St Bartholomew held a morning special service on 11 November from 1920 to 1937 except in 1930, regardless of whether it was a Sunday or not. This became a Remembrance Sunday service in 1938.[44] This service represented the main effort of that particular church for war commemoration during the inter-war years.

During the Second World War years in these parishes the *relative* significance of Remembrance Sunday increased, compared to a general decline in churchgoing. Both St Bartholomew and St Alban saw sharp increases in attendance at Remembrance services during the second half of the war. This could be related to two things. The decline in German bombing restored a sense of normality in urban areas. Probably more significant was that the vast majority of British military fatalities were suffered during the last two years of the war (see Chapter Seven). A small number of grieving or even anxious relatives would easily explain the increase.

Both churches saw a big increase in attendance on Remembrance Sunday both relatively and absolutely after the war ended. St Bartholomew in particular saw a very large attendance on Sunday 11 November 1945. There are two possible explanations available. The coincidence of Armistice Day and Remembrance Sunday in 1945 and the subsequent shift of the national commemoration to Sunday increased the formal role of the church. For 1945 in particular the presence of recently demobilised servicemen seems plausible as an explanation of the high attendance in St Bartholomew. The urge to congregate and commemorate was probably strong in November 1945.

In considering the 'change' to formal commemoration on Remembrance Sunday in 1946, it is important to stress continuity as much as innovation. Church commemoration on the Sunday before Armistice Day was a feature of the inter-war years. After 1939 it became the principal form of commemoration and gained a new relative significance to the church. In her parish of Burleigh on the outskirts of Coventry, Clara Milburn described the service in 1941, 'A raw, cold day for Remembrance Sunday. Church was full of Home Guards, British Legion, schoolchildren and casuals, so regulars took side aisle seats.'[45]

In 1942, Archbishop Temple wrote to the Moderator of the Church of Scotland deploring what he saw as the interference of the Home Office in arrangements for Sunday commemoration, 'Remembrance Sunday has been observed throughout England and, I imagine throughout Scotland for a great many years and has nothing to do with the cancellation of the observance of Armistice Day consequent upon the war.' He went on to endorse local independence, 'Most parishes have their own methods of observing it, and I cannot help thinking the best thing to happen is that we should each of us in our appropriate ways express the hope that Remembrance Day will be observed in accordance with custom.'[46] In 1945 the coincidence of 11 November and Remembrance Sunday effectively merged the two commemorations and as a result the decision to move the Cenotaph service to Sunday in 1946, was in certain respects simply the formalisation of a *fait accompli*, one that was already clear at local level.

Other Churches: Roman Catholics and Methodists

The largest churches in inter-war Britian, other than the Church of England, were the Roman Catholic Church and the Methodist churches.[47] Roman Catholicism was relatively buoyant, still firmly rooted in the Irish immigrant communities of England, Wales and Scotland. The gap between actual and nominal membership of the Roman Catholic Church was far less substantial than for Anglicans, where many who described themselves as 'Church of England' had never troubled the pews of a church. Methodism, by contrast, was beginning its long twentieth century decline, in common with the other 'nonconformists'. In 1919 it was still divided into three main denominations, Wesleyan, Primitive and United Methodist. Reunion of the 'connections' was clearly overdue; the latter body had already united four previously separate splinter groups. Growth, largely through revivalism, could not counter the gradual attrition of active membership in all of the Methodist groups.[48]

The attitudes of Roman Catholics and Methodists to the Church of England were quite distinct, both from each other and from other denominations. Each had inherited the broad Catholic tradition which they shared with the Anglican church, but the very different historical situations of the two churches meant that the relationship with the Anglicans was fundamentally different. For the Roman Catholics, the English state church was bluntly heretical. The only true church in England was the universal Catholic Church, represented by the Roman clergy. Until Vatican II, ecumenical approaches were not merely pointless but positively dangerous, in that they might give spurious legitimacy, aid and comfort to a heretical church and therefore possibly confuse good Christians into risking certain damnation.[49] The Roman Catholic Church wanted reunification but intended to have it on its own terms, either by individual conversion sapping away at the strength of the 'protestant churches' or by the submission of these churches to Roman authority. The fundamental cohesion of the Roman Catholic Church in Great Britain, based on ethnic solidarity, made this position sustainable.

By contrast, the Methodists had a much more ambiguous position in regard to the state church. They had been expelled from the Anglican communion against their will and they had few theological differences with the Church of England. During the nineteenth century, the Wesleyans in particular had been uncomfortable with 'free church' status as they did not consider themselves dissenters, although the other, less hierarchical Methodists had accommodated themselves to the idea. During the last major clash between non-conformity and Anglicanism, the education agitation in 1903–4, the Methodists had sided with the other non-conformists, partly because the long history of local tensions between church and chapel had stored up bitterness, especially amongst Primitive Methodists. Nonetheless, it seems reasonable to say that the long-term project of reunion with the Church of England in an English Catholic Church was meaningful to Methodists, particularly Wesleyans.[50] In this they differed from the other free churches, which were less concerned with universalism although often ecumenically minded in a practical and federal sense.

These positions led to quite different strategies in dealing with a commemoration in which the established Church was inevitably substantially involved. The Roman Catholic Church agreed that there was an important role for religion in the commemoration of the war dead, but was unwilling to participate in a unified commemoration under any other aegis. For example:

> Requiem Mass for the repose of the souls of all Catholic ex-servicemen was offered in St John's Cathedral, Salford on Friday – Armistice Day – and a sermon preached by Fr J. Birch. Dr Casartelli, Bishop of Salford, in asking the clergy to announce the Mass, wished them to warn Catholic ex-servicemen that they were forbidden to attend services held in non-Catholic churches.[51]

This strategy was inimical to the ideology of the ex-service community and its language of comradeship. The Roman Catholic hierarchy was demanding that Catholic ex-servicemen see themselves as Catholic first and veterans second, in opposition to any sense of community amongst veterans.[52]

This position would have been difficult to justify or sustain, if it were not for the particular association of the majority of Roman Catholics with the Irish community. During the Irish war of independence the sympathies of that community, including presumably many ex-servicemen, were divided. The army which was busy brutally suppressing Irish revolt, was also heavily involved with public commemoration. Indeed, the authorities were not adverse to compounding war commemoration with ideological justification for actions in Ireland. The intelligence officers assassinated on the orders of Michael Collins in 1920 were used for propaganda in a way that illustrates the links; their bodies were returned to Britain and paraded through London on the same gun carriage used for the ceremonial burial of the Unknown Warrior.[53]

When the following story appeared in the *Catholic Herald* in 1920, it would obviously have underlined some of the doubts amongst the Irish Catholic community about the message that the silence was intended to convey:

> The following notice was posted early in the week in Athlone.
> "Shop keepers of Athlone are hereby ordered to close their premises on Armistice Day, November 11, in honour of the fallen heroes of the Great War and the police murdered in Ireland. This notice applies to all business houses and factories. Any failure to comply with this order renders the destruction of said premises inevitable." – (signed) BLACK AND TANS.[54]

If the observance was to be interpreted as in some respect a tacit support for the British war in Ireland, it was inevitable that the Roman Catholic church, both in Great Britain and Ireland, would need to keep its distance from participation in official commemoration. On the other hand, there was an imperative to mark the day both to avoid the accusation that the Roman Catholic church and its members were unpatriotic by their nature and because a Catholic church could not avoid dealing with a matter of such emotional importance to its communities.

The church, like its Anglican counterpart, had a nervous attitude towards the idea of a 'civic religion' without a Christian component. In 1921, the *Catholic Herald* attacked the Cenotaph as 'nothing more or less than a pagan memorial' which was 'a disgrace in a so called Christian land', at which, 'Atheist, Mohammedan, Buddhist, Jew, men of any religion or none' could offer homage, as if 'God and his Christ were mere superstition.'[55] It is interesting to note that the *Church Times* attacked the initial inscription on the Tomb of the Unknown Warrior on exactly the same grounds.[56] For the Roman Catholic church, the attack on purely civic religion had the added attraction of being a club with which to beat the established church, undermining its pretensions to represent a Christian nation.

The strategy of separate commemoration was an uneasy, but generally effective compromise, as the need for religious recognition of the importance of commemoration for both the bereaved and the ex-servicemen could not be ignored. Roman Catholics as individuals participated in civic commemoration and as the Anglican Church became more involved in the ritual of Armistice Day, it became important for the Roman Catholic church to respond. On 'Remembrance Sunday' 1923, Roman Catholic churches mounted a series of church-based commemorations: 'The fifth anniversary of the signing of the Armistice was observed in all the Catholic churches throughout the country.'[57] In 1930, 'Armistice Day was celebrated in many Catholic churches throughout the country... In many cases the observances took place on Sunday and in some other towns the ceremony of remembrance has been postponed until tomorrow so that Catholic ex-servicemen will have the opportunity of honouring their comrades in their own churches.'[58]

The most elaborate Catholic commemoration was the annual Mass at Westminster Cathedral for the Roman Catholic ex-servicemen of the Metropolitan Police. This was held a few days after the 11 November. It received official recognition through the presence of the Chief Commissioner of the Metropolitan police, who took the salute in a march-past after the service. Later in the day, a wreath would be laid at the Cenotaph.[59] This service, which incorporated an element of civic pomp and recognition, could stand as a specifically Catholic alternative to the Cenotaph service. It is worth noting that the Catholic press did not specifically attack the incorporation of 'Anglican' elements in the Whitehall Cenotaph service, even though in strict terms the public prayer and hymn singing should have excluded devout Catholics. The clash over Anglican involvement in civic war commemoration came, perhaps unsurprisingly, in Liverpool.[60]

The argument occurred because of the conjunction of two traditions. The city had been extremely slow in building its war memorial. By 1930, when it was completed, it was more likely that such a memorial would be unveiled on 11 November than would have been the case in the early 1920s.[61] At the same time the religious communities of Liverpool had established a tradition of holding their commemorations for Armistice Day along the pattern of the city's great sectarian divide.[62] By 1930, it would have been unthinkable to Anglican clergy that the unveiling of the war memorial on Armistice Day would not be accompanied by a short civic service, such as was normal throughout the country on 11 November. It was equally unthinkable to the Roman Catholic hierarchy that the Anglicans would be able to get away with this in the most Catholic of English cities. Their position was further strengthened by the fact that the Roman Catholic clergy of Liverpool were headed by an Archbishop as opposed to a mere Bishop. On Remembrance Sunday, two days before the unveiling of the Cenotaph, the Anglican Canon Raven attacked the omission of a religious service as 'an act of civic apostasy' and accused the 'Roman Mission' of having blocked such a service. Sir Thomas White, chairman of the Cenotaph committee, denied this, but agreed that his intention had been to avoid denominational controversy in Liverpool.[63] It appears that the controversy was settled by an informal agreement whereby each denomination would be led in prayer by a representative. Archbishop Downey said a *De Profundis* for the Roman Catholics and the former chaplain of the 55th (West Lancashire) Division offered the dedicatory prayer (thus side-stepping the question of precedence). Free Church and Jewish representatives also led prayers.[64]

The argument did not end there because the Anglican Bishop, Dr

David made some harsh comments on the Roman clergy the next day. This drew a response from Dr Downey the day after.[65] Both sides should have understood the reasoning behind their antagonist's position. The Church of England could not forego the right to preside at the ceremony without tacitly admitting the superiority of the Roman Catholics in the Liverpool Diocese because at all the major Armistice Day ceremonies, including that of the capital city, the state church had become a participant. On the other hand, the Roman Catholics could not accept the claims of the state church to universal representativeness in what was one of their major strongholds.

Both sides made specious arguments in appealing to the 'centre ground'. The Anglicans implied that the Roman Catholics were being mean-spirited in not joining them in a simple prayer and some hymn singing 'on a moving public occurrence'[66], yet they must have been fully aware that such activity was specifically condemned.[67] Likewise the Roman Catholics claimed, 'we are not concerned with what arrangements the Anglicans make providing thy are prepared to give freedom to those who are not of their communion – Nonconformists, Jews, the "Roman Mission" and others. The Cenotaph is in memory of all of these and is not the perquisite of any one religious body'.[68] Given the comments made by their press about the Whitehall Cenotaph in 1921, this was disengenous. In reality, this was a classic example of the two denominations sniping at each other whenever the opportunity occurred. Dr David's speech which mentioned the Cenotaph incident was principally concerned with the Catholic Evidence Guild and with priests pressuring partners in mixed marriages. Accusations of civic impiety were a useful stick with which to beat the Catholic Church at that moment. Sectarian politics in Liverpool in 1930 had experienced a brief upsurge over the Labour Education Bill; simultaneously there was a split in the Labour group of councillors.[69] This context probably made a climb down from entrenched positions difficult for both sides and the apparent passion of the argument should, in context, be considered the minimum acceptable rhetoric. The compromise which occurred at the civic ceremony was an indication of the long-term decline of sectarianism which was beginning to occur in the city.

The difficulties of reconciling religious and civic imperatives were further illustrated in Warrington in 1933, where the newly elected mayor, A.M. Crowe, felt unable to attend the 11 a.m. service at the local memorial and instead attended a requiem mass at his local church. Prior to the service he placed a wreath at the memorial, with his chaplain in attendance. The mayor's refusal to participate had angered the local ex-servicemen's organisations which refused to participate in the mayoral procession to celebrate 'Civic Sunday' the following day. More dramatically a young man, apparently a British Legion official, seized the mayor's wreath after the Cenotaph service and hurled it over a parapet into the River Mersey. The mayor described this action as a 'gratuitous insult to the dead, an insult to my official position and an insult to the citizens of Warrington.' [70] In this case the conflict was less between the churches than between the British Legion members' conception of their civic rights and the conscience of an individual mayor.

Although such incidents are interesting, it is important not to overstate their significance. They belong to the tense traditions of Lancashire sectarian politics, rather than indicating a deep rift in British society as a whole. Although the Catholic clergy refused to accept ecumenical commemoration for reasons of principle, outside Lancashire they tended to avoid polemics on the subject. Anglican clergy likewise made little of it as an issue.

By contrast the Methodist churches showed a distinct tendency towards ecumenical co-operation on this point. There was no sacramental reason why they could not co-operate with the Anglicans in this respect (at least from the Methodist side). Nor was there such a stark sociological and ethnic divide between the members of these churches. There were also some obvious reasons why co-operation would be beneficial or even essential. Methodism was less of an urban phenomenon than the Roman Catholic church and had a much stronger rural base, ranging from pit villages in Durham to the farming communities of East Anglia. In such areas small congregations for commemoration would be further diminished by rigid separatism.[71]

In Cornwall in 1923, the first Armistice Sunday in the china clay district was an ecumenical affair aided by the 'strong spirit of unity which exists between the various churches...about fifteen hundred clay workers, their wives and children, came together to worship and remember, the arrangements being carried out by the Vicar of Trebyn'. The vicar shared a platform with the local Methodist minister and the district chairman.[72]

It would be a mistake to see such services as merely a symptom of a developing ecumenicism. In many areas it is quite probable that it was the Remembrance Sunday services which initiated local ecumenical contacts. War commemoration may have played a hitherto unacknowledged role in the significant development of 'local' ecumenism which has been an important feature of mid- and late-twentieth century churchgoing. For example, Lutterworth in 1923 held two services, one at the war memorial and one in the parish church. Although both were presided over by the Rector, Nonconformists were heavily involved; the Congregational minister read the lessons and the Wesleyan minister gave a sermon. Apparently this was the first time that a Methodist minister had ever preached from the pulpit of John Wycliffe, a privilege specially granted for the occasion by the Bishop of Peterborough.[73] At Whiston on the Rotherham Circuit a Methodist minister was invited to preach by the Rector, 'in an effort to promote unity of spirit between his people and those attending the Wesleyan church.'[74]

Not all Anglicans approved. In 1928 the Bishop of Gloucester went so far as to suggest that in combined services on Remembrance Day in parish churches, a Nonconformist Minister ought to be asked to preach as a matter of course.[75] This request produced a strong editorial in the Anglo-Catholic *Church Times* which condemned, 'irregular and unauthorised experiments in reunion'. The editorial went on to condemn Dr Headlam for not appearing to realise that 'if nonconformist ministers and ordained priests of the Church of England have the same divine authority then the repeated claims of the church have no justification'. In the next paragraph the *Church Times* went so far as to call for Armistice Day to be ended because it was 'exploited by hotel propreitors and the ingenious conductors of popular newspapers for their own ends' and 'Armistice Day celebrations are far more calculated to encourage militarism than spread the cult of peace'.[76] It seems clear that the context for this sweeping attack on Armistice commemoration was provided by Anglo-Catholic fears of the excuse provided by the national commemoration for local ecumenical initiatives between the free churches and 'Evangelical' churchmen.

Ronald Blythe in his description of life in 'Akenfield' states that the villagers, despite some deep seated social separations between church and chapel, their congregations had nevertheless 'managed to practise ecumenicism for years, the occasional union being forced upon them by the fact that the war memorial is in the church'.[77] This might imply that the ecumenical power balance was entirely in favour of the Anglicans and that ecumenicism was simply a cover for incorporation. Many small communities probably did have only a single war memorial in the grounds of the parish church or inside it. In such cases this analysis may be correct. In larger communities Methodist churches and chapels were more likely to have their own memorials and it would also be likely that the main community memorial would be a civic one on neutral ground. In such cases the Anglican parish church would not be the automatic choice for an ecumenical service.

In 1928, the *Methodist Recorder* lists a number of ecumenical services. Some, such as the one at Rayleigh, were held in the parish church. Others, such as Rye Hill, were held entirely at the war memorial. In Rochdale a large combined service was held in a hall. Significantly, a number of united services were held on Methodist premises. The single united service at Castleford was held at the Wesleyan church and in Sutton (Surrey) there was a wreath laying ceremony at the war memorial, which was followed by an Armistice service at the Wesleyan church, which included listening to the Cenotaph Broadcast. In Ilford, the pattern was reversed; the morning service was held at the Wesleyan church, followed by an afternoon wreath laying at the war memorial.[78]

In the same way that the Roman Catholics could attain prominence in Remembrance commemoration in areas of particular local strength, Methodist commemoration occasionally took on the nature of 'establishment' commemoration, incorporating civic dignitaries and veterans groups. In Market Rasen, members of the council, magistrates, police, British Legion and 'representatives of other public bodies' attended the Remembrance Sunday service in 1923 which included the unveiling of the Methodist war memorial. The same year in another East Midland market town, Melton Mowbray, Territorials, Yeomanry, ex-servicemen and a detachment of Boy Scouts, headed by the town band, marched from the corn exchange to the Methodist church.[79]

Methodist revivalism was declining, but was not yet a spent force. Where Armistice Day coincided with a revival, it would be incorporated. During the 1923 crusade to the Kentish towns, the revival held a service near the Chatham memorial: 'The evangelists, of course, made the most of an unequalled opportunity to drive home the message of the Cross'. They were possibly aided by the fact that, 'within two miles there were eight hundred widows who had lost their husbands through the sinking of the three cruisers during the early days of the war'.[80] In another revival meeting on

Armistice Day, 'twelve hundred were present and public decisions were made'.[81] The tradition of the open air revival could influence the form of the ordinary commemorative service, such as the one at Paisley in 1922, which was the sole religious observance on Remembrance Day in the town.[82]

The tradition of the revival meeting, with its stress on conversion, was one possible variant model for Armistice Day proceedings drawing on an already venerable evangelical tradition. The Roman Catholic Church had a much more formidable liturgical institution in the form of the Requiem Mass. Where the evangelical approach stressed individual conversion, the Catholic stressed communion, a communion broad enough to encompass the dead. Purgatory was a doctrine with which many might feel uncomfortable as an explanation as to the current location of the deceased, but it had the significant virtue of empowering the bereaved to do something positive for their loved ones.

Conclusions: A Retreat to the Margins

The religious traditions of Evangelicanism and Catholicism exemplified by Methodists and Catholics could be fitted to the practices of Armistice Day, because the commemoration and particularly the discourse that informed it owed so much to these traditions. The Anglican church in its role as *Via Media* had brought both these traditions into public life for many years and the influence of these doctrines spread far beyond those who could have understood them in any formal sense. Three hundred years of evangelical missions, from seventeenth-century puritanism, through Wesley and Hannah More and on to the Salvation Army had familiarised the British people with the idea of personal conversion. The influence of Catholicism was more limited, but arguably more intense; as a vital part of Irish identity it had informed a substantial part of the urban population and as a strand in nineteenth-century Anglicanism, it had been at the forefront of the activity of Christian Socialism in the cities.

There is an absence of powerful anti-clerical and actively irreligious movements in Britain analogous to those of Continental Europe.[83] This has meant that 'civil religion' has never been defined independently of religious perceptions, even if the 'religion' involved has been fuzzy, attenuated and undogmatic.[84] In France the standard form of inscription on war memorials is 'Mort pour La

France'[85] or 'Mort pour la Patrie'. In Britain there is a far wider variety of possibilities ranging from 'For King and Country', variations on 'To the immortal memory', 'To the Glory Of God', 'Lest we forget' and 'Their Name Liveth Forever More'. The iconography of British war memorials is stilted compared with that of France, but the variations of inscription are far wider. In France the cult of 'La Nation' was sufficiently developed to allow a simple reference to dying for the nation to suffice.[86] To die for France was self - explanatory. The reification of the 'Nation' was less advanced in Britain.[87] There might be a sense of a 'deep England'[88] or a problematic sense of identity amongst the Celtic nations, but memorialisation required more. 'They died for England' is a perfectly viable epitaph in theory, yet in practice the temptation to mention Honour, Duty, God, Sacrifice or Immortal Memory was rarely overcome.[89]

The absence of an *abstract* nationhood, goes a long way towards explaining the particular forms of discourse which informed Armistice Day. The centrality of the concept of sacrifice moved this discourse on to a quasi-religious level. Semi-secularised religious concepts stood, therefore, at the back of public discussion.[90] The language of consolation which grew up to comfort the bereaved owed much to Catholic (in the broadest sense) concepts of communion amongst the living, between the living and the dead and amongst the saints. The idea of the redemptive sacrifice of the dead was principally a secularised and perhaps perverted Christology. The language of exhortation used by the ex-servicemen to demand a reciprocity of sacrifice echoes centuries of Nonconformist calls for conversion and reform of behaviour to lead a more godly life. The pacifist exhortations of the 1930s owe a great deal to the same traditions.

To accuse the churches of having hijacked the commemoration of the war dead for their own ends is to miss the point. Church leaders and lesser clergy were well aware of the superficially secularised religiosity of the occasion. They attempted to take this practice of 'folk religion' and restore it to a sound doctrinal footing, ameliorating its potential heresies and uncovering the Christian suppositions it contained. The triumph of 'Remembrance Sunday' in the post- Second World War years gave them the chance to formalise the occasion. Yet the task was impossible; the vitality of Armistice Day rested on its resistance to formal dogma and it thrived on the multi-vocality of the occasion. It could not retain that appeal in a 'Sunday church' atmosphere. Religious impulses, of a broadly defined variety, were widespread, but the habit of churchgoing was not. Secularisation in Britain has been principally a matter of the decline of Church authority, rather than demystification and loss of belief. The church could not enforce a Sunday ritual in the way that public opinion, a diffuse conglomerate of individual wills, could enforce a week-day observance. The habit of commemorating the war by formal observance of the two minutes' silence was lost between 1939 and 1945. Much of the innocent belief in the validity of sacrifice in war was lost as well.[91]

Notes to Chapter 6

1. *Daily Express*, 27 Feb. 1923, p. 6. See also, Lambeth Palace Library (LPL), Davidson Papers, vol. 202, ff. 1–19 for correspondence on this issue.

2. Illustration of this will be provided by J.M. Winter, *Persistence of Tradition* (forthcoming).

3. The established church had contributed to this confusion by uncritically using the rhetoric of sacrifice during the war in its efforts to comfort and encourage. See the perceptive examination of the diary of Rev. Andrew Clark in Trevor Wilson, *Myriad Faces,* p. 170.

4. Horatio Bottomley, in contemplative mood whilst serving his sentence for fraud in Maidstone gaol, penned lines which illustrate the point:

A DOUBLE SACRIFICE
"For God so loved the world", he said,
"His only son he gave
That they who would believe in him
Their souls He died to save."

And whilst he laboured once again
The old familiar text,
I watched with interest the face
Of convict sitting next...

And, after service walking back,
I asked him why he smiled
When hearing how, to save the world, God gave his only child.

And now his answer I will tell –
It thrilled me through and through –
God gave his only son – just so:
But bless you I gave two.

H. Bottomley, *Songs of the Cell*, London, 1928, p. 23. Bottomley wrote no less than three poems on Armistice Day in this volume.

5. *Westminster Abbey, St Martins Day. November 11th 1919. The Anniversary of the Armistice*, London 1919, Pamphlet in LPL: H 5133. 1000. 16. 1.

6. *Service of Thanksgiving and Memorial for those Killed in Action or Died of Wounds during the Great War; November 7th 1920; Being the Sunday preceding the Second Anniversary of Armistice Day.* SPCK 1920. Pamphlet in LPL: G.283.W 21. 20.

7. The sentiments expressed are respectively: 'Have mercy upon us O Lord', 'If it had not been the Lord who was on our side, when men rose up against us', and 'The sceptre of wickedness shall not rest upon the land of the righteous.'

8. The reading from Daniel is the story of Shadrach, Meshach and Abednego who bore witness to the Lord in the face of persecution.

9. The passage in Revelations concludes,'neither shall there be mourning nor crying nor pain anymore, for the former things have passed away.'

10. *Service of Thanksgiving and Memorial for those who were Killed in Action or Died of Wounds and Sickness during the Great War, November 6th 1921; Being the Sunday preceding the Third Anniversary of Armistice Day,* SPCK 1921., Pamphlet in LPL: G 199. 55. 41. The price was 6'6d per 100.

11. SPCK, *Thanksgiving 1920,* p. 3.

12. LPL: Davidson Papers vol. 540/217–228; handwritten draft of sermon to be delivered at Westminster Abbey 11 Nov. 1920, (with Davidson's own emphasis marks and suggested alternative phrasings), p. 226, p. 228.

13. SPCK, *Thanksgiving 1921,* p. 2.

14. Once a religious presence was conceded Curzon made a point of inviting Jewish, Muslim and Sikh religious leaders, apparently to the disgust of Dean Inge. See, PRO: HO 45/15305/657655/40. Minute on religious representation at the Cenotaph, 22 Nov. 1933. Interestingly the religious leader who most frequently attended the Cenotaph ceremony was the Chief Rabbi.

15. LPL: Davidson Papers, vol. 14; diary 1920, (entry dictated 13 Feb. 1921), p. 76. Presumably Davidson had forgotten the original objection a paragraph later.

16. LPL: Davidson Papers, vol. 6/62; letter from John Hilthorpe to Davidson, 18 Nov. 1920.

17. Unfortunately the 'Fulham Papers' which incorporate the papers of the Bishops of London at Lambeth Palace are distinctly patchy and there is very little for Winnington-Ingram in the post war period.

18. *The Guardian,* 16 Nov. 1923, p. 1045.

19. LPL: Davidson Papers, Vol. 14 ; diary 1923, (handwritten entry), p. 243.

20. LPL: Davidson Papers, Vol. 199/176; Cantab to Winton, 1 Oct. 1921. Lord Horne was the chairman of the ex-service ordination fund for whom collections were taken at this time on the Sunday preceding 11 November. The British Red Cross took the collection on the Sunday after the 11 November. The Bishop of Winchester was requesting that Sunday 6 November be dedicated to prayer for the success of the Washington Conference on Naval Armaments, and Davidson was pointing out that the church was already heavily committed that week.

21. *Uckfield Ex-Servicemens memorial service,* LPL: G.199. 55. 35.

22. *Brighton Parish Church (St Peters): A Service for use on the Anniversary of Armistice Day,* LPL: G. 199. M.3.

23. 'Remembrance Sunday in a Village', *British Legion Journal,* December 1927, p. 161.

24 At least this was a general rule, although an account of the Remembrance ceremony in Grimsby, by no means a village, describes the mayor laying a wreath at the memorial transept at the parish church, *Grimsby Telegraph,* 17 Nov. 1928, p. 8.

25. D. Haworth, *Bright Morning: Images of a Lancashire Childhood,* London 1990, p. 145.

26. A.G. Street, *In His Own Country,* London, 1950, p. 254.

27. Ibid., pp. 254–255

28. A. Calder and D. Sheridan (eds.), *Speak for Yourself: A Mass Observation Anthology 1937–1949,* Oxford, 1984, p. 28.

29. *St Agatha's Review,* November 1922, pp. 539–541.

30. E. Short, *I Knew My Place*, London, 1983, pp. 120–121.

31. *Guardian*, 10 Nov. 1939, p. 679.

32. This data was chosen as a balance between convenience and representativeness. There is no such thing as a typical diocese of the Church of England.

33. It is almost impossible to pick an 'average' church Sunday because saints' days, baptisms and events of parish significance distort the picture. For example in many areas the third Sunday of November was 'Civic Sunday'. The first Sunday of December was chosen because the weather would not be too disimilar to Remembrance Sunday and the relative consistency of an Advent congregation would iron out wide variations.

34. My experience as a fieldworker on the 'Rural Church Project' has made me wary of this measure.

35. DRO 51 A/30–31.

36. DRO 53 A/7–8

37. DRO 93/37–38

38. DRO 93/37–38

39. DRO 53 A/8

40. DRO 93/38

41. DRO 53 A/8

42. Not included in the analysis above as it is outside the years available for comparison with the other two churches.

43. DRO 93/36

44. DRO 53 A/7. The service is frequently marked in the Parish Returns as 'Armistice service'.

45. P. Donelly (ed.), *Mrs Milburn's Diary*, London, 1979, p. 113.

46. LPL: W. Temple Papers, vol 55/296; Temple to Moderator of the C of S (J. Baillie), 11 Oct. 1942. His successor Archbishop Fisher would demonstrate a different attitude (See Chapter 7).

47. I have avoided discussion of remembrance in the Church of Scotland. There is work in progress by Fiona Douglas at the University of Edinburgh on the subject. In any case, space would preclude an adequate treatment of the subject which would require a great deal of contextual material.

48. Church membership is a complex question. The only relatively reliable figure for active Anglicanism in Britain, is the number of Easter Communicants. This figure was in the region of two and one-half million in 1920 and 1930, falling to two and one-quarter million by 1940. This contrasts with two and one-half million Roman Catholics in 1920, rising to two and three-quarter million by 1930 and three million by 1940. But the Roman Catholic figure was for the total Roman Catholic population. Active involvement with the church was probably around 50% of these figures during this period. Total nonconformists membership was around two million in 1920 and had fallen to one and three-quarter million by 1940. The total number of Methodists increased slightly from eight hundred thousand in 1920 to eight hundred and forty thousand by 1930 and dropped back to the 1920 figure by 1940. The important points are that Anglican and Methodist churchgoers were shrinking as a proportion of the population and the number of Roman Catholics was growing and that the three churches retained their positions as first, second and third in numbers of active churchgoers throughout the period. See R. Currie, A. Gilbert and L. Horsley, *Churches and Churchgoers*, Oxford, 1977, pp. 31, 164.

49. This is a harsh judgement because considerable stress has been made on ecumenical efforts from Lambeth 1920 onwards through the Malines conversations. It should be remembered that the Roman Catholic Church in Britain was intensely hostile to the efforts of Cardinal Mercier of Malines and ultimately played an important part in getting the Pope to condemn the effort in the encyclical *Mortalium Animos*. See R. Lloyd, *The Church of England 1900–1965*, London, 1966, pp.

412–413. Certainly an examination of the R.C. press shows a continuing hostility to all 'protestant' churches.

50. Scotland was complicated by its own schism between the Presbyterian established church (The Church of Scotland) and the Presbyterian Free Kirk. In Wales, the Anglican church was disestablished after the war.

51. *Catholic Herald*, 12 Nov. 1921, p. 8. This warning was repeated in Salford in 1933, *Catholic Herald*, 11 Nov. 1933, p. 3.

52. British Legion Rule 1(a) stated that the organisation would be non-sectarian, this was placed before the clause disowning political affiliation. See Wootton, *Official History*, Appendix I , p. 300.

53. I would like to thank David Lloyd for this information.

54. *Catholic Herald*, 13 Nov. 1920, p. 5.

55. *Catholic Herald*, 19 Nov. 1921, p. 8. It is interesting to note how the rationale of this attack is almost identical with the justification for what was intended as an *Imperial* war memorial.

56. *Church Times*, 12 Nov. 1920, p. 438. It was also recorded that Dean Inge was deeply angered by the decision to invite Sikh, Muslim and Jewish religious leaders to the dedication of the Tomb. See note above.

57. *Catholic Herald*, 17 Nov. 1923, p. 4.

58. *Catholic Herald*, 15 Nov. 1930, p. 11.

59. *Catholic Herald*, 18 Nov. 1933, p. 1. *Catholic Times*, 12 Nov. 1926, p. 18; 19 Nov. 1926, p. 16.

60. For sectarianism in Liverpool politics see P.J. Waller, *Democracy and Sectarianism; A Political and Social History of Liverpool 1868–1939*, Liverpool, 1981.

61. For the Liverpool memorial, see Boorman, *Going Down of the Sun*, pp. 153–154.

62. For example see, *Catholic Herald*, 17 Nov. 1928, p. 6.

63. *Manchester Guardian*, 10 Nov. 1930, p. 12.

64. Boorman, *Going Down of the Sun*, p. 153.

65. *Manchester Guardian*, 13 Nov. 1930, p. 9; 14 Nov. 1930, p. 4.

66. *Liverpool Review*, December 1930, p. 508.

67. At this time Roman Catholics could attend for personal reasons the services of another denomination, but were banned from participating.

68. *Catholic Herald*, 15 Nov. 1930, p. 1.

69. Waller, *Sectarianism*, p. 325–26.

70. *Catholic Herald*, 18 Nov. 1933, p. 10.

71. Not that urban areas were immune to the appeal, in Newcastle in 1919, a special memorial service was held before the two minutes' silence with two Anglican and six Nonconformist churches co-operating. *Newcastle Daily Journal*, 11 Nov. 1919, p. 6.

72. *Methodist Recorder*, 15 Nov. 1923, p. 25.

73. The issue of Nonconformists preaching at Anglican pulpits had been debated in the Convocation of Canterbury in 1920, an attempt made to prevent the practice was defeated. See the *Chronicle of the Convocation of Canterbury* (Geo V: 3), pp. 162–170, for the debate of 12 Feb. 1920. It seems likely that such ecumenical exchanges originated with the war.

74. *Methodist Recorder*, 15 Nov. 1923, p. 25. See also references to Porton in Wiltshire.

75. *Manchester Guardian*, 10 Nov, 1928, p. 13.

76. *Church Times*, 9 Nov. 1928, p. 531.

77. R. Blythe, *Akenfield*, London, 1969, p. 59.

78. *Methodist Recorder*, 15 Nov. 1928, p. 25.

79. *Methodist Recorder*, 15 Nov. 1923, p. 25. The main memorial in Market Rasen was not built on Anglican premises due to the strength of Nonconformity in this market town (information supplied by the Vicar of Market Rasen in 1989 when I interviewed him for the Rural Church Project).

80. *Methodist Recorder,* 15 Nov. 1923, p. 4. The sinkings referred to are most likely those of the *Cressy, Aboukir* and *Hogue* in September 1914.

81. *Methodist Recorder,* 15 Nov. 1923, p. 6.

82. *Methodist Recorder,* 16 Nov. 1922, p. 21.

83. Militant atheism in the United Kingdom has been frequently dealt with by historians as a variety of religious sect, rather than as a European style anti-clerical movement.

84. Civil Religion in Britain and America represents a quite different phenomenon from civic religion in republican France or the communist Soviet Union where it was as an assault on the prerogatives of the Church. In Britain and in the United States civil religion has incorporated religious ceremony and belief, this is particularly ironic given the former's low level of formal religious practice and the latter's constitutional seperation of Church and State. For Civil Religion in the United States see: R.N. Bellah 'Civil Religion in America', *Daedulus,* 96, 1967, pp. 1–21; W.L. Warner, *The Living and the Dead* New Haven, 1965; and in Britain see E. Shils and M. Young, 'The Meaning of the Coronation', *Sociological Review,* 1. 1953, pp. 63–81; R. Bocock, *Ritual in Industrial Society,* London, 1974.

85. I was struck by the fact that this inscription was even used in Bayonne, the capital of the 'Pays Basque'.

86. See P. Nora, *Les lieux de la memoire,* Paris, 1984.

87. For examples of symbolic representation of the republic see M. Agulhon, *Marianne into Battle: Republican Imagery and Symbolism in France,* Cambridge, 1981.

88. A term I have borrowed from P. Wright, *On Living in an Old Country,* London, 1985, pp. 81–87.

89. See C. Moriarty, 'Christian Iconography and First World War Memorials' *Imperial War Museum Review,* 6, pp. 63–75

90. In discussing First World War poetry Martin Stephen makes a revealing comment, 'It is the very universality of of religious interest that makes it impossible to rope off in a section of its own. Its influence permeates all types and styles of Great War poetry, and in terms of definition 'religious poetry' ceases to have any meaning in the Great War precisely because of the variety of uses to which religion could be put by poets.' M. Stephen, *Never Such Innocence: A New Anthology of Great War Verse,* London, 1988, p. 11.

91. Or was it? In the sermon preached at Washington's Episcopalian cathedral after the dedication of the Vietnam Memorial, The Rev. T.H. Evans described his experience of Remembrance Sunday in Saigon's Anglican church at the beginning of the Vietnam war. He mentions his ambivalence about the service. Yet in concluding his sermon he stated: 'We can be renewed by the sacrifices of those who have given their lives in wars and we can be renewed by Christ's sacrifice which once looked like defeat.' Except for the crucial word 'defeat', this sentiment could have come from any remembrance service from Memorial Day in 1868 to Remembrance Sunday in 1945. The paradigm of redemptive sacrifice has proved extra-ordinarily tenacious even as it looks to be increasingly irrelevant. See, W.Capps (ed.) *A Vietnam Reader,* London and New York, 1991, pp. 249–252.

7

The Restoration of Tradition?

Twenty-six years ago the Armistice was signed, and oh my goodness me what a lot has happened since then! The one thing we did not forsee was this chaotic world, this welter of destruction of property, this wholesale division of families. It is as well we cannot see ahead – our hearts would break.

Mrs Clara Milburn's Diary, 11 November 1944. [1]

Death, Grief, Mourning and the Second World War

It is sometimes argued that the Second World War was a profoundly different experience of mass death for the British people from the First World War.[2] This may be true, but for different reasons than those usually ascribed. One distinction made is the idea that the scale of civilian casualties prevented the alienation between home front and front-line which occurred between 1914 and 1918. Yet British civilian casualties should be kept in perspective. 60,000 civilian dead represented only just over one fifth of the number of military dead (excluding the Merchant Navy from both figures). As a proportion of the military dead, British civilians got off comparatively lightly. China, Japan, Germany, Poland, Yugoslavia, Greece and Holland suffered *more* civilian casualties than military. The same is probably true of the Soviet Union, France and Italy (depending on the definition of 'partisans'). It is only by comparison with the other English-speaking countries that British civilian losses appear significant.

Numbers alone do not tell the whole story. British civilian casualties were remarkably concentrated, occurring mainly during the period September 1940–May 1941. During this time civilian losses far outstripped military losses, and it was during this period that the image of the 'people's war' was created. Yet taken as a whole, the war was marked more by the inequality of sacrifice than

Notes for Chapter 7 can be found on page 223.

by universality. Until the spring of 1943 the human cost of the war had been borne principally by civilians, the Navy and the Merchant Navy[3]. After that point, during the second (and substantially bloodier) phase, the cost was borne principally by the Army and the RAF. Over half of the total military fatalities (one third of the total including merchant navy) occurred during the last 18 months of the war.[4]

The 'people's war' was therefore marked by inequalities in terms of human loss. Civilian casualties were largely urban and concentrated in the areas most accessible to air attack. Greater London and the population centres of the South and Midlands suffered most (although all major centres were bombed).[5]

The high loss rate of the RAF is also worthy of note. Aircrew in Bomber Command, which bore the brunt of casualties, were overwhelmingly middle-class. Almost 40,000 British aircrew were killed in Bomber Command alone[6] (excluding Dominion and allied personnel). These young men were the close equivalent of the 'subalterns' who died in huge numbers in the First World War, but a navigator in 1943 would have envied the life expectancy of a second lieutenant in 1916.

Once the British army became seriously engaged in the war on land, casualties mounted rapidly. The burden of death fell unevenly within the army, perhaps less than 20% of personnel in the Second World War were engaged in a genuinely combatant role, but the experience of those who were was not so greatly different from that of a previous generation. The mythology of a war of movement and liberation has hidden the savage fighting and brutal attrition that occurred on every front in 1944–45.[7] We are familiar with the 'futile' horrors of Thiepval and Passchendaele, but who now remembers Kohima or Walcheren or the bloody battles for the Gothic Line in the autumn of 1944?

Once again it seems that Junior Officers suffered the highest proportional casualties, the British army had nearly three times the number of subalterns per battalion compared to the German army and their leadership role was correspondingly greater.[8] If this is taken together with the middle-class nature of RAF aircrew,[9] it becomes clear that the top echelons of British society suffered *proportionately* more compared with the rest of society in the Second World War, than they had in the First. For example 20% of Etonians who served in the First World War were killed, as compared with 15% in the Second. But the former figure represents 80% greater than average fatal casualties, whilst the latter is closer to 150%.[10] The Angel of Death was as elitist between 1943 and 1945 as he had been in 1915 and 1916. Against all expectations Robert Graves survived the First World War; his eldest son did not survive the sequel.

It may therefore seem surprising that the Second World War did not create a lost-generation myth amongst the social elite. A plausible reason can be advanced; politically such a myth would have jarred with the 'people's war' mythology created in the crucial years 1940–41.[11] The heaviest losses were incurred at a point when the war was clearly militarily won and the nature of the post-war world already foreshadowed in the Beveridge plan. Certain middle-class images of the war have penetrated film and popular fiction since the conflict; for example, the public school ethos demonstrated at Colditz, by the 'Dam Busters' and by Douglas Bader. The decline and fall of the gentry through the war also found its chronicler in Evelyn Waugh. But it was the 'people's war', the war of the Blitz and the Home Guard, that would dominate popular memory.

Likewise the 'myth of war experience' never became prominent in the post war period. The non-combatant roles played by most servicemen and the long periods of home service experienced by the majority, with regular leave and continued contact with family life, prevented a sense of separation between front and home. The conscription of women and the large numbers of WRENS, WAAFS and Army Auxilaries, who performed much the same tasks as the majority of their male equivalents, similarly prevented the accentuation of gender differences. Only the campaigns in the Far East created a real sense of separation, where the Fourteenth Army took a perverse pride in its reputation as the 'forgotten army' and whose veterans still consider the Burma Star to be the most significant of all campaign medals.

The less extreme nature of the separation of front and home and the 'myth' of the people's war with its stress on civilian sacrifice, characterise the principal contextual differences between the First and the Second World War. It is therefore an apparent paradox that Remembrance Sunday after 1945 was to be far more of an ex-service commemoration than the pre-war equivalent. Veterans were (and are) more prominent both at a local level and in the national commemoration at the Cenotaph than they had been between the wars. Of course there are simple practical explanations. As the discussion of Remembrance Sunday in the pre-war years has indicated, ex-servicemen played a much more prominent role in Sunday commemorations of the war than in ordinary Armistice Day commemorations, for entirely practical reasons. In this sense the developments after 1945 represent an extension of a pre-war trend.

At a deeper level the answer is contained in the paradox. The First World War generated an intense 'myth of war experience' based on the gap between the sacrifices of the soldier and the civilian. Yet as has been stressed in previous chapters, the principal rhetoric surrounding Armistice Day was not a product of this myth and the practises composing it were not generally supportive of it. Armistice Day was not a symptom of the 'myth of war experience', but an antidote to it. It stressed civilian, particularly women's, sacrifice through bereavement. It aimed to universalise the memory of the war, to make it the property of the nation as a whole. The ex-servicemen were marginalised in the process.

No such activity was required after the Second World War. The myth of the 'people's war' was well established by the middle of 1941. Civilians had no need to claim equality of sacrifice; it was already assumed. The civilian versus ex-service issue over the burden of sacrifice was heavily overlaid with gender considerations during the First World War. During the Second World War the conscription of women blurred and mediated the dichotomy. As a result, the need to stress the sacrifice of women, as bereaved mothers, sisters and wives, and of civilian men, as bereaved fathers and brothers, was far less in 1945 than it had been in 1919. The 'economy of sacrifice' was apparently sufficiently balanced to allow Remembrance Sunday during the post-war years to concentrate its symbolism on the veterans of the armed forces.

Which Day to Remember?

The decision to institute the Sunday before 11 November as the national day of remembrance appeared to have been taken with remarkable ease. On 12 November 1945, Captain Bullock raised the question of future commemoration in parliament with Herbert Morrison. He asked if 11 November could be made the day of remembrance for both wars and then rather confusingly further suggested that it would be 'much to the advantage of the public if a Sunday were always chosen for the Day of Remembrance'. Morrison stated that the matter was under consideration.[12] In February, Major Digby tabled a written question to the Prime Minister asking him to take into account 'the views held by many ex-servicemen of both the last and the 1914–18 wars who would strongly deprecate any change from 11th November for this purpose.' Attlee pointed out that he was aware of this feeling.[13] After being intermittently harassed by Captain Bullock on a number of occasions to give a firm statement of Government intentions, the Prime Minister finally gave a statement to the House of Commons in June 1946. He told parliament that the Home Secretary had consulted widely amongst 'representative bodies' and that they were 'all agreed that the Sunday before the 11th of November, unless the 11th or 12th of November was itself a Sunday should be known as Remembrance Sunday, should be observed as a National Day of Remembrance for the wars of 1914–18 and 1939–1945 and should be associated with the National observance at the Cenotaph and the Two minutes Silence'.[14]

In fact, the Labour government had been in consultation via the Home Office with interested bodies for some time prior to the first statement in the House of Commons. The process had begun with the preceding governments. On 14 May, a week after the end of the war in Europe, a deputation had attended the Home Office with 'proposals for a National Day of Remembrance endorsed by the churches and the British Legion'. The deputation had consisted of the Bishops of Winchester and Leicester, the Roman Catholic Archbishop of Westminster, the assistant secretary to the Free Church Council and three representatives of the British Legion, General Sir Frederick Maurice, Sir Brunel Cohen and Mr Griffin. The Bishop of Winchester had presented a position paper which stated that the purpose of the deputation was to raise in good time the question of what was to be the future of Armistice Day and Remembrance Sunday. All the concerned groups 'were agreed that it would be most undesirable that there should be two days of remembrance' because it would mean 'as time went on an undesirable division of attention and energy.'

The Bishop went on to outline the advantages of retaining the existing approach: 'The observance of November 11 and the Sunday following is already well established' and 'The British Legion which has so immense a vested interest in the observance of Armisticetide could feel that it would have the force of habit behind it.' Nonetheless, on balance the Bishop recommended a change because, 'November with its short days is not really a good time for public celebrations or public collections' and 'unless some outstanding event in this present war or at the close of it happened or was arranged to coincide with a date in November, there would seem something unreal and almost derogatory to the scale of the present war and the magnitude of the sacrifices made in it if we tried to enfold its commemoration inside the commemoration of the earlier and lesser struggle'. As it seemed improbable that the allied commanders would organise the final offensive against Japan in order to arrange a suitable date in November, 'the Churches and the Headquarters of the British Legion in England as presently advised, would certainly view with favour any policy and any occurrence which would facilitate the observance in England of a Saturday–Sunday in the summer as a National Day of Remembrance, Thanksgiving and Dedication'.[15]

The conclusions of these consultations were reported to Churchill's caretaker Cabinet in July and a Cabinet paper was produced which recommended that 'it would be inappropriate to appoint 11th November as the day of remembrance for the two wars'.[16] This was the situation that James Chuter-Ede inherited on taking up the Home Office.[17] In a Cabinet meeting on the 13 September, shortly after the Japanese surrender, Chuter-Ede gave a briefing on the question of commemoration of the two wars. He gave a brief account of the background, stating that, 'during the war the holding of services on 11th November had been abandoned.' He then went on to brief his colleagues on the present state of Home Office thinking; 'there should not be separate days of remembrance for the two wars.' In the immediate future it made most sense to hold the commemoration on Sunday 11 November in 1945, 'on the usual lines...as a day of remembrance for those who had fallen in both wars' but, 'in the near future some other date would be fixed on which all those who had fallen in both wars would be honoured and remembered'. In the meantime the Home Office would, 'examine with the churches and the British Legion and other interested parties the question of settling a national day of remembrance for future years'. In an interesting reflection on the Atlanticist honeymoon of the first months of the Labour Government Chuter-Ede suggested that, 'if it were possible' a date should be fixed which, 'the United States would also be willing to observe as Remembrance Day.' The suggestion was made of trying to relate the date to the signing of the Atlantic Charter. Consultation with the Dominions was also requested.[18]

A further meeting at the Home Office on 2 October confirmed the decision to celebrate Armistice Day at the Cenotaph on 11 November, because by the start of October the necessary assents had been gathered.[19] The King had been approached on 14 September and had approved the plan on 22 September. The British Legion discussed the question at National Executive level on 22 September and concluded that 'in the event of 11 November not being decided upon' for the next year they would like 'a Sunday in June as first preference.'[20] They replied to a request for co-operation in 1945 on 28 September.[21] The Bishop of London was contacted to conduct the Cenotaph ceremony on 24 September 1945 and replied in the affirmative on 26 September.[22] Armed with this assurance, Chuter-Ede informed the King on 4 October that the ceremony would follow 'strictly' the pre-war pattern and in view of the 'many enquiries' that the Home Office was receiving a short statement would be issued to the press, 'as soon as possible' to be followed by a longer communiqué,' towards the end of October.[23] These statements would cover both the arrangements for 1945 and the government's intentions for a future day of commemoration.[24]The Archbishop of Canterbury was contacted to to contribute his own announcement.[25]

The Home Office began to consider viable alternatives. A memorandum drawn up indicates the remarkable breadth of the possibilities considered. Dates tabled included, 8 May (VE Day), 6 June (D Day), 15 June (signing of the Magna Carta), 4 July (US independence! Perhaps a unique example of a government seriously contemplating celebrating a national defeat), 14 August (signing of the Atlantic Charter), 15 August (VJ Day), 2 September (capitulation of Japan), 3 September (outbreak of War 1939), 15 September (Battle of Britain Day), 2 November (All Souls Day) and 11 November. Serious objections were raised to every single date. The Japanese war was considered insufficiently emotive to the British, the European war dates were considered offensive to Australian national sentiment in what was intended as a Commonwealth wide commemoration, the trans-Atlantic and historical dates were too abstract and All Souls was too religious.[26] 11 November was drifting back on to the agenda by default.

The Cenotaph ceremony was held on 11 November 1945, which was both Armistice Day and Remembrance Sunday. According to James Cameron: 'Along Whitehall, past the Horse Guards as far as it was possible to see in Trafalgar Square the people stood jammed from kerb to kerb.'[27] On that day Chuter-Ede gave a speech at

Epsom stating that he expected that 1945 would, 'be the last Remembrance Aniversary to be held in November.'[28] The following day a consultative meeting was held at the Home Office and it was clear that a lobby in favour of the retention of a November date was emerging. It was a widely consultative meeting with representatives from a range of Government departments, the British Legion and the churches. Both the Scottish churches and the English free churches strongly backed 11 November as a 'day in possession' which men and women now serving in the forces had been brought up to observe. The Foreign Office pointed out that the United States had observed 11 November. The India Office stated that they favoured 11 November for 'climatic reasons'. The Dominion Office stated that Canada liked the idea of D Day, but the other Dominions which had been only marginally involved in that battle had objected strongly. The Bishop of Winchester also felt that the church could not approve the celebration of a battle as a day of remembrance.[29]

The meeting came to no definite conclusion at the Home Office, but it is clear that the churches and the British Legion continued the discussion. On 24 November the Bishop of Winchester sent a letter to the Home Secretary countersigned by the Chairman of the British Legion. In it he remarked that, 'unfortunately the last war has not yielded any one day or season, the commemoration of which would be *generally* felt to have the significance or ground of appeal to that which Remembrance Sunday in November has actually acquired'. Remembrance Sunday has already been movingly and generally observed in 1945, since the conclusion of the last war and evidently has no less strong appeal to those who fought and were bereaved in 1939–45 than to those who had fought and were bereaved in 1914–18.' This is a significant moment in the development of commemoration, because with extreme subtlety the Bishop had changed the date under discussion from 11 November to Remembrance Sunday. The reasons are obvious; as the previous chapter has indicated, both the church and the British Legion had a clear vested interest in maintaining the commemoration on a Sunday. The letter goes on to outline the proposals which would become the basis for future commemoration. The Cenotaph ceremony would be held in future on the second Sunday of November (usually the Sunday before Armistice Day) and the Day would still be known as 'Remembrance Sunday'.[30]

In the meantime the Home Office had begun to receive letters from the general public expressing their opinions on the subject and, as noted above, a question had been asked in the House of Commons. The letters kept by the Home Office indicate a marginal sentiment in favour of a change; 21 suggest a different date as opposed to 15 supporting the 11 November. However, the letters suggesting a change are wildly inconsistent with each other, only two dates, 6 June and 15 September, received more than three letters in support.[31] Furthermore some of the letters favouring 11 November were from representatives of larger bodies; for example, the Federation of Towns Women's Guilds pleaded that, '11 November is Our (the women's) day of Remembrance'. The same point was made by Nancy Poole in support of 11 November, 'who is most entitled to have a say in such a matter, surely the loved ones of the fallen'.[32] These letters were in support of 11 November rather than Remembrance Sunday and tend to support the general thesis that 11 November was the day for the bereaved. In the inter-war period the wishes of the bereaved had been taken as paramount, but in the aftermath of the Second World War the Labour Cabinet (feeling its way on the issue, due to the dispersal of both Home Office records and personnel),[33] had relied heavily on the advice of the churches and the British Legion to a much greater extent than any pre-war Government.

The Cabinet was still a little resistant to the Bishop of Winchester's proposals and some members of the Cabinet communicated their doubts informally to Chuter-Ede before he met a further deputation on the 9 January. By this time both the Bishop and the Chairman of the Legion had hardened their position. The Bishop stated that he felt the link of the observance with 11 November was a matter of 'the soul, rather than historical tradition'. Brigadier General Fitzpatrick was less gnostic, claiming that consultation with his colleagues in the Legion and with, 'younger ex-servicemen', showed general support for an observance on Remembrance Sunday and that the views of the Cabinet were 'not a reflection of public opinion'.[34] The Cabinet were unlikely to face up to a fight with the churches and the Legion on this issue and on 28 January 1946, Chuter-Ede convinced his colleagues agreed to the Bishop of Winchester's view, provisional on Dominion approval.[35]

On 2 March, Clement Attlee wrote to Archbishop Fisher in reply to a letter of 18 February. Fisher had clearly not been kept well informed of developments and Attlee reassured him that: 'We entirely share your views that the two wars should be commemorated on Remembrance Sunday which should be the Sunday *before* the 11th November except when the 11th or 12th of November is a Sunday. For your private information we still have to get the consent of the Dominion Governments.'[36] This consent was forthcoming from New Zealand in February, Australia in March and Canada in May.[37] In late May 1946, 13 motions from branches at the Annual Conference of the British Legion, urged the executive to ask the government to continue to observe Remembrance Day on 11 November.[38] By this time the question was already settled. Attlee was able to make his official announcement in the House on 19 June.[39]

On 26 June, the Archbishop of York contacted Fisher, suggesting that the Church of England should produce a National Form of Service and that the Bishop of Sheffield's liturgical committee, which had been meeting intermittently since early 1944 to discuss commemorative services, should produce such a pamphlet to be printed by SPCK. The Archbishop of York clearly had a very different opinion of decentralising the service from that of the late Archbishop Temple, confiding to his colleague, 'Most of the clergy are completely incapable of composing one for themselves.'[40] Nothing directly came of this suggestion, although a revised version of the 'British Legion' service programme did serve as a widespread guide in this and subsequent years.

The 1946 programme was finalised on 20 September at a Home Office Conference, modelled on the pre-war system. Fisher was asked to preside over the rededication of the Cenotaph which had been inscribed with the dates 1939–1945; the precedent that Davidson had done so in 1920 was cited. The British Legion decided to hold the Poppy Appeal annually on the Saturday preceding Remembrance Sunday and the Festival of Remembrance on the evening of that day, 'since poppy day has always been associated not with the 11 November as such but with the fact that the day was observed as Remembrance Day'.[41]

It is clear that what occurred in 1946 was less a matter of innovation and more a matter of continuity and rationalisation. 11 November had been displaced during the war years, in 1946 the Churches, the Legion and the Home Office simply failed to reinstitute it. The major commemorative elements, the Cenotaph ceremony and the two minutes' silence, were restored but shifted to Remembrance Sunday, a move made easier because they had been officially performed on a Sunday in 1945.

The Shadow of Tradition

Remembrance Sunday since 1946 has never had the emotive power that Armistice Day displayed between the wars. It has become increasingly remote as a ritual for the general population. The reason for this is partly that it has come to be seen as principally the property of the British Legion and the churches, property rights that grew out of the pre-war Remembrance Sunday and which were in effect formally acknowledged by the decision-making processes which revived the ritual in 1945–46. But there may be a deeper reason. Armistice Day was the response to a particular moment of mass bereavement and mass grief. It provided structure and meaning to an unparalleled outpouring of collective emotion. Yet the meanings that it provided, traditional patriotism and idealistic pacifism, had failed each in turn. The mood of 1945 was sceptical of the high ideals and high flown phrases that had marked the year which saw the beginning of the Silence. The disillusionment that had begun during the last years of the 1930s had come to fruition. There was a new silence in 1945, the silence after Auschwitz and the silence after Hiroshima, the silence in which nothing meaningful could be said:

To Mr Attlee   25.10.45.
Prime Minister
Houses of Parliament
Westminster
SW

Dear Sir,
I wish to protest against the proposed 2 mins silence Nov 11th.
I do think it is about time that this form of hypocrisy was put an end to.
My life has been completely 'silent' for the past 2 yrs when I received the dreadful news that my dearly beloved son was 'missing' from a raid over Essen.
Surely there is no need for this 'mechanical' 2 mins silence as many families like my own do not want *reminding* of their grief.
I think that the harm done to such as us is quite sufficient without the need to emphasise it. Many people will undoubtedly show reverence for *2 mins only* at 11 o'clock on that day, but by 1 o'clock this will all be forgotten & the real reverence will come only from such as myself.
I say again we do not need the 2 mins silence.
Dear sir, I leave this matter to your much respected judgement
I am
Yours faithfully
(Mrs) M. Harrison.[42]

Notes to Chapter 7

1. P. Donelly (ed.), *Mrs Milburn's Diary*, London, 1979, p. 250.

2. See for example, J.M. Winter, *The Great War and the British People*, London, 1985, pp. 39–40, 99.

3. All of the Royal Navy's major capital ship losses, HMS *Barham, Hood, Courageous, Ark Royal, Prince of Wales, Repulse*, etc., occurred before 1942. The Battle of the Atlantic was won by the summer of 1943 and subsequent Merchant Navy losses were minimal. The overwhelming majority of bombing casualties (80%) occurred before May 1941. ·

4. Up to April 1944, 120,958 members of the Armed forces had been killed. By September 1945, 264,433 military personnel had been killed. M. Gilbert *The Second World War*, London, 1989, pp. 514, 746.

5. The county of Kent suffered one-seventh of the total civilian casualties in the United Kingdom from bombing (2,974 deaths). Lancashire did suffer more heavily with 4,800 civilian deaths and Warwickshire suffered 3,881. But the casualties in Northern Britain were much lower as a proportion of the population and the Warwickshire deaths were concentrated in Birmingham and Coventry. Similarly, Yorkshire suffered only 2,328 dead compared with the Hampshire figure of 2,176, a huge disproportion by population. London suffered more than half of the bombing casualties. See A. Rootes, *Frontline County: Kent At War 1939–45*, London, 1992, pp. 201–202

6. This *exceeds* the *total* officer casualties of the First World War: J. Terraine, *The Smoke And the Fire*, London, 1980, p. 208.

7. The myth that ground combat in the Second World War was in some way 'better' than during the First World War is thoroughly exploded by the work of John Ellis. On the question of casualties the picture is distorted by the much higher proportion of rear echelon troops; amongst fighting troops the casualty rate was closely comparable with losses on the Western Front 1914–1918. What this means is that there were two substantially different experiences of war in the armed forces between 1939–1945, with the majority of those serving in relative safety and a minority who were at high risk. See J. Ellis, *The Sharp End*, London, revised 1990.

8. Remarkable as it seems, infantry battalion losses of officers were proportionately higher in the Second World War than in the First World War. Ellis, *The Sharp End*, pp. 162–164.

9. See M. Hastings, *Bomber Command*, London, 1979.

10. Fatal casualties as a proportion of total enlistment were roughly 12% in 1914–18 and 5% in 1939–45.

11. See in particular A. Calder, *The Myth of the Blitz*, London, 1991.

12. *Hansard,* HCD, 5th Series, vol. 415, 12 Nov. 1945, p. 1745.

13. *Hansard,* HCD, 5th Series, vol. 415, 6 Feb. 1946, *p. 418.*

14. *Hansard,* HCD, 5th Series, vol. 424, 19 June 1946, pp. 179–180.

15. PRO: HO 45/20696/892217/1. Minutes of Home Office Meeting 16 May 1945. Herbert Morrison, Coalition Home Secretary was in the chair.

16. Cabinet Paper, 12 July, CP 45 (77) in HO 45/20696/892217/4. Sir D. Somervell was Home Secretary. See, A.J.P. Taylor, *English History*, p. 786.

17. Morrison having become Lord President. For Chuter-Ede, a somewhat forgotten figure, see K. Morgan, *The Peoples Peace: British History 1945–1989*, Oxford, 1990, pp. 19, 88, 90, 100, 101.

18. PRO: HO 45/20278/891772/1. Extract of Cabinet Conclusions, 13 Sept. 1945.

19. PRO: HO 45/20277/891772/26. Minutes of Home Office conference, 2 Oct. 1945.

20. BL: National Executive Minutes, 22 Sept. 1945, p. 208.

21. PRO: HO 45/20277/891772/23. Letter from J.R. Griffin to H.A. Strutt, 28 Sept. 1945.

22. PRO: HO 45/20278/891772/15. Chuter-Ede to Bishop of London, 24 Sept. 1945 and reply 26 Sept 1945.

23. See for example, *Daily Express,* 10 Oct. 1945, p. 1

24. PRO: HO 45/20277/891772/26. Letter from Chuter-Ede to Sir A. Lascelles, 4 Oct. 1945.

25. PRO: HO 45/20278/891772/18. Chuter-Ede to Archbishop of Canterbury, 5 Oct. 1945.

26. PRO: HO 45/20696/892217/9. The memorandum is undated and may have been used as an agenda for the conference on 12 November.

27. *Daily Express,* 12 Nov. 1945, p. 2.

28. *Daily Express,* 12 Nov 1945,p. 1.

29. PRO: HO 45/20696/892217/9. Home Office Conference, 12 November.

30. PRO: HO 45/20696/892217/9. Letter from Bishop of Winchester and Brigadier General Fitzpatrick to Chuter Ede, 24 Nov. 1945. The coincidence of a Fitzpatrick being involved in the second key moment of commemoration is extraordinary.

31. PRO: HO 45/20696/892217/11.

32. PRO: HO 45/20696/892217/10. Letters from the Secretary of the Towns Women's Guild, 14 Nov. 1945 and Nancy Poole, 17 Nov. 1945 to Mr Chuter-Ede. See also letter from Mrs Emerson in HO 45/20696/892217/8.

33. PRO: HO 45/20696/892217/6. Letter A.Strutt (Home Office) to C.C. Cunningham (Scottish Office), 17 Sept. 1945.

34. PRO: HO 45/20696/892217/9. Minutes of Home Office Conference, 9 Jan. 1946.

35. PRO: HO 45/20696/892217/22. CM(46), Cabinet conclusions, 28 Jan. 1946.

36: LPL: Fisher Papers, vol. 17, ff. 340–341, Attlee to Fisher, 2 March 1946.

37. PRO: HO 45/20696/892217/21. Communications from Dominion Office.

38. BL: GSC, 'Provisional Agenda for the British Legion Annual Confrence, 1946', p. 24. Unfortunately I have been unable to find whether these motions were carried as phrased, or as seems likely to me, amended to urge the nearest Sunday be adopted, in line with executive thinking.

39. See note 10 above.

40. LPL: Fisher papers, vol 17, ff.344. York to Canterbury, 26 June 1946.

41. *British Legion Annual Report and Accounts, 1946–47,* London 1947, pp. 7–8.

42. PRO: HO 45/20278/891772/44. Handwritten.

Conclusion

And now,
Whenever the November sky
Quivers with the bugles hoarse, sweet cry,
The reason darkens; in its evening gleam
Crosses and flares, tormented wire, grey earth
Splattered with crimson flowers,
And I remember
Not the war I fought in
But the one called Great
Which ended in a sepia November
Four years before my birth

Vernon Scannell (Born 1922)

At the centre of Armistice Day was a silence. Yet paradoxically this silence could only be understood in relation to a language. The memory of the First World War was framed by a language that pre-dated the conflict, a language of sacrifice. The origins and development of this language must be sought in the late nineteenth century, but it seems unquestionable that this language was informed by Christian concepts of redemption through blood. The tensions which were mediated through Armistice Day were the tensions of the 'economy of sacrifice' during the war years, the tensions between the competing claims of those who had suffered directly in combat and those who had suffered vicariously through parting from relatives. Obviously these tensions were closely tied to perceptions of the gaps between the sexes and the generations. During the war, the sacrifice of the combatants was obvious and acknowledged and the hardships of those who, for various reasons, could not fight, were always implicitly belittled. In the aftermath of the war, the belligerent nations had to decide how the war would be remembered and whose sacrifices would be enshrined as central.

The British chose to put the sacrifices of families first. Nevertheless, the sacrifices of the veterans found a place in the commemoration, through the practical expression of solidarity in the Haig Fund appeal. The multivocality of British commemoration helped it to serve as a healing process, defusing the war-time resentments and re-emphasising the essential shared values of society. The contrast with Weimar Germany could not be more obvious. In Britain there was a shared perception of the war's ideal meaning. This was emphatically not a consensus, but it was a limitation on the terms of dissent; the critics of Armistice Day spoke in the same moral language as its supporters. Behind the dissent was a solidarity with the victims of war. In Germany the memory of the war was not underpinned by such a sense of solidarity, ultimately the tensions were resolved by an enforced consensus.

By interpreting slaughter as sacrifice, Armistice Day was inherently idealistic. Sacrifice implied that the war had been purposeful. The problem was that the signs of valid purpose became increasingly difficult to find. There was no 'land fit for heroes' in the 1920s and by the middle 1930s 'the war to end war' was becoming an implausible proposition. The validity of the sacrifice became less an established fact and more of a moral exhortation, a demand that the new generation live up to the high ideals for which it was claimed that a million men of the Empire had been sacrificed. It was up to their successors to provide the redemption. But finally it became clear that 'the world was not renewed'. The conscript of 1940 went to war knowing, to paraphrase Herbert Read's poem, that there was no certain use in all his sacrifice.

The Second World War created a much more complex mythology than the First, a richer popular memory which has pervaded British popular culture for good and ill ever since. It was impossible to encapsulate such complexity into a single date and a single moment in the way that the memory of the First World War had been caught in the Armistice Day ritual. Remembrance Day since 1945 has been a compound of the memories of two wars, but a partial and sectional memory of each. The day no longer carries the mystical conviction that it should be a transforming experience, one that makes sense of all the suffering and which re-dedicates the nation to high aspirations. It is increasingly the memory of a memory. It can survive as long as those who remember what Armistice Day once was survive or in other words, while those who fought a war remembering another war still live. But the language which surrounds the ritual is dead. Without the conviction of a transformative redemption we cannot understand sacrifice; the word becomes part of an empty rhetoric. We can respect the suffering but we can no longer hope to understand it.

Selected Bibliography

1. Archival and Unpublished.

A. Public Record Office (PRO)

Cabinet Papers:
CAB 23/11
CAB 23/22
CAB 23/46
CAB 24/GT 3345
CAB 24/CP45.
CAB 27/99
CAB 27/142

Home Office Papers:
HO 45/11557
HO 45/12329
HO 45/12468
HO 45/12840
HO 45/13091
HO 45/14357
HO 45/14866
HO 45/15305
HO 45/16743
HO 45/17161
HO 45/20184
HO 45/20277
HO 45/20278

B. Lambeth Palace Library (LPL)

Davidson Papers: Vols. 6, 14, 198, 199, 202, 540.
Lang Papers: Vol. 83.
W. Temple Papers: Vol. 55.
Fisher Papers: Vol. 17.

Liturgical Files:
G.283
G.199
H.5133

C. Royal British Legion Central Office, Pall Mall (BL)

Annual Accounts and Reports (Published).
General Secretary's Circulars (GSC). These include other material.
National Executive Minutes.
Miscellaneous material.

D. Peace Pledge Union Office (PPU)

Alternative Remembrance File.
Sponsors' Meeting Minutes.
Miscellaneous Material.

E. Imperial War Museum (IWM)

Programmes of war memorial dedications.

F. Tom Harrisson Mass Observation Archive, University of Sussex (MO)

Special Day Files:
ARMISTICE DAY: 1937, 1938, 1939, 1940, 1941, 1946.

G. BBC Written Archive Centre, Caversham (WAC)

Files:
R. 34/227/1
R. 34/227/2
R. 34/227/3
T. 16/191/1

H. Birmingham Public Library, Diocesan Record Office (BPL: DRO)

Parish Magazines:
DRO 99/70 (St Johns, Sparkhill)
DRO 63A/16 (St Andrews, Bordesley)
DRO 76/95–96 (All Souls, Witton)
DRO 43/104–122 (St Agathas, Sparkbrook)

Parish Returns:
DRO 51 A/30–31 (St Edburgha, Yardley)
DRO 53 A/7–9 (St Bartholomew, Edgbaston)
DRO 58/22–24 (St George, Edgbaston)
DRO 93/33–41 (St Alban, Bordesley)

I. St Mary's School, Tetbury

Log Book.

J. London School of Economics (BLPES)

Materials relating to Womens Co-operative Guild and League of Nations Union.

2.Periodicals 1919–46.

Belfast Telegraph, Birmingham Evening Mail, British Legion Journal, The Caian (Gonville and Caius College, Cambridge), Cambridge Chronicle, Cambridge Daily News, Catholic Herald, Catholic Times Daily Chronicle, Church Times, Contemporary Review, Durham University Journal, Dundee Advertiser, Dundee Jute and Flax Workers Guide, Eastern Daily Press, Eton Chronicle, Evening Standard, The Ex-Serviceman, Daily Express, The Fiery Cross, Glasgow Herald, Granta, Daily Graphic, Grimsby Telegraph, Guardian, The Harrovian, Daily Herald, Isis, The Listener, Liverpool Courier, Liverpool Review, Liverpool Weekly Post, Llanelly and County Guardian, Daily Mail, Manchester Guardian, Methodist Recorder, Daily Mirror, Morning Post, The Nation, National Review, New Statesman, Newcastle Daily Journal, News Chronicle, No More War, Nottingham Guardian, Nottinghamshire Free Press and Derbyshire Chronicle, Oxford Chronicle, Oxford Magazine, Pall Mall Gazette, Peace News, Radio Times, Reynolds Illustrated News, Royal Cornwall Gazette, St Martins Review, Scotsman, Daily Sketch, The Serpent (Manchester University), Spectator, The Student (Edinburgh University), Sunday Express, Sunday Times, Daily Telegraph, The Times, The Veteran, Western Mail, Western Morning News and Mercury, Westminster Gazette, Womens Pictorial, The Wykhamist, Yorkshire Post

Transcripts of Debates

Hansard: House of Commons Debates
Hansard: House of Lords Debates
Chronicles of the Convocation of Canterbury

3. Primary Sources: Fiction, Poetry, Autobiography, Oral History, Pamphlets, etc.

Asquith, H. (Earl of Oxford), *Memoirs and Reflections, 1852–1927*, Vol. 2, London, 1928

Blythe, R., *Akenfield*, London, 1969

Bridgeman, Lord., *Report of the Committee of Investigation of the British Legion, 2 May 1930* . (Pamphlet), London, 1930

Brittain, V., *Chronicle of Friendship; Diary of the Thirties 1932–39*, (ed.) A. Bishop, London, 1986

Calder, A. and D. Sheridan, (eds), *Speak for Yourself: A Mass Observation Anthology 1937–1949*, Oxford, 1984

Carrington, C., *Soldier from the Wars Returning*, London, 1965

Clifford, W. G., *The Ex-soldier by Himself*, London, 1916

Donnelly, P. (ed.), *Mrs Milburn's Diaries*, London, 1979

Drake-Carnell, F.*Old English Custom and Ceremonies*, London, 1938

Ewart, W., *The Way of Revelation*, London, 1921

Gilbert , M., *Winston Churchill, Volume 4 , 1917–1922*, Companion Volume 2 London, 1977

Gore, J., *King George V, A Personal Memoir*, London, 1941

Graves, R., *Goodbye to All That*, London, 1929

Graves, R. and A. Hodge, *The Long Weekend*, London, 1941

Hannington, W., *Unemployed Struggles*, London, 1936

Harcourt, M., *Tubby Clayton: A Personal Saga,* London, 1952

Harrisson ,T. and C. Madge, *Britain; by Mass Observation*, London, 1938, reprinted 1986

Haworth, D., *Bright Morning; Images of a Lancashire Boyhood*, London, 1990

Hibberd, S., *This – Is London...*, London, 1950

Hole, C.,*English Custom and Practises*, London, 1941

Jarché, J., *People I have Shot*, London, 1934

Lauder, H., *Roamin' in the Gloamin*, London, 1928

Magdalene College, *Magdalene College War Memorial; Dedication by the Bishop of Ely, November 11th 1923*, Cambridge, 1923

Mayhew, H., *London's Underworld*, (ed.) P. Quennel, London, 1950

McMillan, J.(ed.), *The Way it Was;1914–34*, London, 1979

Middlebrook, M.,*The First Day on the Somme,* London, 1971

Moult,T. ed., *Cenotaph: A Book of Remembrance in Poetry and Prose*, London, 1923

Muggeridge, M., *The Thirties*, London, 1940

Northcott, R.J., *Dick Sheppard and St Martin's*, London, 1937

Read, H., *Poems 1914–1934*, London, 1935

Redfern, P., *The New History of the C.W.S* ., London, 1938

Reilly, C. (ed.), *Scars upon my Heart: Women's Poetry of the First World War*, London, 1981

Roberts, R.E., *H.R.L. Sheppard, Life and Letters*, London, 1942

Sassoon, S., *The War Poems,* London, 1983
Sayers, D. L., *The Unpleasantness at the Bellona Club*, London, 1928
Sheridan, D., *Among You Taking Notes: The Wartime Diaries Of Naomi Mitchison,* Oxford, 1986
Sherriff, R. C., *Journeys End,* London, 1929
Short, E., *I Knew My Place*, London, 1983
Simpson, R., '81,000 women want to know the reason why', Pamphlet, nd., 1937?
Street, A. G., *In His Own Country*, London, 1950
Taylor, A.J.P., *A Personal History*, London, 1983
Various authors, *The British Legion Album – In aid of Field Marshall Haig's appeal for Ex-servicemen of All Ranks*, London, nd., 1923?
Weintraub, S., *A Stillness Heard around the World,* Oxford, 1985

4. Secondary Works: Books and Articles.

Adams, M., *The Great Adventure: Male Desire and the Coming of World War 1*, Bloomington and Indianapolis, 1990
Addison, P., 'Patriotism Under Pressure: Lord Rothermere and British Foreign Policy', in C.Cook and G.Peale, (eds),*The Politics of Reappraisal 1918–1939,* London, 1975
Addison, P., *The Road to 1945*, London, 1975
Adey, L., *Class and Idol in the English Hymn,* Vancouver, 1988
Agulhon, M., *Marianne into Battle: Republican Imagery and Symbolism in France,* Cambridge, 1981
Anderson, B., *Imagined Communities*, London, 1983
Anderson, O., 'The Growth of Christian Militarism in Mid-Victorian Britain', *English Historical Review*, 86, 1971, 46–72
Annan, N., 'Remembrance Sunday', *Theology* , 64 , 1961 , 442–445
Aries, P., *Western Attitudes towards Death from the Middle Ages to the Present*, London, 1976
Bailey, E., 'The Folk Religion of the English People', in P.Badham (ed.), *Religion, State and Society in Modern Britain,* Lampeter, 1989, pp. 145–155
Bellah, R .N., 'Civil Religion in America', *Daedalus*, 96, 1967, 1–21
Bellah, R .N., *The Broken Covenant*, New York, 1975
Bennet, D., *Margot,* London, 1984
Berton, P., *Vimy,* Toronto, 1986
Birn, D. S., *The League of Nations Union*, Oxford, 1981
Blake, R., *The Unknown Prime Minister*, London, 1955
Bloch, M., *The Reign and Abdication of Edward VIII*, London, 1990

Blythe, R., *The Age of Illusion*, London, 1963

Bocacz, T., ' "A Tyranny of Words"; Language, Poetry and Anti-Modernism in England during the First World War', *Journal of Modern History*, 3 , 1986, 643–668

Bocock, R., *Ritual in Industrial Society*, London, 1974

Bond, B. (ed.), *The First World War and British Military History*, Oxford, 1991

Boorman, D., *At the Going Down Of the Sun: British First World War Memorials*, York, 1988

Bowen, E. J., 'Sussex Peace Groups 1914–45', *Journal Of Southern History* , 9 , 1987, 141–157

Boyle, A., *Only the Wind Will Listen: Reith of the BBC*, London, 1972

Bracco, R. M., *Merchants of Hope; British Middlebrow Writers and the First World War 1919–39*, Oxford and Providence, 1993

Briggs, A., *The Golden Age of Wireless*, Oxford, 1965

Cannadine, D., 'War and Death, Grief and Mourning in Modern Britain', in J.Whaley (ed.), *Mirrors of Mortality; Studies in the Social History of Death*, London, 1981, pp. 187–252

Cannadine, D., 'The Context, Performance and Meaning of Ritual: The British Monarchy and the "Invention of Tradition", c1820–1977', in E.Hobsbawm and T.Ranger (eds), *The Invention of Tradition*, Cambridge, 1983

Cannadine, D. and S. Price (eds.), *Rituals of Royalty: Power and Ceremonial in Traditional Societies,* Cambridge, 1987

Capps, W.(ed.), *A Vietnam Reader,* London and New York, 1991

Ceadel, M., 'Interpreting East Fulham', in C. Cook and J. Ramsden (eds), *Bye Elections in British Politics*, London, 1973

Ceadel, M., 'Popular Fiction and the Next War,' in F. Gloversmith (ed.), *Class ,Culture and Social Change*, Brighton, 1980

Ceadel, M., *Pacifism in Britain: 1914–1945,* Oxford, 1980

Ceadel, M., *Thinking about Peace and War*, Oxford, 1987

Chadwick, O., 'Armistice Day', *Theology* , 79, 1976, 322–329

Charmley, J.,*Chamberlain and the Lost Peace*, London, 1989

Clark, J., M. Heinemann, D. Margolies and C. Snee (eds),*Culture and Crisis in Britain in the 30's,* London, 1979

Clarke, I. F.,*Voices Prophesying War 1763–1984*, Oxford, 1966

Connerton, P., *How Societies Remember*, Cambridge, 1989

Cook , C. and G. Peale (eds),*The Politics of Reappraisal 1918–1939*, London, 1975

Cook, C. and J. Stevenson, *The Slump*, London, 1977

Coppin, R.,'Remembrance Day', *Theology*, 63, 1965, 525–539

Cordingley, P. and S. Limb, *Captain Oates: Soldier and Explorer,* London, 1982

Cressy, D., *Bonfires and Bells: National Memory and the Protestant Calendar in Elizabethan and Stuart England,* London, 1989

Croucher, R., *We Refuse to Starve in Silence: A History of the National Unemployed Workers Movement,* London, 1986

Cutforth, R., *Later Than We Thought: A Portrait of the Thirties,* London, 1976

Darnton, R., *The Great Cat Massacre and Other Episodes in French Cultural History,* New York, 1984

Douglas, R., *1938: In the Year of Munich,* London, 1977

Durkheim, E., *The Elementary Forms of Religious Life,* 1984 Edition, London, 1915

Edwards, D. L., *Christian England, Volume 3,* London, 1984

Eksteins, M., *The Rites of Spring,* London,1989

Ellis, J., *The Sharp End,* London, Revised edition 1990

Feldman, D. and G. Stedman Jones, *Metropolis London,* London, 1989

Fuscher, L.W., *Neville Chamberlain and Appeasement,* New York, 1984

Fussell, P., *The Great War and Modern Memory,* Oxford, 1975

Gaffin, J. and D. Thoms, *Caring and Sharing; The Centenary History of the Co-operative Womens Guild,* Manchester, 1983

Garrett, R., *The Final Betrayal: Armistice 1918...And Afterwards,* Southampton, 1989

Geertz, C., 'The Way We Think Now: Ethnography of Modern Thought', in C. Geertz, *Local Knowledge,* New York, 1983

Geertz, C., *The Interpretation of Cultures,* London, 1975

Geertz, C., *Negara – The Theatre State in Nineteenth Century Bali,* Princeton, 1979

Giddens, A., *The Nation State and Violence,* Cambridge, 1987

Gilbert, A. D., *The Making of Post-Christian Britain,* Oxford, 1980

Gilbert, M. and R. Gott, *The Appeasers,* London, 1963

Gilbert, M., *The Roots of Appeasement,* London, 1966

Gilbert , M., *The Second World War,* London, 1989

Girouard, M., *The Return to Camelot: Chivalry and the English Gentleman,* New Haven and London, 1981

Gloversmith, F. (ed.), *Class, Culture and Social Change,* Brighton, 1980

Godwin, H., *Cambridge and Clare,* Cambridge, 1985

Gorer, G., *Death, Grief and Mourning in Contemporary Britain,* London, 1965

Grainger, J. H., *Patriotisms: Britain 1900–1939,* London, 1986

Graves, R. P., *Robert Graves: The Assault Heroic 1895–1926*, London, 1986

Hastings, M., *Bomber Command*, London, 1979

Hibberd, D., *The First World War*, London, 1990

Hinton, J., *Protests and Visions: Peace Politics in 20th Century Britain,* London, 1989

Hobsbawm, E. and T. Ranger (eds), *The Invention of Tradition*, Cambridge, 1983

Homberger, E.,'The Story of the Cenotaph', *Times Literary Supplement*, 12 Nov. 1976, 1429–30

Houlbrouke, R . (ed.), *Death, Ritual and Bereavement*, London, 1989

Howard, M., *War in European History*, Oxford, 1976

Huntford, R., *Scott and Amundsen,* London, 1979

Huntington, R. and P. Metcalfe (eds), *Celebrations of Death: The Anthropology of Mortuary Ritual,* 2nd edition, Cambridge, 1991

Huppauf, B., 'Langemarck, Verdun and the Myth of a New Man in Germany after the First World War', *War and Society,* 6:2, 1988, 70–104

Hynes, S., *The Auden Generation*, London,1976

Hynes, S., *A War Imagined: The First World War and English Culture,* London, 1990

Inglis, K. S., 'The Anzac Tradition', *Meanjin Quarterly* , 100: 24: 1, 1965, 25–44.

Inglis, K. S.,' Anzac Day in Australia and New Zealand', conference paper, Peronne, 1992, publication forthcoming

Jackson, A.M., *The Redding Pit Disaster,* Falkirk, 1988

Jalland, P., 'Death, Grief and Mourning in the Upper Class Family 1860–1914,' in R.Houlbrouke (ed.), *Death, Ritual and Bereavement.*, London, 1989, pp.171–187

James, E., 'I Vow to Thee My Country,' *Bulletin of the Hymn Society of Great Britain and Ireland*, 135, 10:1, 1982, 4–5

Kee, R., *1945: The World We Fought For*, London, 1985

Kertzer, D., *Ritual, Politics and Power*, New Haven, 1988

Kübler-Ross, E., *Living with Death and Dying*, London, 1982

Kübler-Ross, E., *On Death and Dying*, London, 1970

Kyba, P., *Covenants Without Swords: Public Opinion and British Defence Policy*, Ontario, 1981

Lane, C., *Rites of Rulers: Ritual in Industrial Society – The Soviet Case*, Cambridge, 1981

Lawrence, J., 'Class and Gender in the making of Urban Toryism 1880–1914' unpublished paper, cited with author's permission,

Leed, E. J., *No Mans Land: Combat and Identity in World War 1*, Cambridge, 1979

Lévi-Strauss, C., *Structural Anthropolology*, New York, 1963

Lifton, R.J. and E. Olson, *Living and Dying*, London, 1974

Lloyd, R., *The Church of England 1900–1965*, London, 1966

Loraux, N., *The Invention Of Athens: The Funeral Oration in the Classical City*, trans. A. Sheridan, London, 1986

Ludlam, H., *Captain Scott: The Full Story*, London, 1965

Macdonald, L., *Voices and Images of the Great War*, London, 1988

Mackenzie, J. M., 'In Touch with the Infinite, the BBC and Empire, 1923–53', in J. M. Mackenzie (ed.) *Imperialism and Popular Culture*, Manchester, 1986, pp.165–192

Marwick, A., *Britain in the Century of Total War 1900–1967*, London, 1968

Marwick, A., *The Deluge: British Society and the First World War*, London, 1965

Marwick, A., 'Middle Opinion in the Thirties', *English Historical Review*, 79, 1964, 285–298

Masterman, C.F.G., *England After the War*, London, 1922

McKernan, M. and P. Stanley (eds), *Anzac Day: Seventy Years On*, Sydney, 1986

Middlemas, K., *The Diplomacy of Illusion: The British Government and Germany 1937–9*, London, 1972

Middlemas, K and J. Barnes, *Baldwin: A Biography*, London, 1969

Miller, S.I. and L. Schoenfield, 'Grief in the Navajo: Psycho Dynamics and Culture', *International Journal of Social Psychiatry*, 19, 1973, 187–91

Moley, R., *The Story of the American Legion*, New York, 1966

Montgomery-Hyde, H., *Baldwin*, London, 1973

Moorhouse, G., *Hell's Foundations: A Town, its Myths and Gallipoli*, London, 1992

Morgan, K., *Consensus and Disunity: The Lloyd George Coalition Government 1918–1922*, Oxford, 1979

Morgan, K., *The Peoples Peace: British History 1945–1989*, Oxford, 1990

Moriarty, C., 'Christian Iconography and First World War Memorials', *Imperial War Museum Review* 6, 1992, 63–75

Mosse, G., *Fallen Soldiers: Reshaping the Memory of the World Wars*, Oxford, 1990

Mosse, G., 'Two World Wars and the Myth of War Experience', *Journal of Contemporary History*, 21, 1986, 491–513

Mottram, R. H., *Through the Menin Gate*, London, 1932

Mowat, C. L., *Britain Between the Wars 1918–1940*, London, 1955

Moynihan, M., *God On Our Side: The British Padre in World War One*, London, 1983

Nasson, B., 'The Great Divide: Popular responses to the Great War in South Africa,' unpublished Faculty seminar paper, University of Capetown. cited with the author's permission

Newell, V., 'Armistice Day: Folk Tradition in an English Festival of Remembrance', *Folk-Lore*, 87, 1976, 226–229

Nicholson, H., *King George the Fifth*, London, 1952

Nora, P. (ed.), *Les lieux de la memoire, 1. La Republique,* Paris, 1984

Nora, P. (ed.), *Les lieux de la memoire, 2. La Nation,* Paris, 1984

Northcote Toller, T., *An Anglo Saxon Dictionary*, Oxford, 1972

Panichas, G. (ed.), *Promise of Greatness: The War of 1914–1918*, London, 1968

Parfitt, G., *Fiction of the First World War: A Study*, London, 1988

Parker, P., *The Old Lie: The Great War and the Public School Ethos*, London, 1987

Porter, R., *Myths of the English,* Cambridge, 1992

Prochaska, F., 'Philanthropy', in F.M.L.Thompson (ed.)*The Cambridge Social History of Britain*, vol. 3, Cambridge, 1990

Prost, A., *In the Wake of War: 'Les Anciens Combattants' and French Society.* Oxford and Providence, 1992

Prost, A., *Les anciens combattants et la société Française*, 3 vols., Paris, 1977

Pugh, M., 'Pacifism and Politics in Britain 1931–1935', *Historical Journal,* 23, 1980, 641–656.

Purcell, W., *Woodbine Willie*, London, 1962

Reese, P., *Homecoming Heroes: An Account of the Re-assimilation of British Military Personnel into Civilian Life*, London, 1992

Rootes, A., *Frontline County: Kent At War 1939–45*, London, 1992

Rowse, A.L., *All Souls and Appeasement*, London, 1961

Salt, G. (ed.), *Of Whole Heart Cometh Hope: The Centenary History of the Co-Operative Womens Guild,* London, 1983

Samuel, R. (ed.), *Patriotism: Volume 1: History and Politics*, London, 1989

Samuel, R. (ed.), *Patriotism: Volume 3: National Fictions*, London, 1989

Scannel, P. and D. Cardiff, *Serving the Nation: A Social History of British Broadcasting Volume One 1922–39*, Oxford, 1991

Scott , C., *Dick Sheppard*, London, 1977

Serle, G., 'The Digger Traditon and Australian Nationalism', *Meanjin Quarterly,* 101, 21:2, 1965, 149–158

Seymour-Ure, C., 'The Press and the Party system', in C.Cook and G.Peele, *Politics of Reappraisal,* pp. 232–258

Sharpe, M., 'Anzac Day in New Zealand 1916–1939', *The New Zealand Journal of History,* 15:2, 1981, 98–115.

Shepherd, R., *A Class Divided,* London, 1988

Sherry, N., *Life of Graham Greene,* London, 1990

Shils, E. and M. Young, 'The Meaning of the Coronation', *Sociological Review,* 1, 1953, 63–81

Shils, E., *Tradition,* London, 1981

Shweder, R.A. and R. A. LeVine (eds), *Culture Theory: Essays on Mind Self and Emotion,* Cambridge, 1984

Sillars, S., *Art and Survival in First World War Britain,* New York, 1987

Skinner, Q., *The Foundations of Modern Political Thought,* vol. 1, Cambridge, 1978

Solomon, R. C., 'Getting Angry: The Jamesian theory of emotion in Anthropology', in R. A. Shweder and R. A. LeVine (eds), *Culture Theory: Essays on Mind Self and Emotion,* Cambridge, 1984

Stedman Jones, G., *Languages of Class,* Cambridge, 1983

Stephen, M. (ed.), *Never Such Innocence: A New Anthology of Great War Verse,* London, 1988

Stevenson, D., *The First World War and International Politics,* Oxford, 1988

Stroebe, W. and M. Stroebe, *Bereavement and Health,* Cambridge, 1987

Stromberg, R.S., *Redemption By War,* Lawrence, Kansas, 1982

Summers, A., 'Militarism in Britain before the Great War', *History Workshop Journal,* 2, 1976, 104–124

Taylor, A.J.P., *English History 1914–45,* Oxford, 1965

Taylor, L., *Mourning Dress, A Costume and Social History,* London, 1983

Terraine, J., *The Smoke And the Fire,* London, 1980

Terraine, J., *The Right of the Line: The Royal Airforce in the European War,* London, 1985

Thomas, J., *The North British Railway,* vol. 2, London, 1975

Thompson, F.M.L. (ed.), *The Cambridge Social History of Britain,* vol. 3, Cambridge, 1990

Thomson, D., *Scott's Men,* London, 1977

Turner, V., *Drama, Fields and Metaphors,* Ithaca, 1974

Turner, V., *The Forest of Symbols; Aspects of Ndembu Ritual,* Ithaca, 1967

Van Gennep, A., *Rites of Passage*, Chicago, 1972

Waller, P.J., *Democracy and Sectarianism: A Political and Social history of Liverpool 1868–193,*. Liverpool, 1981

Ward, S., 'Intelligence surveillance of British Ex-servicemen 1918–1920', *Historical Journal*, 16, 1973, 179–189

Ward, S., *The War Generation: Veterans of the First World War*, New York, 1975

Warner, W. L., *The Living and the Dead*, New Haven, 1965

Watkins, K W., *Britain Divided: The effect of the Spanish Civil War on British Political Opinion*, London, 1963

Weber, M., 'The Development of Bureaucracy', in *Weber: Selections in Translation*, trans. E. Matthews (ed.) W.G. Runciman, Cambridge, 1977, pp. 341–354

Whalen, R. W., *Bitter Wounds, German Victims of the Great War 1914–1939*, Ithaca and London, 1984

Wilkinson, A., *The Church of England and the First World War*, London, 1978

Wilson, T., *The Myriad Faces of War*, Oxford, 1986

Winter, D., *Death's Men: Soldiers of the Great War*, London, 1978

Winter, J. M., *The Experience of World War I*, London, 1988

Winter, J. M., 'Spiritualism and the First World War', unpublished paper delivered to Cambridge Social History Seminar, Spring 1992

Winter, J. M., *The Great War and the British People*, Cambridge, 1985

Winter, J. M., *The Persistence of Tradition*, forthcoming

Wohl, R., *The Generation of 1914*, London, 1980

Wootton, G., *The Politics of Influence*, London, 1963

Wootton, G., *Official History of the British Legion*, London, 1956

Wouters, C., 'Changing regimes of power and emotions at the end of life: The Netherlands 1930–1990', unpublished paper, cited with author's permission

Wright, P., *On Living in an Old Country*, London, 1985

Wrigley, C., *Arthur Henderson*, Cardiff, 1990

Yamamoto, J., 'Cultural factors in Loneliness, Death and Separation', *Medical Times*, 98, 1970, 177–83

Ziegler, P., *Crown and People*, London, 1978

Dissertations

Kimball, C., 'Ex-Service Movement in England and Wales 1916–1930', PhD. Stanford, 1986

Styrker, L., 'Languages of Sacrifice and Suffering in England during the First World War', PhD. (1 Cambridge, 1992)

Index

Index

Index

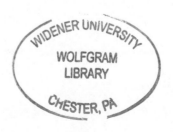